THE RISE OF
TRUE CRIME

THE RISE OF
TRUE CRIME

TWENTIETH CENTURY MURDER AND AMERICAN POPULAR CULTURE

Jean Murley

Westport, Connecticut
London

Library of Congress Cataloging-in-Publication Data

Murley, Jean.
   The rise of true crime : 20th-century murder and American popular
culture / by Jean Murley.
      p. cm.
   Includes bibliographical references and index.
   ISBN 978–0–275–99388–7 (alk. paper)
   1. Crime in popular culture—United States—20th century.   2. Violence in popular
culture—United States—20th century.   3. Crime in mass media.   I. Title.
   HV6789.M87   2008
   302.23′4—dc22   2008020453

British Library Cataloguing in Publication Data is available.

Library of Congress Catalog Card Number: 2008020453
ISBN: 978–0–275–99388–7

First published in 2008

Praeger Publishers, 88 Post Road West, Westport, CT 06881
An imprint of Greenwood Publishing Group, Inc.
www.praeger.com

Printed in the United States of America

The paper used in this book complies with the
Permanent Paper Standard issued by the National
Information Standards Organization (Z39.48–1984).

10 9 8 7 6 5 4 3 2 1

For Joel

CONTENTS

ACKNOWLEDGMENTS

Before I thank individuals who have helped make this work possible, I need to acknowledge a crucial and difficult fact: this book takes as its subject the murder of real people. As I've done the research and writing, I have tried never to forget that, and it is my sincere wish that my work illuminates and honors rather than obscures the lives that have been lost to homicide.

I am indebted to many people who have helped and supported me, directly and indirectly, over the years of working on this project. Marc Dolan advised my dissertation and encouraged me when I most needed it; I wouldn't be the same scholar without his care and patience. William Kelly and Morris Dickstein were wonderful teachers at the CUNY Graduate Center and thoughtful readers of my early work on this subject. My editor at Praeger, Daniel Harmon, was instrumental in shaping the form of this book and in guiding me through the production process. Staff at the Library of Congress were most helpful in tracking down the obscure true-crime magazines that hadn't seen the light of day for forty years; Patterson Smith generously opened his exceptional magazine collection to me on a memorable January afternoon, and has kept me stocked with magazines since. Jill Leovy, Ann Rule, and Paul LaRosa were helpful and generous with their time and ideas, as were Carolyn Strange and William Straw. The PSC-CUNY Research Foundation gave me financial support in the form of three separate grants for the completion of this work, and my colleagues in the English Department at Queensborough Community College—Beth Counihan, Susan Jacobowitz, Richard Tayson, and especially Sheena Gillespie—were unwavering in their support of my work.

Friends and colleagues, including Susan Falls, Barbara Adams, Nelson Lowry, Barrie Cline, Chris Franko, David Peppas, Maryl Swick, Maria Cabrera, Hester Guido, Catherine Silburn, Cory Einbinder, Kalle Macrides, Peter Eide, and Olga Akselrod, listened and talked, helped nurse my obsessions into writing, and read drafts throughout the process. CUNY Graduate

Center colleagues, including Diana Polley, Tom Cerasulo, Kim Engber, Duncan Faherty, and Roger Rawlings, were early supporters of my ideas and good friends. Pamela Harris heroically and helpfully read the first draft manuscript. My parents, Curt and Penny Murley, encouraged me every step of the way, as did the rest of the Murley and Griffin families. Finally, this work would not exist in its present form without the care, encouragement, patience, and humor of my loving husband, Joel R. Griffin, to whom this book is dedicated.

INTRODUCTION

> Rosenberg's First Law of Reading: Never apologize for your reading tastes.
>
> —*Genreflecting: A Guide to Reading Interests in Genre Fiction*

This book began with a question, or rather, a series of questions, which I've been trying to answer since I picked up my first true-crime book as a teenager: "What *are* these books? Why are they so popular?" And, perhaps most important, "Why can't I stop reading this horrifying story?" That book was Ann Rule's *The Stranger Beside Me* (1980), a pillar of true crime for many reasons: its subject matter (the infamous serial killer Ted Bundy), Rule's personalized perspective on the events, and her expert use of the conventions of the true-crime genre. In the 1980s and 1990s, true-crime texts were hugely popular, and like many readers, I consumed the volumes like candy: *In Cold Blood, Helter Skelter, Zodiac, Fatal Vision*—I couldn't get enough. True crime was more than just another formula, another genre, another story—it was about real things that had happened to real people, and the stories of murder were both terrifying and oddly reassuring. No matter how dreadful and devious, the killers were always caught and punished. The genre spoke in a visceral and graphic way about acts of human evil, and the writers never minced their terms: the killers, predators, and sexual psychopaths of true crime were called monsters, madmen, beasts, and sadists, murderers without conscience or even recognizable humanity. Their existence, and their stories, insisted that in the American middle-class 1980s and 1990s, a world where nearly everything had been made safe and comfortable, a gnawing undercurrent of unmitigated evil was still present.

Reading and shamelessly enjoying true crime over the past twenty-five years, and getting a Ph.D. in English along the way, I've come to realize the interconnectedness of my original questions by studying the circumstances of the genre, reading scores of the books, and talking to many true crime fans. My questions have been slowly sketched in while becoming slightly more nuanced: what is the appeal of this genre at this particular point in time? Why is this type of murder narrative so fascinating and flexible, while also being rigid, formulaic, predictable, and almost boring? When—and why, and how—did true crime become the market force that it is now? How have true-crime texts informed other popular culture representations of murder? What kind of cultural work do these murder narratives, in various media forms, do? *The Rise of True Crime* contains my answers to these questions, and it describes and explores the origins, growth, and cultural impact of true crime in twentieth- and early twenty-first-century American popular culture. This book maps out the rhetorical, technical, and cultural dimensions of true-crime magazines, books, television programs, films, and Internet material.

Although murder narratives and nonfiction crime writing have a history that spans centuries, modern true crime made its earliest appearance in the pages of *True Detective Magazine* during the 1940s and 1950s, as a new way of narrating and understanding murder—one more sensitive to context, more psychologically sophisticated, more willing to make conjectures about the unknown thoughts and motivations of killers—emerged. More than a single popular literary genre or even a set of technical narrative conventions, true crime has become a multifaceted, multigenre aesthetic formulation, a poetics of murder narration. True crime is a way of making sense of the senseless, but it has also become a worldview, an outlook, and a perspective on contemporary American life, one that is suspicious and cynical, narrowly focused on the worst kinds of crimes, and preoccupied with safety, order, and justice. True crime has brought a tabloid sensibility into high culture, and has illuminated the sordid with beams of truth: in its best exemplars, true crime questions its own motivations and reason for being. The cultural work of true crime, in its various pop culture manifestations, is important, compelling, and often misunderstood or ignored entirely.

But true crime in its current iteration also raises a host of difficult moral, ethical, and cultural questions, questions that are largely ignored by its mainstream producers and consumers: Why is there such an easy acceptance of murder as entertainment? Why are we so preoccupied with sexual violence against women, and what is the appeal of the genre for women, who make up the majority of its audience? Why do the vast majority of true-crime depictions deal with white, middle-class killers and victims, thereby ignoring the real dimensions of homicide in America, which is statistically more prevalent in urban communities of color? Since the 1960s, the genre and its practitioners have withstood accusations of misogyny, racism, and moral bankruptcy, with some choosing to tackle the tough issues, others deciding to duck for cover. An analysis of the "rise" of true crime—its enormous popularity and appearance in multiple media forms—reveals a populist grassroots perspective on the formidable issues that have emerged since the 1960s in American society. Atavistic in its intensely gendered appeal and misogynist subject matter and avoidance of race and multiculturalism, true crime can be read as a countercurrent to the social progress and cultural changes—feminism, multiculturalism, political correctness—that have transformed American life in the past four decades.

True-crime depictions appeal to many different people, for reasons ranging from vicarious and perhaps prurient interests in the untimely demise of "innocents" to the genuine desire to understand a mysterious and sometimes tragic death (or, more commonly, a *series* of deaths). We read true-crime books and blogs and watch the television shows and films because they promise to furnish answers to serious questions about human behavior, because they're formulaic and therefore as addictive and soothing as old-fashioned mystery novels, because of our insatiable human curiosity about the macabre and forbidden, and because of our late twentieth-century hunger for nonfiction, part of the gluttony for information that Americans have indulged since the 1970s. True-crime depictions have formed a momentous cultural response to a frightening rise in violent, seemingly random crime in our society between the 1960s and the present. Part of that response has been to reinvigorate and reinvent the language of evil and monstrosity, and in the late twentieth century, true crime was one of the only sites in American culture—barring evangelical Christianity—where the rhetoric of evil was used without ambiguity, irony, or postmodern questioning of absolute moral categories.

During the 1970s, with skyrocketing American crime rates and the appearance of a frightening trend toward social chaos, the true-crime worldview made sense of such phenomena as the Charles Manson crimes and the widening threat presented by psychopaths in books, films, and television programs. In the 1980s and 1990s, true crime both created and assuaged fears about serial killers, and it educated consumers of pop culture about forensics, profiling, and highly technical aspects of criminology. We have become a nation of violent crime pseudoexperts, with many ordinary people able to speak intelligently about blood-spatter patterns and "organized" versus "disorganized" serial killers. The true-crime worldview and narrative poetics confirms the reading public's shifting and often paranoid fears about violence in America, bringing the reader or viewer into closer relationship with real killers by drawing us "into the minds" of such people, while simultaneously distancing us from the possibility of random violence and death. In true crime, the killers are usually incarcerated or executed at the end of the story, reassuring us with a good old-fashioned reordering of the chaos wrought by crime. Through representational strategies which posit certain kinds of killers as "monstrous" or outside the realm of normative human morality, the emergence of the figure of the sociopath/psychopath, the creation of a textual and visual landscape of paranoia and fear of "stranger-danger," and by portraying these conditions as reflective of ordinary American reality, the true-crime aesthetic both managed and helped create fears of crime and violence. True crime is also the site of a dramatic renegotiation and revaluation of the rhetoric of evil, and is one of the sites in American public discourse where that rhetoric is used without irony, and where notions and definitions of evil are presented without ambiguity. When seen within its proper historical context, true crime emerges as a vibrant and meaningful strand of popular culture, little understood and often devalued as lurid and meaningless "pulp" reading and viewing.

In the 1970s and 1980s the true-crime literary genre rose to prominence and became the dominant form of nonfiction murder narration in America. In the 1980s, true crime became a consumer-driven publishing industry category, garnering huge profits for mass-market paperback publishing houses that have continued to grow. In the decade of the 1960s, there were approximately thirty-seven texts that treated single cases of contemporary murder and/or the activities of single murderers. In the 1970s, there were seventy-eight examples of the same; in the 1980s, there were 145, and in the 1990s, the number rose to 165.[1] Entire careers—that of Ann Rule, for example, whose work regularly appears on bestseller lists—have been spawned and nurtured by true crime, and large booksellers such as Barnes and Noble devote entire shelves to the genre. Since Capote, textual true crime has acquired a specific set of generic conventions, narrative techniques, and assumptions about audience, which its writers have adhered to, creating a coherent body of texts that narrate real murder and posit a consistent way of understanding it. Those same techniques are used in visual representations as well, with the addition of new trends and amplification of others, such as the dramatic reenactment and the creation of a noir-inflected visual landscape.

True crime has created and brought to life an important pop culture icon, the socio-psychopath. Although psychopaths and sociopaths differ significantly to mental health professionals, in popular media representations the two categories are often blurred together. The sociopath is popularly understood as a person who has no conscience but can function in society, while the psychopath is conscienceless, prone to violence, and has paranoid, grandiose, or schizoid delusions, making it hard for him to function 'normally' in relationships, in employment, and in general society. Not all psycho- or sociopaths are killers, but throughout this book, I will use the terms to signify the murderers whose stories are told in true crime, and whose actions have become landmarks in the American popular imagination. People like Ed Gein, Charles Manson, Ted Bundy, John Wayne Gacy, Jeffrey Dahmer, Aileen Wuornos—these are primal socio-psychopathic American icons, whose stories have granted them the kind of cultural capital usually given only to celebrities. (For more on this phenomenon, see David Schmid's *Natural Born Celebrities: The Serial Killer in American Culture,* 2005.) True crime was instrumental in securing for such people a place in an American celebrity culture of infamy, which, while not explicitly glorifying serial murder itself, fetishizes, romanticizes, and traffics in the "careers" of such killers. The serial killer has become the container and symbol for a contemporary understanding of evil in popular culture, one that posits evil as hidden, persistent, and spectacularly gruesome.

Literary forms, or genres, both reflect and contain a perspective on their cultural moment; just as the eighteenth century "rise" or creation and popularity of the novel corresponded to the realities of emerging market capitalism and social and political changes in England and the emergence of a consciousness of the self, true crime as a genre rose in America during a period of drastic and rapid social upheaval, the advent of New Journalism, and a dramatic and frightening upsurge in violent crime. In this book, I reveal and articulate the strategies true crime uses to make meaning out of violent and irrational acts in contemporary American society, and I show that true crime responds to murder with both irrational fear and compelling fascination. True crime, although laying strong claims to factuality, truthfulness, and realistic representation of actual events, is driven by and preoccupied with themes of an updated, contemporary gothic horror, and it is marked by a carefully constructed rhetorical style that inspires horror. This horror is personified by the presence of the psychopath, paranoia, and hidden threats lurking in a seemingly innocuous environment, domestic and romantic betrayals and reversals, and extreme, graphic, sexualized violence against women. Within a social and cultural context of rising murder rates, increasing sexual freedom for men and women, and greater social freedoms and significant economic advances for women, true crime responded with an intense, gruesome, and paranoid counterstory, repeated endlessly—serially—through its narrative framework and strict conventions.

Such conventions include the depiction of one murder event, a narrative focus on the killer through exploring his or her history, motivations, and unique psychological makeup, some degree of fictionalizing or speculating about events, and a great deal of tension between emotional identification with and distancing from the killer. In true crime, repulsion vies with attraction, murder is rife with suspense and mystery, and the graphic destruction of bodies is commonplace. True crime is obsessed with full-on visual body horror: autopsy footage, close-ups of ligature marks and gunshot wounds on bodies, bruises or lividity on flesh, and blood pools, stains and spatters in the physical spaces where murder has occurred are all depicted in the genre, with varying visual intensity, causing some critics to refer to true crime as "crime porn." The overwhelming majority of true-crime stories portray white killers and victims, with a heavy emphasis on both serial killing and murder in the domestic sphere, and the "missing white woman of the week" is vastly overrepresented in major media forms like cable television news and their Internet affiliates.

Contemporary murder narration in the form of true crime did not spring fully formed into existence, and modern true crime shares some important characteristics with its predecessors. The true-crime narrative poetics are surprisingly similar to nineteenth-century depictions, relying largely on horror and a rhetorical distancing of the killer through the language of monstrosity. Popular early twentieth-century murder narratives in the work of Edmund Pearson show a Modernist sensibility, with a self-mocking ironic tone and a witty, almost sarcastic narrative style. The hard-boiled style used in crime fiction found its way into murder narratives in the 1930s and 1940s, and in the 1950s, after two world wars and in reaction to the "teenaged threat" of that era, murder narratives began a significant change that culminated in the formation of true crime. Before delving into the annals of contemporary true crime, the following paragraphs sketch out the historical trajectory of murder narration in America and offer a condensed overview of the cultural work that murder narratives have effected in American life.

TRUE CRIME AS MURDER NARRATIVE

Very simply, a murder narrative is a story—the story of real events, shaped by the teller and imbued with his or her values and beliefs about such events. Narratives can be textual, visual, aural, or a mixture of the three. In addition, murder narratives are also shaped by the means of their production—under deadline for a newspaper story, with great attention to research and accuracy for a high quality book, or brought to life by actors in a televised dramatization or film. The ways that real murder is narrated, and therefore understood by any given culture, change through time and with differing historical circumstances. Different stories, interpretations, emphases, and perspectives on any single case of murder abound. An 1892 account of the Lizzie Borden murder events reads differently, employs a different rhetoric, examines and emphasizes different elements of the actors and actions than a modern retelling of the same set of events. In her book *Murder Most Foul: The Killer and the American Gothic Imagination*, cultural historian Karen Halttunen writes that "Any story of murder involves a fictive process, which reveals much about the mental and emotional strategies employed within a given historical culture for responding to serious transgression in its midst."[2] Because murder narratives are constructed and are always somewhat fictive, no matter the reality of the event being discussed, they reveal the underlying preoccupations and perspectives on "serious transgression" in ways that other texts—stories about sports, say, or dance—do not. The trajectory of American nonfiction murder narration both responds to and reflects its context and historical circumstance, showing changes and shifts in widespread religious beliefs, philosophical understandings about crime, definitions of insanity, and shifting perspectives on the meaning and mystery of radical evil.

In the seventeenth and eighteenth centuries, the story of murder was told very differently than it is told now, and was circulated in society mainly through broadsheets, pamphlets, and execution sermons. Early American murder narratives, primarily execution sermons, focused on the spiritual condition of the murderer. Typically, a minister would spend weeks or months with the convicted killer, conversing, eliciting the confession, acting as spiritual advisor, and writing the sermon, which would then be read to the entire community either on the Sunday before the killer's execution or at the actual event. Rather than relating the shock and horror of murder and details about the crime, execution sermons related the spiritual transgression that led to murder, and (hopefully) described how the murderer's soul was then saved by his or her minister before execution. These narratives also posited a view that violent transgression, although shocking, was not entirely beyond comprehension because of widespread acceptance of the Christian doctrine of innate depravity and fallen human nature.

From the Calvinist and Puritan perspective, everybody was subject to various forms of sinning, whether it was lying, drunkenness, adultery, infanticide, or homicide. Lesser forms of sin were understood to lead into greater transgressions, and one important function of the execution sermon was to relate the progression from relatively minor spiritual difficulties, which resulted in such small sins as lying or laziness, to more serious breaches, which, if left unchecked, could culminate in murder. The sermon had two specific and highly focused goals: to bring the murderer back into the human community in a metaphorical sense, and to ask the community "to look sin in the face—the face of the convicted criminal before them—and see in that face a mirror image of themselves, with their rages and lusts, wayward impulses and vicious inclinations, small sins and great."[3] In the Puritan context, the murderer was spiritually redeemable, not beyond the pale and certainly not expelled from the moral structures of the larger society. Rather, he or she was seen as a common sinner, spiritually wayward but not monstrous, inhuman, or beyond redemption. The sinner was given the ultimate punishment, but physical death did not negate the spiritual progress that the killer had hopefully made during the period of confinement.

During the turn from the eighteenth into the nineteenth century, execution sermons, with their focus on the spiritual condition of the killer and the absence of graphic descriptions of the crime, began to change slightly to include more biographical details about the killer. Gradually, an interest in who the killer was—his personality, experiences, motivations, and behavior—emerged within the most popular forms of murder narrative. This preoccupation with biographical details of killers and the newly emerging and fast-growing forms of crime narratives in printed material would lead to the formation of a new genre, the sensational account. Writing about this much earlier shift, Halttunen finds that "the new murder accounts evinced a great interest in the narrative act of defining the individual person by his or her distinguishing characteristics and tracing personal development over time."[4] Changing narrative forms such as newspaper accounts, books, trial transcripts, and killer's biographies, would eventually replace the execution sermon, as they more capably handled a new and growing fascination with and interest in the figure of the killer. Simultaneously, killers began to be portrayed with a set of "Gothic horror" conventions, including a preoccupation with domestic crimes, an increasing emphasis on gore and more graphic violence, and a depiction of murder as mystery. The language of murder narration changed tone and register dramatically during this period, as the more rhetorically ornate and abstract language of the execution sermon dropped out of the accounts, and a more physical, embodied, and horror-inflected rhetoric took over.

In the early nineteenth century this change in the ways that murder was narrated reveals a cultural and ideological shift into viewing murderers as "moral aliens," and as entirely beyond the boundaries of human experience and understanding. The increasing popularity and dominance of Enlightenment ideas about the supremacy of rational thought and behavior helped to shift the focus of the murder narrative onto the utter irrationality and horror of interpersonal violence. In the sensational accounts, differences between the killer and the reader were emphasized with a rhetoric which stressed moral monstrosity, "barbarity, unknown among savages or beasts," in the words of one account from 1804.[5] Enlightenment ideas stressed the basic goodness and rationality of human nature, ideas that were necessary for the growth and maintenance of a healthy new democratic society. The necessity for having faith in one's fellow man in order to create a stable and viable society left no room for the bizarre, the irrational, or the unjustified in human behavior. Fears about hidden moral corruption and ideological rot were expressed through murder narratives, for the murderer embodied individual instances of the irrational and senseless. Murderers were now depicted as hideously outside the moral boundaries of humanity, not, as in the execution sermons, as having fallen into sin and the free expression of impulses which lurked within us all. They had to be seen so, for to admit otherwise would mean that democracy could not, would not, flourish, and "mobocracy" or anarchy would overcome young and vulnerable American government institutions.

The melodramatic generic conventions of the sensational account—killers as monstrous moral aliens, an exaggerated sense of horror and moral outrage, murder as titillating gothic mystery—dominated nonfiction murder narratives throughout the nineteenth century. Different representational vogues came and went, each expressing passing social concerns or anxieties, adding complexity and nuance to the narratives: the murder of prostitute Helen Jewett in 1836 prompted an outpouring of support for the killer, a young man who was depicted as naïve and duped by an experienced and sexually dangerous woman, and a large number of murder narratives reflected the various perspectives on the gender and social class issues contained within this crime. The antebellum "penny press"—most notably New York's *Sun, Herald, Tribune,* and *Transcript*—made crime reporting a staple of working class news, the more sensational the better. With the aplomb and finesse of a first-rate nineteenth-century confidence man, these papers expertly negotiated the tension between exploitation and truth-telling, titillation and responsible journalism, while adding an element of political rivalry and class-consciousness, which appealed to the increasingly literate journeymen, mechanics, and laborers of the larger cities. Scholar David Ray Papke writes that between 1830 and 1900, "an immense variety of crime-related products traveled every avenue into the cultural marketplace. Journalists published thousands of broadsheets, pamphlets, articles and columns concerning crime. Writers of fiction created crime novels, detective stories, and serial crime thrillers. Police chiefs, detectives and criminals composed memoirs, confessions and crime-stopping kits."[6] In most of these accounts and however varied the media, melodrama was the prevailing narrative mode, served with a heaping appeal to the reader's sense of disgust, pity, and sympathy.

Apart from the penny press news dailies, one nineteenth-century publication stands apart as offering coverage of crime and criminals exclusively: the *National Police Gazette*. This weekly publication had its origins in two British publications: the *Newgate Calendar*, a regularly published collection of criminal biographies, confessions, and accounts of crimes, investigations and executions, and the *London Police Gazette*, which furnished descriptions of fugitives mostly for local police forces. Beginning publication in 1845, the American *National Police Gazette* filled the growing demand for a codified selection of crime reporting and narration in tabloid form, and during the period from the mid-nineteenth century into the early twentieth century, it traces the arc of popular murder narration from gothic horror to scientific, ironic detachment. Its early incarnation relied on sensationalism and headlines shouting about "horror" and "fiends," and the *Gazette*'s writers employed the standard conventions of melodrama and sensation to narrate murder. But as the century progressed, advances in science and forensic techniques fostered a new depiction of homicide as a scientific and sociological problem. During the turn of the century, killers begin to be of much greater interest to science.

As advances in criminology and new theories about human psychology became more well known, a rhetoric of medical deviance began to infuse murder narration, with the result that killers were no longer portrayed as moral monsters, but as moral deviants with physical, measurable differences from "normal" people. Courtroom battles over legal definitions of sanity and insanity raged, as alienists debated the limits of legal reason and moral will. Changes in understandings about the causes and "cures" of crime included the theories of late nineteenth-century European criminalists Cesare Lombroso and Alphonse Bertillon, who both believed that the bodies of criminals gave clues about their deviant intentions and that different criminal "classes" could be parsed and studied. Bertillon developed a photographic categorization system, which was used to measure, classify, and record the physical features of known criminals in the belief that such a system could help police agents both predict and control crime. In addition, the increasing professionalism and proficiency of policemen, detectives, and prosecutors, new understandings about psychology, and advances in forensic science and detection techniques, were all written into nonfiction murder narratives in the decades of the late nineteenth and early twentieth centuries.

A story from January 1905 exemplifies this trend: the case of a young man who killed his entire family is headlined "Sensational Murders in California Baffle All the Experts: Remarkable Case of the Boy who is Accused of Killing Father, Mother, Sister and Brother." Rather than demonize this killer, the text of the article medicalizes him: the first sentence reads, "There is a twenty-year-old boy in the Placer County Jail, at Auburn, Cal., who would be a study for criminologists."[7] The killer is now an object of scientific study to a range of unnamed "experts," rather than a moral monster who should be disposed of physically and whose soul should be prayed for. The distance between reader and killer remains, but is achieved through a scientific approach to homicidal acts rather than the traditional one of placing killers in a separate-but-still-human moral category. A 1905 article entitled "Marks on Criminals—There Are Many Telltale Signs—Detectives Look For," reprinted in the *Police Gazette* from a London tabloid, describes some rudimentary forensics techniques as well as indulging in the "science," created by Lombroso and Bertillon, of categorizing criminals by their physical attributes. The article goes on to describe early forensic scientists using teeth to identify a burned murder victim's remains, and a case in which bite mark evidence was used to successfully identify and convict a killer.[8] Looking forward to twentieth-century forensic science and its great popularity in both textual and visual representations, we can see in these early accounts the appeal of forensics and the hope that minute, mysterious, and previously invisible or illegible physical evidence can somehow unravel the mystery of how and why people kill each other.

Other significant shifts in murder narration during this period include the introduction of the textual re-creation of the crime within the narrative, perhaps a result of the emerging scientific understanding of murder, where minute examination and explication of evidence demanded re-creation or reenactment of the crime. This kind of intimate description of action that couldn't possibly have been witnessed by anyone other than the killer and victim wouldn't become standard within murder narration until the true-crime era, nearly 100 years in the future, but it began to appear sporadically in the murder stories of this period. Depictions of the murderer and his fate become more systematic during this period, more routine, and subject to a more regular set of conventions, which causes them to blend together and present a unified and blunted threat rather than that posed by the individual souls or single fiends of earlier periods. In addition, as reporters began to get their stories from the police and not the courts as previously, social critiques within murder narratives became rarer in the crime press, and stories in the *Gazette* neither critique nor challenge murder events, but merely report them. Popular murder narration begins a drift toward the maintenance of the status quo with a law-and-order bent, a feature that would become all-too-common in the late twentieth century.

One effect of the scientific approach to criminality is a cooling of rhetoric and a more objective tone within the narratives. Murders that would once have been described within a moral and emotional register, with lurid and blood-soaked language, are now given more objective, detached, and pared-down treatment, such as this one, described simply as "A Murder In Kentucky":

> At Sharpesville, Washington county, on the afternoon of Jan 26, Lud-low Cornish, a dissipated fellow of 30 years, called at the house of John Green, a respectable farmer. At the time the only persons about the house were Mrs. Green and her two daughters, Lulu, aged 18, and Jennie, aged 16. Cornish entered the sitting room and engaged the women in conversation . . . [Mrs. Green leaves the room and Cornish shoots one of the girls.] The frantic mother rushed into the room, and found the bleeding form of her eldest girl stretched upon the floor. Cornish stood in the middle of the room with a smoking revolver in his hand, and as the mother entered he raised it and fired a third shot, the ball penetrating Mrs. Green's hand.[9]

This account is surprisingly removed and unemotional, without excessive descriptions of gore, terror, or an aggressive and melodramatic appeal to the reader's emotions. Distance from the killer, formerly enacted with and through a language of monstrosity, is now written into the accounts as emotional distance from the act of murder itself. Rather than being metaphorically invited into the murder scene and asked to gaze upon the horrible tragedy and streaming gore, *National Police Gazette* writers began to offer the dioramic description, as if viewed from a scientific, objective remove and using precise and flattened-out prose. This type of account would gradually replace the hyperbolic, diabolic, overinflated prose of earlier murder narratives, ushering in a new age of ironic detachment and an increasingly sardonic perspective on acts of murder. Although writers would continue to craft blood-soaked and melodramatic accounts, a competing mode of murder narration became increasingly popular after World War I, epitomized in America by the work of Edmund Lester Pearson.

Pearson wrote mostly short, article-length murder narratives, brought together in collections of his work, although he did devote one entire text to the Borden case. This aspect of his work coincided with popular taste in murder narratives, for most early twentieth-century true-crime books were collections of cases, and not until the 1950s would writers regularly begin to publish entire books about single nonsensational murders. High profile cases, such as the Leopold and Loeb murder and trial (1924), produced many textual treatments, both case study books and inclusion in collections or anthologies. Some examples of earlier twentieth-century murder narratives include Edwin H. Porter, *The Fall River Tragedy: A History of the Borden Murders* (originally published privately in 1893, reprinted in 1985 by King Phillip Publishing Company); Frank P. Geyer, *The Holmes-Pitezel Case: A History of the Greatest Crime of the Century and of the Search for the Pitezel Children* (Publishers' Union, 1896), a text about early serial killer H.H. Holmes; Benjamin H. Atwell, *The Great Harry Thaw Case, Or, A Woman's Sacrifice* (Laird & Lee, 1907); C.P. Connolly, *The Truth about the Frank Case* (Vail-Ballou, 1915); Thomas Duke, *Celebrated Criminal Cases of America* (1920); Osmand Fraenkel, *The Sacco-Vanzetti Case* (Alfred A. Knopf, 1931); Craig Rice, *45 Murderers: A Collection of True Crime Stories* (New York: Simon & Schuster, 1952); and Charles Samuels, *The Girl in the Red Velvet Swing* (Fawcett, 1953).

Some of the writing in these texts invokes Pearson's ironic sensibility, some is in the muckraking mode, and some is of the older, sentimental variety. Collections of real case studies were common into the 1920s, 1930s, and 1940s, with writers and editors continually reviving interest in such enduring figures as Jack the Ripper and Lizzie Borden. But until the 1950s, book length murder narratives varied widely, and there was no single genre or set of conventions that dominated the way that the story of murder was told in books. Magazines were another story, however, and pulp magazines such as *True Detective Mysteries, Master Detective,* and *Real Detective Tales* dominated murder narration and were the genesis of the modern true-crime mode.

From the 1920s to the 1950s, the murder narratives offered in the pulp nonfiction magazines, tinged with the rhetoric of noir and mystery fiction, were the primary form of American murder narration. One giant in this field was *True Detective Mysteries*, which was created in 1924 by publisher Bernarr Macfadden, who had founded such magazines as *True Story* and *Physical Culture*. The magazine began publishing mystery fiction, then gradually changed to nonfiction entirely when, in the 1930s, Macfadden discovered the popularity of real stories. Public appetite for real crime stories was astonishing, and during the 1930s and 1940s, *True Detective* was reportedly selling two million copies per month. *True Detective Magazine* (Macfadden dropped the *Mysteries* from the title in 1941) ceased United States publication in 1995, after changing hands several times and surviving enormous changes in both crime and publishing.[10] *True Detective* and its sister publications (*Master Detective* and *Official Detective*) created and popularized the pithy, formulaic, objective, lightly fictionalized journalistic murder narrative that we recognize today as the essence of true crime, and in its pages the metamorphosis from noir mystery to true crime is visible.

There has been an enormous outpouring of true crime since the mid-twentieth-century, and I have had to make difficult choices about which materials to analyze. One major challenge raised by the genre as a whole is the muddy distinction between the true, the real, and the fictional in murder narration. True crime is a genre that claims a strict and tidy relationship with "reality" or "truth," and many of its creators and consumers believe it to depict "just the facts." The genre does present factual material about crimes that have actually occurred, and some of its creators and consumers believe true crime is uniformly honest and truthful. But true crime always fictionalizes, emphasizes, exaggerates, interprets, constructs, and creates "truth," and any relationship to the facts is mediated and compromised. I am fascinated by the terms of that mediation, and have investigated it by choosing specific artifacts that highlight changing trends, themes, and preoccupations within the genre, charting the evolution of true crime as a genre through major works in popular mediums.

It follows then that not all of my subjects of analysis are technically "true-crime," a category that I define as a murder narrative whose truth-claims are unchallenged by its audience and taken as "real," and whose producers deploy a widely used set of narrative conventions and strategies. There are many other categories of popular entertainment or genres related to true crime, including the book or movie "based on" a real crime, such as the book and film versions of *Looking for Mr. Goodbar*, the police procedural form, or the forensics-based television programs such as *CSI* or *Law and Order*. In popular culture, different genres inform and inflect each other, and some of these are part of the true-crime story. The magazines surveyed in Chapter 1 represent a tiny portion of surviving and accessible copies, but they provide insight into true crime in the pretelevision age; such bestselling texts as *In Cold Blood*, *Helter Skelter*, and the huge volume of work by Ann Rule anchor the chapter on books. Television programs presented unique challenges of genre-blurring and selection: programs were selected for their historical importance or the way they have furthered or enriched the conventions of true crime, so my analysis does include some crucial fiction programs. Similarly, the huge number and range of films on true-crime topics necessitated some difficult choices and the inclusion of some "docudrama" films; Internet material was chosen for its salience and innovations in the genre.

Trying to figure audience demographics and readership presented challenges as well. Without undertaking a full-scale (and lengthy) ethnographic study of readers, viewers, producers, and authors, I hesitate to make any definitive statements about the true-crime audience; however, some observations about audience and readership are well known and documented. Contemporary true crime attracts a largely female fan base, for reasons that are explored in Chapter 2 and the Conclusion. The Nielsen television ratings system, while arguably unreliable and narrow, shows a similar preponderance of women viewers for some true-crime programming, and a more gender-neutral or male-dominated audience for others; information on age is similarly split, with Court TV attracting an older audience generally, but younger male viewers for some programs. Statistical information on race is elusive, but because of its vast popularity, the true-crime audience must be massive and diverse. Much more work needs to be done on the issue of the genre's viewers and audiences, particularly around questions of taste, preference, and the experiential qualities of true crime. I view this book as the starting point for an in depth, serious, and thorough body of scholarship on true crime as a significant part of contemporary popular culture, for many questions about the genre remain to be explored.

chapter one
MAGAZINES

No fiction writer pounding out machine-made plots can equal the truth itself—the truth of bizarre crimes committed by cunning men who leave no clues behind them; of detectives, clever, brainy and brave, who take the tangled knot of circumstances into their hands and slowly, patiently unravel all its twistings and windings, until finally the great secret is disclosed and the criminal brought to justice.

—Excerpt from Bernarr Macfadden's 1924 prospectus for *True Detective Mysteries* magazine

We can see nothing of any possible value to society in these magazines, but they are as much entitled to the protection of free speech as the best of literature.

—Excerpt from the 1948 U.S. Supreme Court opinion on the legality of true-crime magazines

American true-crime magazines were published for eighty years; they flourished for forty years; they were the dominant form of crime and murder narration in popular culture for thirty years. The "golden age" of true-crime magazine publishing and circulation was between the 1930s and the 1960s, before the television era and the widespread availability of slick and cheaply produced paperback books. The very first true-crime magazine, *True Detective Mysteries*, evolved from a hybrid detective fiction/nonfiction mystery magazine in the mid-1920s, and the last American true-crime magazine, *Startling Detective*, was printed in 2000 (the form survives in scattershot fashion, with occasional publications and some produced in countries outside the United States, mostly in the United Kingdom). During the magazine heyday, between the end of World War II and the early 1960s, more than 200 different titles saw publication, and the genre became the primary site within American culture for the dissemination of crime news, both lurid and no-nonsense. The most popular and mainstream titles within the genre, such as *True Detective* and *Master Detective*, posited a law-and-order ethic and became arbiters of "taste" within a largely tasteless tabloid tradition, forging a sensibility of fear and its containment, of crime and justice, which would inform and shape true-crime depictions in later genres such as books and television. The magazines reflected and recorded the vast changes in American life that occurred during their period of publication, with particular focus on shifting sociological understandings of criminality, the figure of the criminal, and women as both victims and perpetrators of crime.

In his book *Cyanide and Sin: Visualizing Crime in 1950s America*, Will Straw suggests that:

> The richness of the true crime magazine lay not in its uniqueness, but in its unrestrained absorption of countless elements from the culture around it. In the first forty years of its existence, the American true crime magazine soaked up the styles of tabloid journalism, film noir, New York street photography, Surrealism, American urban realist painting, revolutionary montage and innumerable other currents crisscrossing American culture between 1920 and 1960. True crime magazines reassembled these styles within dynamic juxtapositions of image and text.[1]

The true-crime magazines were ubiquitous and numerous during those forty years, and in their entirety form a rich repository of American popular visual history, distinct from that of the pulp fiction magazines such as *Black Mask* and *Weird Tales* because of their stated representation of "truth." But the magazines offer much more than a document of changing visual styles, for they chart the enormous changes that occurred in representations and narratives of American crime during the period in question, both textually and visually. From a 1920s and 1930s hard-boiled style, which borrowed heavily from the rhetoric of pulp fiction writers such as Dashiell Hammett and Raymond Chandler, to the emergence in the 1950s of a true-crime style that emphasized context and criminal biography, to the modern true-crime period beginning in the 1960s that is preoccupied with contemporary killers as gothic monsters and extreme sexualized violence against women, the magazines offer a record of the shifting emphases in twentieth-century American true-crime representations. From the cover paintings (and cover photographs beginning in the early 1960s) through their stories, to the advertisements in the back of the books, the true-crime magazines offer one slice of American reality, highly stylized and even fantasized, which was involved with reporting, shaping, and documenting crime for an imagined white working-class readership.

Information about magazine readers from eighty years ago is notoriously unreliable, especially regarding the true-crime magazines. Because of prejudicial assumptions at the time that readers were young, barely literate, working-class men who read the magazines for entertainment or worse, titillation, the audience was devalued, undermined, and not seriously studied. The magazine editors themselves probably held some of the same assumptions as the librarians and English teachers who complained and fretted in the pages of academic journals about the reading tastes of their students.[2] The most reliable information about who actually read the magazines comes from surveying the advertisements. Although there are serious methodological problems with imagining an audience from the advertisements they were exposed to, Erin Smith suggests that "examining a large body of successful ads for resemblances in the appeals they make does tell us something about what was important to readers of that magazine."[3] The advertisements give clues about what the magazine's editors imagined their readers to be, and it is true that if an ad didn't work, it didn't last. The accumulation of ads for goods (better trusses, improved cosmetics and personal hygiene products) and services (increased skills for a higher-paying skilled labor job, a matching pair of pants for any suit jacket) gives a picture of idealized readers as both male and female, working and middle class, and probably white, a conclusion that complicates the conventional wisdom about pulp and "down market" slick magazine readers as strictly male and working-class.

An examination of ads from the 1920s indicates that during its initial period of publication, *True Detective Mysteries* was searching for an audience: appeals to men, women, and working- and middle-class readers abound. There were no appeals to black readers—the publishers of the true-crime magazines apparently imagined an all-white world, as they very rarely printed any articles or stories featuring people of color, apart from the appearance of black faces in "The Line-Up" or similar "most wanted" features.[4] Except for the preponderance of ads for facial-lightening creams, a popular product with blacks at the time, nothing in the ads indicates any awareness of race. This was not unusual for the period, for black consumer presence and power was still years away from mainstream culture in the 1920s; what was unusual was the apparent confusion about the gender of its core readers as indicated by the ads. Ads for men and women were present in equal numbers in the early editions until the 1930s, when the ads indicate a mostly male market, with many fewer female-targeted products and services. The class question is also complex, as ads in the early magazine for music lessons, living room furniture, and "This 6-Room Aladdin Home for $689" speak to more middle-class concerns, although the notion of striving to improve social status through the acquisition of more "up-market" goods and services may explain the presence of such ads. What is clear is that in the early years, Bernarr Macfadden's *True Detective Mysteries* wasn't entirely sure who its market was; beginning an entirely new venture, Macfadden seems to have hedged his bets and waited to see how readership for the new magazine would shape up. By the mid-1930s, the full-page, colorful ads targeting women had been replaced with small print black-and-white ads for masculine goods and services, a signal that the readership was predominantly male, although the mix of ads appealing to members of varying social classes persisted.

A huge number of titles saw publication in the boom years of the crime magazine; some researchers believe that up to 200 different titles were circulated at some point between the 1930s and the 1960s.[5] Bernarr Macfadden's *True Detective Mysteries* (*TDM*), born in 1924 as a mixture of fact and fictionalized "true" stories, started the genre; because *TDM* was such a hit, a few years later he created *Master Detective*, and many competing titles sprang up in the wake of Macfadden's success. Like their counterparts in the pulp fiction magazine market, the true-crime magazines are thought to have had a largely working-class readership, and probably a very large crossover audience; that is, people who enjoyed the crime fiction pulps such as *Black Mask* and *Dime Detective* would have found a similar aesthetic and sensibility in the true-crime magazines, and were courted by the same advertisers in the back of the books. Because few copies of some of the smaller titles have survived in archives and records, it is difficult to determine print runs for many of the titles. *TDM*, as the forerunner of the genre, was considered the most reliable and best-quality book; others had very small print runs or lacked the consistency or characteristics that readers wanted. Among the different titles there were disparities in such qualities as the style of writing, sloppiness or attention to detail, layout and quality of photographs, the use of pseudonyms and highly fictionalized stories, and the number of articles and advertisements, but the overall look or style of the different magazines was similar.

Each monthly edition offered a colorful front cover featuring a painted or (later) photographed scene that portrayed some aspect of one of the lead stories, however tangential or sensationalized. When photographic covers became common, in the later 1950s and early 1960s, models were used and the scenes posed, adding a seamless artificial quality to the veracity of the stories. Most covers depicted women, but some, particularly during the earlier years of the magazines, featured men. Paper quality was in general slightly better than that of the "pulps": most true-crime magazines used smooth stock with neatly cut edges and thicker, colored paper for the covers, and the major titles were considered "downmarket slicks" rather than pulps. Each issue cost between 10 and 25 cents in the early years, depending on quality (*TDM* was the costliest, other titles cheaper). The table of contents for each magazine differed slightly, with some divided into separate categories such as "Smashing Fact Stories" and "Thrilling Short Features." *Master Detective* ran "MD Headline Stories" and an "MD Mystery of the Month."

Feature stories—the most sensational, lurid, or timely—were headlined on the cover, and they always included several black-and-white photographs that displayed the range of characters, scenes, and objects involved in the crime. The magazines sometimes included photographs of corpses from the official crime scene material, unposed and presented as the body was found or discovered. In some cases, autopsy photographs were printed, although this was a rarity. The practice of printing corpse photos endured and increased markedly from the 1980s onward, although true-crime books usually eschew corpse photos, preferring the dramatically whitened-out outlines of corpses (most famously in the book *Helter Skelter*, with the outline of pregnant Sharon Tate offering more horror through innuendo); perhaps issues of sensitivity to victim's families and the possibilities of lawsuits have trumped the desire to show real gore, although there is plenty of visual gore available in other media, most notably on the Internet.

Unlike the fiction pulps, the true-crime magazines have yet to see their day with popular culture and literary critics, and they are largely ignored in scholarly treatments of pulp magazines. As hard-boiled pulp fiction gained critical recognition in the 1970s and 1980s, its creators were tracked down to their earliest productions in the pages of *Black Mask* and similar publications. Dashiell Hammett, Raymond Chandler, Carroll John Daly, Earle Stanley Gardner, and Cornell Woolrich are names that now loom large as important American crime writers; no such names, with the possible exception of Ann Rule and Edmund Pearson, have been resuscitated from the annals of the true-crime magazines (although one of the first editions of *TDM* contains a Dashiell Hammett story called "Who Killed Bob Teal?"). The true-crime magazines may yield literary-historical treasures, and they have yet to achieve the recognition as important cultural products that other pulp forms have rightly claimed. Their value as historical documents is undeniable, for the magazines contain detailed accounts of a huge number of both little known and notorious crime cases that do not exist in any other form.

The magazines experienced one major legal battle during their period of greatest popularity, in the case of *Winters v. New York*, decided by the U.S. Supreme Court in March of 1948. Since 1884, New York (and many other states) had outlawed the possession or sale of printed matter "principally made up of criminal news, police reports, or accounts of criminal deeds or pictures, or stories of deeds of bloodshed, lust or crime."[6] *The National Police Gazette* had presumably gotten around this law by publishing material other than crime news, such as celebrity gossip and show business stories. The law was challenged by a bookseller named Murray Winters, who had been fined $100 in 1942 for selling copies of *Headquarters Detective*. The New York Court of Appeals decided against Mr. Winters; the U.S. Supreme Court ruled, 6–3, in his favor. In the majority opinion, the justices wrote that they could not "accede to New York State's suggestion that the constitutional protection for a free press applies only to the exposition of ideas," responding to the State's argument that lurid fact stories had no right to first amendment protections. And in an intriguing statement that has had far-reaching consequences for American popular culture and entertainment, the Court said that "the line between the informing and the entertaining is too illusive for the protection of that basic right."[7] Having won the right to be entertained by tales of bloodshed and lust, readers continued to enjoy the magazines and sales stayed strong until the post-World War II period.

One aspect of the true-crime magazines that defies easy understanding is their complete refusal to register the significant racial conflict in American society or the racial components of crime. In fact, reading the magazines from their inception, one would think the country was uniformly white. That certain types of crimes were never covered by the magazines—racially motivated lynchings in the 1920 and 1930s, for example—demonstrates that the editors shaped criminal reality for the readers, ignoring certain uncomfortable truths, while packaging others for quick and easy consumption. The careful choice of crimes with a focus on white perpetrators, and the construction of a white readership interested solely in crimes perpetrated by other whites, marks the beginning of a long-standing convention not just in the magazines, but in true crime generally, which would continue throughout the twentieth century in various media forms. True crime's intense focus on the intersection of whiteness and violence is at odds with statistical reality, where in 2006, African Americans made up 12.5 percent of the total United States population, but 49.5 percent of its murder victims.

THE EARLY YEARS: 1920s–1930s

From the inception of the form, the magazines got their stories by soliciting policemen and journalists to send them in. On a back page of the December 1940 edition of *Real Detective*, a half-column box in the middle of the page reads: "You Write—We'll Pay! If you are a newspaperman or a policeman you must have dozens of good, punchy cases in your locker. Why not send them to us?"[8] The magazines solicited stories from the public and used their professional writers to turn raw facts into spicy and compelling narrative. Indeed, many of the stories from the 1920s and 1930s feature two by-lines, usually a policeman and a writer. The by-line for "Who Killed Jean and Virginia Simmons?" a story in the March 1934 *TDM*, reads "By Edgar A. Casey, Chief of Police, Lebanon, Indiana, as told to Frank A. White."[9] The magazines all had their steady professional writers, but unlike newspapers, the writers often got their stories by mail, in addition to the old-fashioned journalistic work of making and using contacts in local police departments. Authenticity and authority were guaranteed with such police collaboration, as readers were eager for the "official" story on any crime, high or low profile. The policeman or journalist provided photographs as well (from about 1930 onward, the magazines wouldn't accept stories without them), which is one explanation for the preponderance of crime scene black-and-whites that accompanied each story.

A sample of tables of contents reveals the types of stories that typically appeared in the early magazines: the October 1936 *Startling Detective* contained eight full-length stories, and six "short features." Titles for the longer stories include "Love Secrets of California's Rattlesnake Romeo," "The Mystery of the Slain Wife," and "'I Was a Karpis-Barker Gang Moll,'" (written by Edna Murray from her home in the Missouri State Penitentiary). Many of the shorter stories in this magazine were one-page descriptions of unsolved cases. The titles may read like a fictional mix of Nancy Drew stories and British "cozy" mysteries, but most of the stories were real, and included large photographic spreads. Even the seemingly fictional cases—the "Rattlesnake Romeo" is a good case in point—turned out to be true. That story involves a man named Robert James, executed in 1942 for killing his pregnant wife, Mary Busch James, by tying her to a chair and putting her foot in a box with two live rattlesnakes, then drowning her in a bathtub when the venom didn't work quickly enough. The tale is "told" to the writer Mark Gibbons by Deputy Sheriff Virgil P. Gray of the Los Angeles Homicide Detail, and is written in a hard-boiled first-person narrative style, with plenty of embellishment and dramatic comments by the narrator. That story was so convoluted and lengthy that it was continued into the next month's issue, guaranteeing continued sales and readers for the November edition.

Early issues of the magazines presented a mixture of fact and lightly fictionalized stories, mostly contemporary American tales from within the past ten years with a sprinkling of older narratives and stories from other countries. The magazines regularly used pseudonyms for its writers and subjects, for as Bernarr Macfadden writes in his prospectus for *TDM*, "In certain instances it is and will be imperative that we take liberties with the facts in order to protect the reputation of the individuals. We shall sometimes find it necessary to change names and places, and to alter situations, so that the characters cannot be identified."[10] The mixture of fact and fiction narratives may reflect the trepidation of editors to throw their entire magazine into largely unexplored true crime territory. The success and popularity of the fiction pulps was well-known and proven in the 1920s, and fact crime magazines appear to have piggybacked from H. L. Mencken's *Black Mask*, the most famous hard-boiled fiction magazine, which debuted in 1920. Fiction pulp titles such as *Detective Fiction Weekly*, *Detective Story*, and *Dime Detective*, and true crime titles *Master Detective*, *Real Detective*, and *Startling Detective* quickly followed, with some confusing results for the researcher. One case in point is that of *Real Detective*, which preceded *TDM* in print, but started out publishing fiction exclusively. Crime pulp fiction and nonfiction magazines evolved during the same period of time, and probably shared readers (if not writers). Like the fiction crime pulps, true-crime magazines were sold at newsstands, drugstores, train stations, and bus depots, and had circulation numbers in the hundreds of thousands.

Because it was the first and one of the longest-lived, *TDM* is the progenitor of the form. One of this chapter's headings is an excerpt from Bernarr Macfadden's prospectus for the magazine, a document that appeared in the first edition (May 1924), articulating his motivation for launching it and suggesting the editorial philosophy that drove the endeavor. He writes that the magazine is "based on a principle that should be the foundation of all our publications; a principle that we have found unfailing—the principle that truth is stranger than fiction."[11] Macfadden's expertise at turning ordinary life into high adventure was already well established by the time he started his magazine. Macfadden is perhaps best known as the father of "physical culture," an early proponent of bodybuilding, strenuous physical exercise, and healthy eating. One Web site devoted to his biography states that "Virtually all bodybuilders of the first half of the twentieth century had some connection with Macfadden."[12] His first magazine, begun in 1899, was *Physical Culture*, and it was a tremendous success. His follow-up was 1919's *True Story*, which published stories of love and romance, purportedly by "real" people, not professional writers. With *True Story*, Macfadden hit on a wildly popular formula, and he quickly brought out *True Romances*, *True Ghost Stories*, and *True Detective Mysteries*, along with many other titles. *TDM* is almost certainly the only title in that series that contained accounts of factual events, as the others were largely fiction masquerading as fact.

Although his greatest interests were in the areas of physical health and advocating the benefits of exercise and nutrition, Macfadden was not uninterested in making money. The same Web site notes that:

> At first glance, the "confession" magazines that Macfadden published may seem to be out of character for a man who championed natural health methods. However, above all else, Macfadden was dedicated to presenting the truth—to stripping away all pretensions, artifices, and hypocracies. The magazines showed people as they really were—they gave people what they were really interested in—they reflected the topics that were part of the average person's everyday conversation and gossip.[13]

Macfadden's editorial ideals—the notion of "truth" without artifice, the desire to narrate extraordinary facets of ordinary lives, to feed the "average person's" appetite for such stories—would inform and shape the genre of true crime for decades to come. His magazines gathered and presented the "transcripts from the bewildering records of the great courtroom of life," an authentic true-crime impulse, which now resides with the producers of television programs and the writers of true-crime books.

A strong moralist, Macfadden's editorial goals remained consistent even as he published the tawdry or tabloid material of true crime: he wanted to show the truth of human behavior, good and bad, noble and corrupt, beautiful and ugly—and he discovered that great numbers of people wanted to read about the truth as he found it. His moral vision is most visible in the pronounced emphasis on the efficacy of law enforcement and the swift and sure apprehension and punishment of criminals in the pages of *TDM*. That magazine rarely printed a story unless the perpetrator had been caught, and the publication was strongly pro-law enforcement, printing regular columns by criminal justice figures such as J. Edgar Hoover, Anna M. Kross, Estes Kefauver, and others. The magazine introduced a popular monthly feature called "The Line-Up," which was an early version of the FBI's "Most Wanted List" and a precursor to the *America's Most Wanted* television program. The murder narratives in *TDM* emphasize the work of detectives ("clever, brainy and brave"), policemen, judges, and juries, and the writing valorizes that work as effectively fighting the forces of encroaching disorder and chaos in society. In early depictions from the 1920s and into the 1950s, murder in the pages of the true-crime magazines, although lurid and gruesome, was placed into a context of containment and order. Although it changed hands during that period, the magazine remained clear in its commitment to depicting crime as a force that was being held at bay by strong and capable policemen, even as the "post-war crime wave" and juvenile delinquency gained prominence and power in both American society and the popular imagination. But that would change in the 1960s, as rates of violent crime escalated and social and political youth movements challenged authority in unprecedented ways.

TDM (and many of the other publications, to varying degrees) juxtaposed a sharp emphasis on law enforcement and apprehension of criminals with an equally strong but opposing impulse to sensationalize crime and make it more interesting to readers. This facet of the magazines perhaps served to reassure their audience about the ultimate and inevitable restoration of social order, for although the pictures tell one story, the text tells another; the pictures often capture the act of violence, while the stories quite literally capture the actor. The magazines draw the reader in with the tension between the act and the apprehension of the actor, between action and consequence, crime and retribution. In their study of 1940s-era Canadian true-crime magazines, Carolyn Strange and Tina Loo note that "No one glancing at true crime magazine covers would have guessed the conservative messages tucked within. This is one of the key features of true crime—its mixture of sexiness and moralism."[14] The true-crime magazine publishers were expert at luring readers in with the false promise of sexual thrills on their covers; once inside, however, the deal was strictly business. The sexy and beautiful cover girls, rendered in full-color in various compromising, terrified, or aggressive poses, would yield to ordinary looking real women, both victims and perpetrators, in black-and-white photos on the inside of the magazine. Compared to their imagined cover counterparts, the real women (and men) whose stories were told were often overweight, dumpy, plain, mean looking or frowsy, without the glamour and drama bestowed by the artist's paintbrush or the model's beauty. The stories, although the writers give them the sheen and glow of sensation, are sometimes dull re-hashings of the plodding and tedious work of detection, but the pictures capture the imagination with dramatic re-enactments and women in lurid, provocative, vulnerable, or challenging poses. Sexual mores of the day dictated more modest covers in the early years, and men were often front-cover subjects; but the covers always seemed to promise drama (usually sexual) and action. But the "real" action depicted in the text often consisted of dry treatises penned by police captains and attorney generals such as "The Public Enemy and Crime Suppression," or "Massachusetts Declares War!"[15]

As with the pictures, so with the text, for the appeal of crime depicted on the covers—screaming headlines and sexy, attractive people wielding power and taking matters into their own hands—gave way to stories that depicted the horrors of gun violence, the anguish of parents of murdered children, and, most importantly, the dreadful end of the line for criminals, either rotting in prison or in that terrifying final trip to the electric chair or scaffold. The June 1928 edition of *TDM* includes a one-page editorial feature called "Where Is It?" that explores the question about the "thrill" of criminal deviance, and readers' interest in it:

There is such a thing as getting a thrill out of committing a crime, if one is to believe certain fiction writers. It's the big gamble. It is win or lose all—with the stakes high. From that comes the thrill. But—is it so? The world's best-known woman crook, or ex-crook, wrote a letter to us the other day and in her letter stated that some persons still seem to think the criminal gets a thrill out of pulling a "job." She said, in commenting on this: "It's the bunk." Down in our hearts we all know "it's the bunk." Another ex-criminal writes us: "It's not 'thrills' one gets—it's 'chills.'" He's right, too—at least, he speaks out of a rich experience in that line, having spent ten years in crime, and double that time in prison. He ought to know. Taken all in all, it seems to be the person who reads about the criminal's exploits who gets the thrill, if any.[16]

This cleverly crafted piece gives a tri-part message: it undermines fiction writers, thereby making a back-handed claim for the benefits of nonfiction; it refutes the romantic notion about the pleasures of the criminal life, furthering the status of the magazine as deeply anticrime and pro-law enforcement and orderly civic life; and finally, it claims that true-crime readers, not the actual actors, get the greatest thrills from crime, both flattering and reassuring its audience that reading true crime is fun, healthy, and wise. Clearly, the magazines had an interest in having their cake and eating it too—in depicting crime as both unspeakably horrible and incredibly, justifiably interesting.

The same issue begins with a long story called "The Millionaire Waiter," about the escape of Charles Ponzi, originator of the infamous "Ponzi" get-rich-quick financial pyramid scheme, and his attempted flight back to Italy in 1926. This story serves to illustrate the concepts elucidated above, for it narrates a "thrilling" fugitive chase that ends with the restoration of order and the triumph of the police, pitting the devious (but somehow still endearing) foreigner Ponzi against Police Inspector John F. Mitchell, a hard-as-nails detective with a reputation for "always getting his man." There are many tensions inherent in such a story: anxieties about a loose immigration policy that allowed criminals to invade America from exotic locales like southern Italy, fears about economic insecurity during an era of vast and unfettered financial speculation, and unease about the ability of a professional detective force to police a nation that was rapidly expanding as a result of greater mobility and ease of transportation. The story of Ponzi's disguise as a waiter onboard a European-bound luxury liner out of Galveston, Texas, is described as "a romantic story with a genuine thrill." One wonders if that is the thrill spoken about in the passage above, which appears just before the Ponzi story.

The magazines always gave a thoroughly mixed message, one that offered a confusing commentary on the nature of criminal violence. These twin messages—that crime is both terrible and fascinating—are, of course, the essence of human responses to violence, and in one sense the magazines were simply articulating and amplifying that response for the magazine-reading consumer. But the early magazines were also articulating the conflicted ethos of the times, as outlaw bandits such as John Dillinger and Pretty Boy Floyd became working-class heroes. The magazines were a part of the interest in the expansion of organized crime that was a feature of American life in the 1920s and 1930s. With the advent of Prohibition in 1920 and the increasing availability of reliably functioning guns and cars during that decade, organized crime and gun violence became more threatening to civil order—and, consequently, much more interesting to many more ordinary American citizens. Readers could (and did) consume the magazines for a variety of conflicting reasons: to feel a vicarious thrill by reading about the daring deeds of criminals who operated outside mainstream Taylorized, starched-and-ironed, middle-class American life; to be reassured by the strong words and judicious plans that law-enforcement officials used to deal with such threats; or to simply feel a delicious, perhaps judgmental and self-righteous sense of disgust about the apparently declining civility and order of American society. *TDM* had something for everyone, and the popularity of the magazine—a reported two million copies sold per month by the mid-1930s, as reported on the magazine's masthead—seemed limitless.

Interest in the exploits of such famous outlaws as Al Capone, John Dillinger, the Ma Barker gang, or Bonnie and Clyde certainly helped drive magazine sales, but those stories—like the killers they describe—had a limited life. Such working-class outlaw heroes, knocking over the banks that in the depressed economy and before the FDIC were foreclosing on homes and sucking up people's life savings, had huge appeal; but most stories in the magazines dramatized ordinary tales of more mundane crimes. Regular readers would have been equally engrossed by the smaller stories that happened in smaller places, those towns and cities where readers actually lived. 1920 is the watershed year of modern American life, when it was determined that more than half of the population now lived in urban, and not rural, locations. As barometers of real trends in American crime, the magazines registered social and cultural anxieties, while capitalizing upon the use of sex as a marketing tool. Like their descendants, the true-crime books, the magazines created an imagined yet verifiably "real" landscape of crime and deviance, giving the reader a fixed location for an unmoored and free-floating fear of violent crime. The magazines in particular, with their many images (both photographic and painted) provided a catalogue of real places on which to pin anxieties about social disorder that violent crime produced. The most common sites of crime and danger changed with demographic, societal, and cultural shifts: in the early decades of the magazines, when the influence of detective fiction on the nonfiction magazine stories was still very strong, cities and urban locales were more heavily represented and depicted as the location of violence. Smaller cities were also favored, and a survey of stories from the 1930s reveals a preponderance of crimes set in the Midwest, in such places as Kansas City, Detroit, Indianapolis, Cleveland, and Chicago.

The rhetoric of the early stories resonates equally with the detective fiction printed during the same period and with more Victorian-era syntax and vocabulary borrowed from British amateur detective fiction. Stories from the 1920s and 1930s illustrate the back-and-forth flow between an older, *Police Gazette* rhetorical style, and the emerging hard-boiled gumshoe detective slang that was beginning to appear in the fiction pulps. Sentences crafted by the writers, like "Tragedy lurked in that house of mystery . . . Death tagged his footsteps" compete with the dialogue of the detectives in the stories, more slangy and informal, such as "the boy was a pretty tough customer but deserved another chance" (both from March 1934 *TDM*). Killers and their actions were described with a decorous and formal-sounding vocabulary, and writers regularly employed the euphemisms of the day such as "outrage" and "criminal assault" for rape, as well as gentler phrases like "bandits" and "desperadoes" instead of the heated gothic-inflected rhetoric of later depictions to describe criminals. The majority of stories were penned in the first-person, narrating events from the policeman or detective's perspective. Consistent with this approach, and with the use of the rhetorical styles of fictional crime narratives, many scenes are imagined and narrated with an impossibly realistic fly-on-the-wall flourish. Details of scenes where nobody but the killer and victim were present are related as though the writer were there, overhearing all the dialogue and viewing every minute gesture, gasp, and circumstance. This was an innovative and major departure from straight murder reportage of the time, as in stories from *The Police Gazette*, which were sensational but not fictionalized.

The magazines fulfilled some unorthodox educational and informational functions as well, as readers learned about the intricate working of the criminal justice system and the complex, often tedious procedures of good (and bad) police work. Every issue also included articles and advertisements about such topics as fingerprinting and criminal identification technology and how-to manuals on becoming a private detective. The March 1934 issue of *True Detective Mysteries* opens with an announcement of a "$1,000 Cash Prize 'Phony Alibi Contest,'" which relates a fictitious kidnapping scenario, prints the prime suspect's alibi, then asks contestants to "Find Flaws in this Alibi Statement and Win Some Easy Money." In the articles, features, and advertisements, the magazines dramatized police work and made it appealing to the imagined audience of mechanics, draftsmen, and factory workers, whose everyday working lives lacked the drama and danger of tracking down killers and gangsters. Certain aspects of police work may have been boring and tedious, but the magazines gradually began to skip over the dull parts and elaborate on the exciting elements.

The crime-control features in each issue did serious cultural work as well, as they both provided the model for a new kind citizen-crime-stopper, and put some measure of power and control back into the hands of people who may have felt powerless in the face of random violence and certain menacing trends in society. Economic woes of the period centered on the fear of burglary or robbery and the predations of confidence men in the true-crime magazines, and murder is often depicted as a consequence of money struggles. *TDM* tapped into the public need to manage anxiety about such crimes by introducing the popular monthly "Line-Up" feature, a precursor to the *America's Most Wanted* phenomenon, in July 1931. By the 1940s, many of the other magazines ran similar features. Each issue contained a two-page photographic spread that showed and described between eight and twelve fugitives, usually murder and robbery suspects. The March 1934 "Line-Up" contains a description of John Dillinger alongside seven other nonnotorious garden-variety crooks, each offering a $100 reward for his capture and giving details about what to do with the fugitive if captured: "If arrested, hold and wire Don L. Sarber, Sheriff, Lima, Ohio," (for Dillinger) or "If arrested, hold and wire Frank R. Boyd, Inspector of Detectives, Police Department, Pittsburgh, PA" (for a murderer named James Farroni). The copy beneath the photos reads, "The Line-Up is a free public service," and "Fifty captures have been made to date, including twenty-eight murderers." On the next page, those captures are detailed in the "Line-Up Captures" section, silent evidence that the "service" really works and that ordinary readers can play a significant role in the apprehension of dangerous criminals, making their own communities safer in the process. "*True Detective Mysteries* presents the Line-Up (see preceding pages) in co-operation with police departments throughout the country. Fifty important captures have been made up to the time this issue goes to press, a short description of each being given below."[17] By encouraging such direct reader participation, the magazine was constructing (and instructing) its readers as warriors in the 1930s "war on crime," offering a tantalizing sense of power and control over an environment that was being undermined by crime.

The construction of the true-crime reader didn't rest solely with the articles and features; publisher inducements and requests sought to engage readers as well. Readers were regularly asked for their opinions about the stories in inexpensive market-research ploys, and the June 1928 issue of *TDM* asks for readers to send in their critiques of that issue's stories. The copy reads "Cash For Opinions. When you have read this issue of *True Detective Mysteries Magazine*, let us know what you think of the stories it contains. Which story is best? Which do you like the least? Why? Have you any helpful suggestions in mind?"[18] This was standard practice of the day in magazine publishing, and the fiction pulps employed the same tactics to register reader opinions accurately. In her book about the crime fiction pulp magazines, Erin Smith writes that the editors "were forever surveying their readership about their likes and dislikes in order to create a more marketable product."[19] *TDM* ran reader's letters beginning in the 1930s, and later editions of *True Detective* (*TD*, after the 1941 name change), beginning in the 1940s, would print a regular reader's feedback column that relayed both the praise and criticisms given by the magazine's readers. The true-crime magazines appeared to have taken very seriously their readers' opinions and abilities, schooling them about detection and charging them with helping to stop criminal activity on their own. Perhaps because of the air of authority lent by collaboration with police agencies, or because they published nonfiction and narratives of real crimes, the true-crime magazines constructed a reader who was serious-minded, worldly, and capable. In short, the magazines targeted and constructed a masculine readership; surprisingly, that's not what they got.

THE 1940s: ANTI-AMERICAN VILLAINS, SPIES, AND CRIME AT HOME

The 1940s true-crime magazines registered the effects of World War II on the culture in both expected and surprising ways. The war years saw many more stories that featured accounts of spying and espionage centered in the United States, more covers with a decided masculine presence, and an emphasis in the rhetoric and features on nationalism and patriotism. The ads reflect a preoccupation with manliness and masculinity, while certain stories and features reverse the shopworn tropes about 1940s men as the "greatest generation" and nostalgic ideas about the nation uniformly and selflessly coalescing around the war effort. National crime rates may have dipped slightly in the war years, but crime certainly did not stop: the faces in the August 1942 "Line-Up" are just as hardened and the charges just as brutal as in the prewar features. The number of readers, estimated from the claim at the bottom of the "Line-Up" page that "More than 2,000,000 persons will read this issue," was probably at its height during the 1940s, although such a claim is difficult to verify; because of its placement on the "Line-Up" page, such a claim may have been a combination of scare tactic directed at the criminal readers and encouragement for the citizen-crime-stopper. Apart from some superficial changes such as wartime paper rationing and the use of older or recycled stories, the magazines retained their look and feel, and emerged from the war unscathed by censorship or a declining audience.

In 1941, *True Detective Mysteries* dropped the "*Mysteries*" from the title and became simply *True Detective*, a symbolic acknowledgement of the magazine's commitment to nonfiction and abandonment of "mystery" detective stories, which were by then firmly associated with the established pantheon of fiction pulp magazines and writers. By the early 1940s, *True Detective*'s core readership, as constructed or imagined by the publishers and reflected in the advertisements, was composed largely of young white men working in low-paying or low-status jobs. Health ads target the aches and pains of the working classes, and the most numerous and ubiquitous advertisements are for trusses: "Ruptured? Get Relief This Proven Way." Although the gender issue had been resolved—*TD* clearly believed its audience to be mostly male by the early 1940s—the editors were bucking the tide of opinion in courting middle-class readers. Perhaps they were acknowledging something that the cultural critics and high school teachers didn't—interest in crime, however sordid or lowbrow it is thought to be, transcends social class boundaries.

During the war years, there was a decided and predictable emphasis in both the stories and the ads on strength, fearlessness, and readiness. Such depictions of combat heroics and selfless service vie with accounts of more negative and embarrassing consequences of the war, as certain men who stayed on the "home front" found new ways to cheat, steal, and scam a population now preoccupied with fighting and winning the war. A June 1944 feature written by John Edgar Hoover (identified as "Director, Federal Bureau of Investigation, United States Department of Justice," even though he needed no such description to regular *TD* readers), called "Betrayal of the Faithful" warns the reader to be wary of a new confidence game perpetrated by men who identify women whose husbands and sons are at war by the "service star" placed in the window of the home. The piece says that such a woman is easy prey for these "traitors to the human race," who "suffer no tweak of conscience in telling the wife of a fighter missing in action that he is safe and will be reunited with her at an early date." Once he gains the woman's confidence, the "operator" then asks her for a loan or to endorse a check, or "some other scheme is brought up to defraud the serviceman's loved one."[20] The text is overshadowed by a drawing that shows a woman waving her two young children off to school, while an enormous sinister-looking man looms over the house, his clutching hand drawing near as the kids skip merrily away. Stories such as this offer a dark counternarrative to the mainstream notion that all American citizens unselfishly rallied behind servicemen and women in the 1940s and that crime on the home front was virtually nonexistent.

The conflict in Europe and Asia found its way to American shores chiefly in the form of espionage and spying, producing an atmosphere of suspicion and cynicism that meshed neatly with the magazine's subject matter. Consequently, stories like "G-Men Trap the Nazi Master Spies," an account in *TD* from July 1942 of the infiltration of a German spy-ring in Manhattan by FBI operatives, is followed by a story of homegrown nefarious deeds in "Pinkertons Smash the Race-Track Dope Ring." The magazine's writers, skilled at coaxing drama from the mundane with the right mix of dash and adverb, were perfectly positioned to spin compelling narratives from the international spy stories that already contained drama and intrigue. A new feature that ran throughout the period introduced some levity and the lure of celebrity presence, tempering the real threat of Nazi aggression and the possibility of losing the war with homespun American humor. The "Favorite Crime Thriller" feature showcased a famous entertainer's "favorite" true-crime story from the past and pictured the celebrity on its cover, posed in some slightly humorous manner. The October 1941 cover is a photograph of a startled Bob Hope looking directly into the camera and holding the previous month's magazine, giving the impression that he is reading it intently. July 1942 features Fred and Gracie Allen looking through an open window, concerned gazes cast downward as if watching a murder or some criminal fracas in the street below. Certain reader-response features began during this period as well, including the "True Detective Forum," which published letters from readers describing "matters pertaining to crime and for the relating of personal experiences—preferably the latter, because actual experiences interest our readers more." The November 1944 *TD* includes a short section entitled "What Shall We Do With the War Criminals?" that prints letters from readers exploring that subject. More reader involvement and feedback may have been effected to bolster audience morale and increase communal feelings, thereby contributing to the joint war effort.

The rhetoric and style of the 1940s stories was still firmly rooted in the hard-boiled fiction tradition, a writing style that transformed very slowly after the war, beginning in the 1950s. "Girl Killer," a story published in *True Detective* in October 1949, illustrates the rhetorical gulf that separates contemporary depictions of murder and killers from the immediate postwar era. Edward Ralph was a serial rapist and killer who attacked twenty-five women and murdered one in Cleveland, Ohio, during 1929 and 1930. Convicted for attempted murder, Ralph was released in 1943 only to rape and murder a five-year-old girl in Cleveland, a crime for which he was executed. Today, we would recognize Ralph as a serial-rapist/killer and a sexual psychopath, and his story would reverberate with the rhetoric of evil, as it narrates his gradual increase in violent attacks from assault and rape to murder. The pathos and tragedy of the victims, the horror of sexual assault and murder, the fear of women in Cleveland while the killer was on the loose, and the depravity of Edward Ralph would all figure prominently in a modern true-crime treatment of his actions.

In October of 1949, however, *True Detective* told his story through concentrating on the work of the detectives involved in his capture and an emphasis on righting the social order. The magazine story gives the names of the detectives and patrolmen, prints the photos of two judges, the Cleveland city manager, one "scientific crime detection" expert, and one policeman, and prints quotations from these pillars of law and order that frame the story. The writer describes the actions of the policemen as closely and carefully as the actions of the murderer, using nearly the same amount of space in the narrative to describe each. The prose is flat and objective, and contains very few sensational exclamations or adjectives, which elevate the sense of horror, instead using the staccato rhythms and tough-guy tone of gumshoe fiction:

> "Did they find the girl?" he inquired blandly.
> Story nodded. He gestured to the bloody shirt and trousers in the unwrapped package on his desk.
> Ralph opened his eyes wide and stared in a puzzled manner.

"They're mine all right," he grudgingly admitted. Suddenly he began to glare with suspicion at Story. "You're trying to railroad me," he charged angrily. "I had nothing to do with it."
He then clammed up and would say nothing further.[21]

The tone, language, and emphasis of this passage are representative of this period, and they reflect a shaping of the true murder narrative along the lines established by the hard-boiled school of crime fiction writers. The work of the detectives is emphasized, the horror of the sexual attacks is described euphemistically, and the killer is portrayed as a tough and dangerous lunatic, not an incomprehensible moral monster and sexual predator. The postwar period saw a change in the way murder narratives were handled in the magazines, with the presentation of crime in a more casual and cynical manner, perhaps because of the impact of the war. The challenges and privations of facing global threats and dealing with the atrocities of Nazis, fascists, and Japanese imperialists left no room for overt emotionality in depicting individual American murders.

THE 1950s: THRILL-KILLING ACROSS AMERICA, THE JUVENILE THREAT AND SEX MANIACS

As early as 1946, *TD* was publicizing the threat of increased crime associated with the masses of returning war veterans and the children who had lived through the war period. In a column from the March 1946 edition entitled "America's Costliest Crime Wave," John Wooster Martin writes that "The post-war period of outlawry is upon us. As these words were written, it appeared certain official records would show that crime in all categories throughout the nation increased at least 15 percent in 1945 over 1944. When all the figures are in, the percentage may climb to 25 or higher."[22] The postwar crime menace would become more pronounced as the 1950s dawned, and the magazines preemptively trumpeted a frightening rise in rates of violent crime, particularly sex crimes. The 1950s magazines also reflected the rise of automobile culture and the ensuing mobility of American life, which corresponded neatly with the perceived social restlessness and anonymity thought to contribute to crime. Coverage in the magazines during the period upped the ante on terror, fear of violence, and the rhetoric of gothic horror, and the 1950s ushered in the modern true-crime period in myriad ways.

A February 1952 story in *TD* exemplifies the strategies of representation the magazine used in depicting the juvenile threat. "Jerry the Wildcat" opens with two full-length black-and-white photos of the teenaged perpetrators, Evelyn Williams Donges ("Jerry the Wildcat") and Tom LaFave. "Jerry" is the girl, blue-jean-clad, unsmiling and smoking a cigarette, with the caption

"'I've seen a lot of tough people in my life, but she's the worst,' said veteran crime investigator," while Tom sports an innocent half-smile, with the caption "Life was very boring—till he helped knock off a drunk and finance the getaway with a few holdups." The story is fairly typical for the period: Jerry, Tom, and two teenaged friends, bored with their lives in slowpoke Miles City, Montana, rolled a drunk and stole his wallet, beating him to death in the process. The foursome then embarked on a Western interstate journey that included several stolen cars, knocking off a gas station, and a dash of prostitution. Three of the kids are sixteen, one is fifteen, and they did not intend to kill their victim; in fact, they didn't realize they were wanted for murder until they were arrested. Bad kids, but something less than the "murderous gang" depicted in the blaring headlines of the narrative. The story is a mash-up of stereotypes and titillation, skillfully deployed shock value and exploitation of certain key facts.

Jerry fills the role of a disarmingly and provocatively tough young woman, with "flaming red hair and a mule skinner's vocabulary." Sexually attractive and experienced—she was married to a soldier in service overseas—she also "had a juvenile record of more than a dozen arrests and had, again and again, proved her extraordinary capacity for violence and invective," although we don't get any details about her past transgressions. Tom is the smirking sidekick, masculine but overshadowed by the "Wildcat," even though he and the other male juvenile proved to be the actual killers. Together, they exemplify the restless boredom that defined the dark side of teenaged life in the 1950s, as the catalyst to their crime spree was a conversation about "their mutual dissatisfaction with their dull and boring life in Miles City." Looking for adventure, they cook up a plan to make a cross-country tour, and embark on the crimes to finance their fun.

One aspect of depictions of killers that would come into prominence during this period is the lack of conscience, usually understood and represented as a facet of the psychopathic or sociopathic personality. In this story, Jerry the Wildcat/psychopath embodies the conflicting qualities of fascination and horror that would make the psychopath a fixture of true crime, with the added thrill of sexual titillation because she is a young woman. The narrative focus rests with Jerry, and the story pops with fascination about her. She is portrayed as the mastermind behind the crime spree, and is brutal, cold-hearted, and sexual: "the Wildcat had no difficulty in luring the 38-year-old ranch hand to a dark street." Her clothing is a subject of great interest—she is seen in "levis and a plaid shirt," fancy "ranch-style clothing," and "flashy cowboy outfits." A description narrated from the victim's perspective reads, "Her dude ranch outfit contrasted oddly with her feminine seductiveness." Most chilling, however, is her utter lack of conscience, completely at odds with "normal" female qualities of nurturance and care. Jerry is a new kind of woman, utterly cold-blooded and conscienceless, fearsome and terrifying to men and women alike (when incarcerated, her female cell mates request that she be removed to a private cell).[23]

The setting of this particular story—rural Montana—is typical of magazine coverage in the 1950s. In this period, the larger cities—New York, Chicago, Los Angeles—are no longer the unquestioned and reigning sites of American violence; rather, the smaller cities and suburbs are depicted more often and with increasing regularity. The 1950s predated the vaunted "white flight" from American cities into the suburbs that exploded in the 1960s and 1970s, but the postwar suburban expansion shows up in the true-crime magazines as a shifting focus onto unfamiliar and burgeoning places. The true-crime magazines offered unexpected and useful geography lessons about unfamiliar American locales and the contours of small communities. With the passage of the Federal Highway Act of 1956, the expanding interstate highway system increased possibilities for more comfortable long-distance automobile travel, and people wanted to learn about unknown and unexplored American towns, villages, and cities. The compendium of place names is endless, and no town is safe from random violence: from Roanoke to Billings to Pensacola. There is a curious emphasis on desert locations and rural, outdoor sites, where grisly discoveries give rise to such stock phrases as "bleached bones" and photos of detectives or criminals pointing out the vegetation-tangled site of a shallow grave. As a geographical guide, 1950s true crime is extraordinary and richly detailed, and the country emerges as a murder-studded map. As in Jack Kerouac's *On the Road*, written in 1951 and published in 1957, the country itself is a character, capable of sustaining multiple interpretations and nurturing conflicting impulses.

Oddly reassuring, each story begins with a statement about place, locating and anchoring the criminal activity in time and space that are at once familiar and menacing. The March 1950 *TD* story "The Mark That Betrayed" is typical, and begins with these words:

> Christ Episcopal Church rises in the midst of a conservative, well-to-do southwest residential neighborhood in Roanoke, Virginia. Its rough-hewn gray fieldstone walls are blanketed with ivy and its lead-paned windows look out on streets graced with stately trees in the old Southern tradition. Deep shadows lay across its walks and lawns on the morning of May 9th, 1949, when Alexander Roland, 51-year-old church janitor, opened its massive oak side door.[24]

In the pages of the true-crime magazines, the idea of "America" emerges as a multifaceted, multidimensional nation of darkness and shadows, lurking dangers for (mostly) women, of dynamism and action for men, of humdrum daily lives interrupted and sometimes ended by the sudden appearance of homicidal violence. In reading the magazines one could embark on a vicarious cross-country wild ride, visiting and viewing a plurality of American places and spaces, exteriors and interiors, women and men, the living and the dead, people sane and insane. Although the stories occur in recognizably real places, the textual reenactment of crime dramatizes and transforms them into fantasized locations, imaginary sites of real horror. As Clive Bloom writes about pulp fiction and nonfiction forms, "Here fiction and fact are both fantasy. Here the *Police Gazette* meets the *National Enquirer* and neither fact nor fiction can any longer be trusted."[25] These places become "realer than real," American locations and American crime staged for entertainment, sites of infamy and banality, murder and everyday life, the unimaginable and the prosaic.

The 1950s covers are dramatic yet carefully controlled, expressive, tense, emotional but cool, and they use a visual iconography that signals sexuality, danger, and secrecy—not necessarily violence. This visual language includes seductive women, eyes shot to the sides of the frame, closed and unsmiling faces, tight and revealing outfits, high heels and fishnet stockings, red lips on white skin, clutching hands and fingers, confrontational or furtive poses. This is the familiar territory of the dangerous woman, the "femme fatale" from the pages of gumshoe fiction and the images of film noir, seemingly borrowed wholesale from those competing pop culture forms. Many of the covers depict stories about pornography, as Estes Kefauver and his various Senate Subcommittees worked to uncover depravity and obscenity and unravel the blossoming porn industry. Another popular theme that was dramatized by beautiful pouting pin-up girls was the reform-school problem, typified by the January 1956 *TD* story, "Are Our Jails Schools for Crime?" This cover pictures a steely eyed, bejeweled, cigarette-smoking blonde, fur coat tossed carelessly over her shoulders, stiletto heels on seductively crossed legs, relaxing on a jailhouse cot. Juvenile delinquent or early *Playboy*-era cheesecake model? Let the reader decide.

The best 1950s stories are those that illuminate the tension between the horrific and the banal. Two such stories are the November 1957 discovery in Wisconsin of Ed Gein's crimes (murder, grave-robbing, and corpse-defiling) and the November 1959 Clutter family massacre in rural Kansas. Gein's case, because of the magnitude and bizarre nature of his crimes, would become notorious in American criminal and pop culture history, and would become the basis for numerous book and film treatments, including both book and movie versions of *Psycho* (Robert Bloch and Alfred Hitchcock) and Thomas Harris's *The Silence of the Lambs*. The Clutter murders would become famous in Truman Capote's *In Cold Blood*, a book that would become the prototype of the entire genre of modern book-length true-crime narratives. Both cases received lengthy coverage in the true-crime magazines, but each was treated as simply another American murder-horror story. The Clutter case was depicted on the cover of *Front Page Detective*, which often used photos and photomontage techniques instead of the "pin-up girl" style. Gein's story was headlined on the March 1958 cover of *TD* as "House Full of Skulls, The Plainfield, Wis., madman who shocked the nation," but the cover illustration depicts a woman reaching for a gun in a darkened toolshed, an image unrelated to the Gein case.

In their original true-crime contexts, these cases were each just another story of random violence and murderous insanity, and not the defining murder archetypes of our times that they became in later treatments. The disparity of treatment in the magazines, books, and movies signals the differing emphases and meanings given to crime narratives at different moments in history; in the 1960s, Ed Gein graduated from the lowly ranks of oddball madman to being the prototypical and iconic psychopath of the day, and the excessively violent and random Clutter murders continue to fascinate readers and viewers, most recently as the story of how Capote got his story in two films, *Capote* and *Infamous*. The 1950s true-crime writers and their readers were more interested in crimes that had roots in perceived social problems of the day; consequently, the Charles Starkweather case, with its teenaged spree-killing and hard-driving, interstate lovers-on-the-run protagonists, was the iconic 1950s crime, not that of the psychopathic cannibal/ghoul Ed Gein.

The terms "psychopath" and "sociopath" became part of the popular vernacular after 1941, with the publication of Hervey M. Cleckley's *The Mask of Sanity: An Attempt to Clarify Some Issues About the So-Called Psychopathic Personality*. Cleckley's text, a combination of psychological theory and case studies, made the concepts and language of psychiatric criminal deviance accessible to nonprofessional readers. The book was popular during the period, and was reprinted in 1950, 1955, and 1964. Another concept that entered popular consciousness during the 1950s was that of the "sex fiend," or "sex psychopath," the man who, because of some disorganization in his mind, was unable to control his sexual impulses and posed a significant threat to the perceived weakest part of American society, women and children.[26] The psychopath also appeared in highbrow literature of the time; in his 1957 essay, "The White Negro: Superficial Reflections on the Hipster," Norman Mailer says that the hipster is a "philosophical psychopath," and that "the psychopath may indeed be the perverted and dangerous front-runner of a new kind of personality which could become the central expression of human nature before the twentieth century is over."[27] Emotionally cool, uncaring, lacking feeling, the hipster would become a quintessential mid-twentieth-century icon, and the cold-blooded killer in the pages of true crime, his dark double.

Covers that dramatized female sexuality as alluring, dangerous, and powerful competed with those depicting women as threatened and vulnerable, as in the October 1951 *TD* cover story "66 Women and the Marauding

Monsters," which features five women's faces, each wearing an expression of terror, and one woman being forced into a car by a man in a suit and hat with his back to the viewer. This type of cover, and its accompanying story, would become more common as the decade wore on and the "sexual psychopath" became a regular figure in the magazines. As early as June 1950, the "sex fiend" killer was emerging as a new kind of threat, depicted in a *TD* article titled, "Today's Challenging Terror." In this piece, Sid McMath, then governor of Arkansas, details the "rising number of crimes by degenerate sex offenders," which had recently been declared by J. Edgar Hoover. In the passage below, McMath outlines Hervey Cleckley's description of the psychopathic personality:

> A person who appears to be physically and mentally normal but who is emotionally sick, possesses what the psychiatrists term a psychopathic personality . . . Court records disclose that a large number of sex crimes are committed by this type of psychopath. He has gentle manners and an engaging smile. Often young women learn to their sorrow, when they are alone with him in his car along a lonely road, that he is a beast in human form.[28]

This is one of the earliest descriptions in popular culture of a figure that would become, sorrowfully, much more familiar in the years to follow: the psychopath. The idea of a person (nearly always male) who could masquerade as normal, victimize women at will, and remain undetected for long periods of time, was new in 1950, but during the following decades would emerge as the primary and most frightening threat to vulnerable victims in the pages of the true-crime magazines, books, television programs, and films. The picture drawn by McMath—a young woman who is suddenly presented with the "Mr. Hyde" side of a "normal-seeming" man, alone in his car with the gothic-horror "beast,"—presages a thousand such scenes to come in pop-culture murder narratives. Such a figure, in many different incarnations, would appear regularly in the 1960s magazines, driving fear and tension, displaying aberrant sexual appetites and behaviors, and fueling newer, competing popular forms to represent him.

THE 1960s—SEX, VIOLENCE, AND THE PSYCHOPATH

The 1960s brought many changes to American society, changes that are readily seen in the true-crime magazines. Technological changes in printing made color photographic covers easier and cheaper to reproduce, so painted covers faded into obscurity; major censorship battles about obscenity in literature were won, and such rulings trickled down to the crime magazines in the form of an increasing portrayal of violent sexual perversity in both images and text; the "hippy" youth movements and accompanying relaxation of social mores and codes of behavior translated into more stories about drug use and wild sexual behavior, with sometimes wacky results within the somewhat reactionary and conservative milieu of the magazines; crime rates began to skyrocket in the decade, producing an unmistakable atmosphere of menace and fear in the magazines; and finally, the early women's rights movement began to take hold, challenging gender roles and increasing women's social and political power. Women's challenges to the existing sexual and power dynamics perhaps resulted in many more stories in the magazines about women being violently and emphatically controlled: "co-eds" were regularly slain, hitchhikers were found dead in ditches, casual sex with strangers held fatal consequences. These social forces combined with the simple reportage of actual events, culminating in the emergence of the sexual psychopath as a dominant figure in the new American landscape of crime and violence.

By 1960, the psychopath was already known to law enforcement, and the magazines were eager to tutor their readers about this new criminal type. An October 1960 article in *TD* titled "Case of the Careless Pickup" details the discovery of a slain prostitute in a cheap Los Angeles hotel room. At first, the investigating detectives think the case is a "run-of-the-mill alcoholic homicide," but they soon discover otherwise:

> "A sadist," was Sergeant Jack McCreadie's tight-lipped verdict. "This was no ordinary drunken brawl."...The veteran Los Angeles homicide men well knew the implications of a sadist on the loose, an ever-recurrent nightmare to police of big cities. A woman of loose morals, possibly a prostitute or barfly, tortured and slain in a transient room, is an old story and a grim one, inevitably bringing back echoes of Jack the Ripper and the London horrors of 80 years ago. By the time the body is found, the psychopathic killer is usually a long jump ahead of the police. And he is the criminal type whose egotism and murderous lust, once he has tasted blood and gotten away with it, drive him to strike again and again.[29]

This bit of omniscient narration, describing the detectives' reactions to and thoughts on this murder, informs the reader about who and what a psychopathic sex killer is. The early 1960s reader needed such overt instruction because the figure of the psychopath was not yet well known as a pop culture icon (or as much of a real threat, either), and the true-crime magazines filled the role of teacher in this regard. From the 1960s onward, the figure of the psychopathic sex killer would intrigue and fascinate consumers of pop culture crime stories, both fiction and nonfiction, and the magazines were one of the first sites that both tracked and helped create the emergence of the psychopath as a figure of violent threat and social disorder.

Covers in the 1960s dramatized the psychopath and illustrated his predations on women. Whereas covers in previous decades, especially the 1950s, had often shown women in positions of power and as perpetrators of crime, not simply victims, 1960s covers tended toward the sexy damsel in distress motif. The scantily clad models are shown in various violent situations with looks of terror and helpless fear on their faces; they are being strangled, bludgeoned, stabbed, grabbed, or held at gun- or knifepoint by menacing masculine figures. Sometimes the model is depicted as a corpse being lifted out of a car trunk, dragged away, or buried. The September 1964 cover of *TD* depicts a dead blond woman in a slip, cleavage spilling out over the lacy front, with a rope tied around her neck and squeezed into a steamer trunk. An iconography of sexual violence is shaped during this period, and images of women in bondage, of dead or dying female bodies, and more graphic implications of torture and suffering become common.

The theme of voyeurism appears as well, and the motif of watching or being watched emerges in two intriguing *TD* covers: March 1965 shows half a woman's face, her lipsticked mouth open in a scream, her aviator-style sunglass lens reflecting a blond male maniac wielding a hatchet. May 1966 features an extreme closeup of a dark masculine eye and the image of a terrified young woman with long blond hair reflected in the iris, one hand up as if to deflect blows or slashes inflicted by the man whose eye we see. These covers in particular implicitly invite and accept voyeuristic enjoyment of viewing violence against women, and they form a conscious acknowledgment about the ways the cover art was experienced by some readers. Voyeurism, perception, and violence were subjects of many films during this period as well, including the British *Peeping Tom* (Michael Powell, 1960) and *Psycho* (Alfred Hitchcock, 1960). Policemen feature prominently on some covers, but it is unclear whether the cop is a figure of salvation or further brutality. The September 1964 cover of *Inside Detective* positions the viewer inside a home looking out a window as a blond woman is being held forcibly against the glass by a cop. Her face registers indifference, but her hands are pressed against the glass in an attitude of panicked helplessness or self-defensive reflex; the cop's gun is drawn and held next to her rib cage, as his other hand clenches her upper arm tightly. The message is clear: even the police, male and armed, offer a threat to female vulnerability and powerlessness; furthermore, viewing such vulnerability offers a voyeuristic thrill.

The emotional effect of such covers is less clear: the predominance of depictions of violence against women may have created more fear of violence, a numbness to such violence, or titillation and arousal. Some infamous killers of the period claimed that reading the detective magazines incited their bloodlust or gave them ideas about perpetrating their own crimes, and the mixture of violence and sex on the covers was routinely criticized by media watchdogs and feminists alike. In a recent online essay, the true-crime blogger Laura James observes that:

> Some time in the 1960s, they [the magazines] began to change their focus to more lurid crimes where photos of naked victims were available (a reflection of the general trend in media to focus on illustrations above content; witness CNN at any given moment; but maybe the Internet will change that). With the new focus on photos of dead women, gone were the aesthetics of the study of murder. It didn't matter whether the crime was a pedestrian husband-on-wife killing or a genuine unsolved and complicated mystery.[30]

Although photos of nude corpses in the magazines were rather rare during this period, still the emphasis had shifted, with the resulting diminishment on the "aesthetics" or flourishes of rhetorical style applied to the study of murder, replaced with a new focus on acts of rape, torture, sadism, and shock. James identifies the birth of so-called "crime porn," presenting the sexual aspects of crime in such a way as to blur the already complicated boundary between prurient and "innocent" interest. The 1960s covers tell a tale of increasingly sexualized and disturbingly commonplace violence toward young women, a phenomenon seemingly borne out by the rising murder rates and trends during that period. A closer look at the statistics would show that, as always, most homicide victims are young men, but never mind: the true-crime magazines tapped into—and encouraged—a taste for graphic, sensationalized, sexual assaults against attractive young women. After all, the "Case of the Butchered Baby Sitter" is much more titillating than "Man Slain in Drug Deal Gone Wrong."

Perhaps the most disturbing aspect of the 1960s covers is that they depicted women as depersonalized and sexualized bodies, physical selves without an emotional or intellectual dimension (except for the expression of terror), a new one available each month, symbolic white women serially violated and available for fantasies of violence. The objectification of women was at its height on the true-crime magazine covers during the 1960s and 1970s, and inside the magazines as well. This is really nothing new, for women have always been objectified and sexualized in popular culture imagery; however, never before had real crimes been so heavily sexualized and depicted with such emphasis and attention to the graphic display of brutality. These were representations of actual events, indicating violence that had been inflicted upon real people. If the magazines didn't narrate real murder, displays of violence upon women's bodies wouldn't be as morally vexed. But as the sexual psychopath and serial killer period in American crime began in the 1960s and 1970s, the magazines offered their own series of paper cutout victims, juxtaposing the real and the unreal, the ugly with the glamorous, photos of real dead women with sexually appealing living ones. Mixing fact with fictionalized, dramatized violence blunts the horror of the fact and underscores the playacting quality of the fiction, ultimately trivializing the reality of violent crime. Set against the backdrop of the women's liberation movement of the 1970s, the creation and rise of "crime porn" can be seen as a powerful, sinister counterforce in popular culture, an insistent voice, strident in both textual and visual representations, against women's sexual and social freedom.

The depiction of certain types of crimes and perpetrators allowed the magazines to create a fantasized version of American criminal activity, different according to decade and emphasis. Racial conflict, particularly in the 1950s and 1960s, was a part of reality that received plenty of coverage in the mainstream press, and the true-crime magazines covered and constructed a different kind of reality for their readers. The racial and demographic makeup of the readership, along with perceptions about readers' interests, probably helps explain why certain kinds of crimes were deemed more "interesting" or "readable" than others. The magazines published material that they felt best appealed to their white working-class readership, perhaps imagining that a portrait of an all-white American criminal reality was preferable to their readers than presenting the mixed-up, messy, emotionally difficult and uncontrollable reality of racial conflict. An escape from such a reality, more violent and with more immediate dire consequences, would also have appealed to black readers. In their glossing over certain social conditions, the magazines offered an escape that masqueraded as crime "news," paving the way for the "crime infotainment" television shows that would dominate true crime from the 1980s to the present.

EPILOGUE: TELEVISION MURDERS THE TRUE-CRIME MAGAZINES!

The role of the true-crime magazines in the larger and more widespread media phenomenon of shaping criminal reality and marketing it as entertainment has been little understood and largely unexamined. Throughout the decades that followed the 1960s, the attention of true crime consumers gradually and inexorably turned from print media to television and book length treatments of crime. In the 1970s, readership fell off dramatically and the magazines attained true tabloid status, with all the class and commerce implications that accompany that designation. The true-crime genre in paperback publishing gained prominence and market share in the 1970s, and television began to compete with such true-crime programming as *America's Most Wanted*, *Cops*, and *Unsolved Mysteries* in the 1980s. During the 1970s and 1980s, the magazines began to fully develop the rhetoric of evil and monstrosity, a way of narrating murder that would reach maturity in true-crime books during the 1980s. Coverage was still focused on sex crimes, particularly sexually motivated murders of young women, and one notable writer emerged during this period. Ann Rule began writing for *TD* using a male pseudonym, "Andy Stack," in 1970. She attained genre "crossover" status in 1980 with her first book, the masterful text about Ted Bundy, *The Stranger Beside Me*. Rule continued to publish stories in *TD* until the early 1980s, when her books began to sell well enough that she could concentrate on longer works rather than the shorter magazine pieces. She is now the best-selling true crime writer in the world.

The magazines struggled on until the bitter end, finally selling out to European and U.K. publishers in the 1990s and 2000s. *True Detective* is still published in the United Kingdom, but with entirely different ownership; the magazine now presents a mélange of European, Australian, United Kingdom, and American cases, with equal coverage of old and contemporary murders. The heyday of true-crime magazines in this country is long past, and a strange nostalgia surrounds some of the older magazines now, evidenced by this entry on a Web site called "detective-magazine.com." The homepage reads:

> Remember those covers of detective magazines long ago of women tightly bound and gagged in inescapable rope bondage? Are you tired of that mamby-pamby posed bondage of today where the bondage is nice and neat and you know the models are only doing it for the money?
>
> I am.
>
> I long for those beautiful women of the '40s through the '80s, Serena, Renee Bond, Annie Owens and all the others we grew up with who filled our heads with visions of real women struggling in real bondage.[31]

A bizarre instance of cultural amnesia indeed, for the models were always only "doing it for the money." What was once real, terrifying, gruesome, and graphic crime now seems quaint, dated, and retro-chic. But the legacy of the true-crime magazines lives on in the tabloid television programs and books that now feed the American public's appetite for murder narratives.

chapter two
BOOKS

Writers of book reviews, sixty to eighty times a year, begin their articles with the grave inquiry: Why do people like to read about murder? After a discussion, in language that at least seems to be the result of profound thought, they come to the conclusion that people like to read such books because they like to do so.

—Edmund L. Pearson, 1928

The truth is that great novels are often inartistic compared with the great works that retell great crimes.

—Jacques Barzun, in Albert Borowitz's *Blood and Ink: An International Guide to Fact-Based Crime Literature*

One thing you don't read true crime for is the truth.

—Marilyn Stasio, *New York Times Book Review*, October 1991

In one of its most popular and widely known forms, true crime is a literary genre. Thick, colorful paperback true-crime volumes—with the requisite "16 pages of shocking photos!"—are typically found in such places as airport magazine and bookshops, but also on the shelves of respectable middlebrow booksellers such as Borders and Barnes and Noble. Literary true crime as a distinct genre has deep rhetorical and stylistic roots in the prose of the true-crime magazines, with some significant differences. Because of space and time limitations, the magazine writers had fewer opportunities to immerse themselves in a case or see it through the trial and execution stages. The book authors had the time to form a relationship with the killer, a crucial evolution that marked the emergence of the true-crime style in book form. In true-crime books, killers were given lengthy biographies, with an exploration of psychopathology and personal history that the public first responded to and eventually came to demand. Building on the success of the magazines, true crime as a literary formula found early expression in some 1950s texts, sprang seemingly *sui generis* from the pen of Truman Capote in 1965, and came into full flower during the 1970s and 1980s. Although murder narratives and nonfiction crime writing have a history that spans centuries, modern American true-crime writing began in the 1950s, as a new way of narrating and understanding murder—one more sensitive to context, more psychologically sophisticated, more willing to make forays into emotional identification with killers through novelistic techniques— emerged. Although formulaic and often devalued as pulp, true-crime literature does valuable cultural work, as it contains multiple and (often) contradictory messages about violence, gender, and fear in American life.

True crime has become a pop culture juggernaut in publishing and a cultural barometer that registers shifting fears about crime and violence in America. From its inception and formation as a distinct genre, true-crime literature has created a nonfiction American landscape of paranoia and danger, random violent crime and roaming serial killers, of mortal threats to women and children from sociopathic husbands, serial rapists, and predatory child-killers. Paradoxically, the genre also assuages such fears, because most true-crime narratives present cases that have been cleared or solved, thereby reordering the violently disrupted social world and reassuring readers that horrifying criminals do not escape punishment, although normal life is regularly and radically altered by acts of extreme violence. True-crime books remain intensely popular, although sales have fallen off somewhat since a high point in the late-1980s, perhaps a result of the prevalence of true-crime television programs and the easy availability of quality true-crime material on the Internet.

The formula for modern American true-crime texts is characterized by a set of technical and thematic conventions that became standardized during the 1970s and 1980s. Such conventions include a depiction of one crime or criminal; preoccupation with certain kinds of crimes—domestic, sadistic, or sexual murders, serial killings, or the crimes of the rich and famous are overrepresented in the genre; a narrative focus on the personal history and psychology of the murderer; a simultaneous distancing from and identification with the killer; depiction of the social contexts and ordinary life details of both victims and killers; the skillful deployment of fiction masquerading as fact (most often used as dialogue or the imagined thoughts of characters related in the narrator's voice, known in literary study as "free indirect discourse"); a writer who is positioned as an "insider" on the events, someone privy to special information about the case and willing to form a relationship with the killer; a middle photographic section; and a four-part structure of events: murder/background/trial/execution or imprisonment, although some texts narrate unsolved crimes.

The single most important narrative innovation in modern true crime has been the prominence and portrayal of the writer/killer relationship. The defining texts within the genre—Truman Capote's *In Cold Blood* (1965–1966), Joseph Wambaugh's *The Onion Field* (1973), Vincent Bugliosi's *Helter Skelter* (1974), Norman Mailer's *The Executioner's Song* (1979), Ann Rule's *The Stranger Beside Me* (1980), and Joe McGinniss' *Fatal Vision* (1983)—each embody and portray an intense and intricate relationship between the writer and the killer. These relationships interrogate different kinds of alignment to killers, whether of love and regard, professional and career-making interaction, of mutual financial benefit, or betrayal of trust. Although the genre is a formula, it is also flexible, for the best true crime engages with questions about the motivation of murderers and our queasy interest in them by presenting differing types of identification with the killer.

SOCIAL CONTEXTS

Formulaic genres, such as true crime, which follow specific rules and conventions and treat specific subject matter in definable ways, both reflect and define some of the beliefs about that subject matter held by many of its readers. In other words, when dealing with popular literary formulas, there is a relationship between the conventions of the formula and the expectations, desires, and beliefs of its audience. True crime follows certain rules because the 1960s and 1970s reading public responded favorably to the depictions of crime and criminals in its pages, and the literary genre developed along lines first staked out during its formative period. The murderer in true crime is often depicted as a stranger to his victims, a loner (or a pair of loners), a person from an abusive or violent background, alienated from most normal social ties such as friends and family, and most fundamentally, as a person lacking a conscience. In the domestic murder scenario that was a later development within the genre, the killer is controlling, jealous, avaricious, and sociopathic. Each of these features correlates to some element in the larger culture that caused anxiety or distress, and the killer in true crime became the receptacle for both real and imagined American fears.

Real fears were exploited and exaggerated in the pages of true crime. One undeniably real trend was an escalating murder rate. Since 1931, the FBI has compiled yearly statistics about crime in the United States. These statistics, known as the Uniform Crime Reports, are gleaned from state and countrywide police agency reports about all known crimes. Uniform Crime Reports are published yearly by the FBI, and they record the actual numbers of homicides committed in a given year, as well as details about the race and gender of victims and killers, relationships between the two, the circumstances of the crime, the kinds of weapons or means used in homicides, and the clearance rate, or how many murders are solved by arrest. Further extrapolations produce the murder rate, or the number of homicides committed per 100,000 citizens per year.

In the 1960s, after a long downward trend, the murder rate underwent a dramatic upward surge. Roger Lane, in his book entitled *Murder in America: A History*, writes that

> As television replaced newsprint as the major source of information, new and heinous kinds of murder, including assassinations and killings for ideological reasons far more complex than those of the Civil War era, were publicized more graphically than any before. The result was to lift questions involving the causes of criminal violence and the effectiveness of legal procedures out of scholarly journals and the several states into national politics and the public arena.[1]

In the decade between 1964 and 1974, the American murder rate doubled, from 5.1 to 9.8 homicides per 100,000 people per year. During this same period of time, Lane says that issues of criminal violence and justice found their way into the "public arena," an arena that includes and is informed by the genre of true crime. True crime rapidly evolved into a public and accessible way to manage fears of violent crime, for as murder rates rose, the genre expanded in tandem, and more killers were metaphorically caught and punished in its pages.

Another significant change occurred not just in the dramatic upswing in the murder rate, but in the types of homicides being committed. In the 1960s, stranger-killings—that is, homicide between two persons unknown to each other—became much more statistically significant. Equally important, the clearance rate for murder was dropping; in the 1950s, the clearance rate for homicide was about 90 percent. In 1974, it was 80 percent, and it's been dropping steadily ever since. These two changes are related, for stranger-killings are much more difficult to solve than homicide between relatives or friends; as the rate of stranger-killings rises, the clearance rate drops. A rising murder rate, an increase in the number of stranger-killings, and a corollary increase in the number of unsolved homicides all registered in true-crime narratives as an emphasis on the unknown, unknowable, morally incomprehensible psychotic killer. There was a huge difference in the types of real crimes being committed in 1960s America, a change that would be explored—and exploited by—true crime.[2]

During the period when true-crime books established a standardized formula (the 1970s and 1980s), there was a dawning recognition first of the rise in violent crime, specifically random-seeming sexual or sadistic crimes against women, and then a secondary recognition that punishments for such crimes weren't nearly severe enough. A response to these two facts came in two forms: the formation of the literary genre, which both expressed and managed fears about violent crime, and real, rapid, drastic change in sentencing guidelines and criminal justice procedures. During the 1960s a series of rulings by the liberal Warren court brought about an unprecedented focus on the rights of defendants and suspects in criminal cases. The *Gideon v. Wainwright* (1963), *Escobedo v. Illinois* (1964), and *Miranda v. Arizona* (1966) rulings said that all defendants had the right to a court-appointed attorney; that confessions gained by bullying or brutalizing suspects could not be used in court; and that suspects' rights must be protected while in police custody. In 1972, *Furman v. Georgia* declared the death penalty, as it was then administered, unconstitutional, a ruling that was reversed in 1976 with *Gregg v. Georgia*. *Time* magazine, in a July 1965 article, declared that the Warren Court had "done more than any other in U.S. history to bolster the rights of the individual against 'ignoble' government power. In so doing, the court in recent years has wrought a revolution in criminal justice."[3] This "revolution" also wrought a perception that the system was letting hardened, dangerous criminals literally get away with murder.

The kinds of killers treated in true-crime books changed during the 1960s, largely due to the change in the most sensationally gruesome crimes being committed, and the growth of a large media-machinery that could hype and inflame fears about such crimes. Fears about marauding "bushy-haired strangers" (the term used by Dr. Sam Shepard—accused wife-killer made famous through the television series "The Fugitive"—to describe the alleged killer of his wife in 1955), "lust-killers" such as Albert DeSalvo (the Boston Strangler, 1962–1964), and Richard Speck (the Chicago nurse-killer, 1966), and mass killers like Charles Whitman (the University of Texas tower sniper, 1966), were increased by heavy media coverage of these crimes. At the same time, there was a growing fascination with the killer who had an inconspicuous and impeccably "normal" façade. One of the most popular framing devices for killers in true crime would be that of highlighting the seeming normalcy of the killer, and then trying to uncover and understand the monstrously aberrant personality that lurked just beneath the surface. In this way, killers came to be framed as both hideously outside the boundaries of normal humanity, yet pretending to respect and abide by those same boundaries. The shift in the narrative construction of killers was undoubtedly influenced by changing categories of mental disturbance within the discipline of psychiatry, fueled by such books as Hervey M. Cleckley's *The Mask of Sanity: An Attempt to Clarify Some Issues about the So-Called Psychopathic Personality*, as the psychopath quickly became a fixture in true crime.

One aspect of the true-crime book phenomenon that is difficult to trace in any detail is the demographic contours of the genre's audience or readership, particularly during its formative years. At present, true crime is a female genre—it attracts more women readers and fans of particular writers and types of true crime, although women comprise 60 percent of readers of all genres combined. The evidence of readership is anecdotal because tracking gender (or race, or any other demographic category) for book sales or library borrowing trends with accuracy is challenging. True-crime authors know that women comprise the majority of fan-letter writers and attendees at book signings, and evidence from Internet true-crime fan sites and Web logs with comment functions bolsters the theory that the genre has a largely female readership. But there is much that remains unknown and unexplored about who reads true crime, and how the readership understands the genre. Do women and men read the genre differently? Are there ethical problems, as some critics suggest, with the power true crime has to titillate or give information that can be used in other crimes, particularly when it narrates sexual crimes against children? Have there been demographic changes in the readership since its beginnings in the 1970s, and why? Is true crime popular with African American, Asian, or Hispanic readers, and how does its emphasis on murder as a white phenomenon inflect its reception among those readers? Are there any meaningful differences among true-crime readers and viewers, or does the genre maintain its appeal in various mediums to the same people? These questions, among many others, could best be examined through a large-scale ethnographic study, along the lines of Janice Radway's work on the romance genre in her book, *Reading the Romance: Women, Patriarchy, and Popular Literature* (1984), which takes ordinary readers' experiences of and interactions with texts seriously.

THE BOOKS: TRUE-CRIME PREDECESSORS

One of the early twentieth-century writers whose work forms a bridge between the nineteenth century gothic or scientific sensibility in murder narration and the modern true-crime style is Edmund Lester Pearson, who wrote "fact-crime" stories prolifically between 1924 and 1936. Pearson was a librarian, court reporter, journalist, and essayist, and he published countless articles and six books about both contemporary and older British and American murder cases. Pearson's work is significant within the genre for his total elimination of gothic horror conventions and sentimentality and the introduction of irony into the American murder narrative. With his detached, cool, urbane tone, Mencken-esque attacks on the follies and foibles of modern man, his witticisms and snide remarks about the failings of American jurisprudence, and his selection of cases—he was particularly enamored of the Lizzie Borden case, returning to it again and again throughout his true-crime career—Pearson crafted a new response to murder. In his major collections, *Studies in Murder* (1924) and *More Studies in Murder* (1936), Pearson does to death any notion of murder as isolated, romanticized gothic evil, instead offering a cynical view of homicide as a snappy and efficient way to solve a problem, eliminate a domestic difficulty, or elevate one's position in the world. For him, the story of murder always rested within a social context, and he was one of the first major crime writers to draw details about homicide at a level that twenty-first century readers would recognize. At the same time, Pearson never loses his grip on a strong moralism that guided his depictions and prevents his work from sliding into the queasy and sordid glorification of murderers through an awed emphasis on their personalities. Pearson, in the words of scholar Roger Lane, "anticipated Truman Capote and Norman Mailer in bringing a touch of class to a form that needed it."[4]

Trained as a librarian, Pearson's true calling was writing, and he published several books on various subjects before turning to crime writing. As editor of publications for the New York Public Library, he wrote for *The New Yorker* and *Vanity Fair*, but his most popular works were his murder stories: *Studies in Murder* (1924), *Murder at Smutty Nose* (1927), *Five Murders, and a Final Note on the Borden Case* (1928), *Instigation of the Devil* (1930), *More Studies in Murder* (1936), and *The Trial of Lizzie Borden* (1937), nearly all of which were collections of previously published articles. Out of print from his untimely death in 1937 until the early 1960s, Pearson's popularity during his own time ended as his style passed out of favor: notably elitist, a vigorous proponent of the death penalty, and deeply opinionated, his writing style quickly became dated within the context of American progressivism, the Great Depression, and (later) World War II. He eschewed any forgiveness for killers at a time when increasingly loud public voices called for critical reforms of the criminal justice system, more emphasis on rehabilitation for convicts, and a greater elasticity in understanding psychological motivation and personal responsibility for crime. Referring to the nineteenth-century Constance Kent case, wherein a woman killed her half-brother and confessed five years later after a religious conversion, Pearson articulates his disdain for modern tendencies to soften responsibility and take the killer's contexts into account when he writes that "even then there was no whining plea for mercy in the name of Freud and Nietzsche and the distorted psyche. Modernism likes to dance but not to pay—it prefers to hire an alienist to help cheat the piper of his fee."[5] Pearson was as unmerciful to his murderers as to his contemporaries who felt that advances in the understanding of human psychology should mediate the simpler, more old-fashioned eye-for-an-eye approach to criminal justice.

Chief among Pearson's virtues was his talent for drawing engaging depictions of contexts, attendants, auxiliaries, precedents, and antecedents to the crimes he wrote about. His accounts were full of details, comparisons with earlier cases, observations about the character and personality of his subjects, and a careful attention to the humdrum and more mundane aspects of any murder event. His powers of observation and his writing abilities were great, shown in this passage from the 1924 "Borden Case," where he describes Lizzie Borden's uncle, John Vinnicum Morse, returning to the murder house on the morning of the crimes, before he is aware of what has taken place:

> He went through the side yard, to the rear of the house, picked up two or three pears, and began to eat them. Pears enter this case more than once, and to all who are familiar with the region and the time of year, they suggest the atmosphere of an old New England garden in August. Perhaps Mr. Morse, as he thought of dinner, foresaw a recurrence of the mutton-soup and was fortifying himself against the blow, but in any event we should not begrudge him his pears, nor the two or three peaceful moments he spent with them, before he went into the house. It was to be a long time before he was to know peace again, or go mooning about Fall River and its vicinity upon his innocent errands.[6]

These four sentences do much work: they both describe and create a moment and a mood, while bringing the reader face to face with the juxtaposition of the mundane and the horrible, always a fascinating feature in the murder narrative. The use of "we" in the third sentence forces the reader to observe the "scene" right along with Pearson, forging an amiable intimacy with the writer. We are there with Pearson the expert, watching the unfortunate actor in this play imbibe his last innocent pleasure, as the dramaturge bestows a wonderfully light touch of dramatic irony on this peaceful domestic scene; not until Capote would there be as much art put into such a description.

For Pearson, the Lizzie Borden case was something of an obsession; it was, after all, the "O. J. case" of its time, complete with a hideous and bloody crime (two elderly people hacked to death with an axe in their home), purely circumstantial evidence brought out at trial, and an obvious killer who was acquitted amid swirling controversy and public opinion, which held that no woman was capable of producing such bloodshed—at least, no woman of Borden's upper-middle-class stature and standing in her community. This crime brought together many of the themes that Pearson explored in his writing, and which absolutely fascinated his readers: murder in the domestic sphere, committed by a woman of blameless character and for financial gain. Pearson strongly believed that Borden was guilty—he wrote that the acquittal was a "vile miscarriage of justice, brought about by a biased court and maudlin public sentiment"—and continued to mull over the case, in print, for years.[7] The case and his writing about it defined Pearson's career in much the same way that in the 1980s, the Ted Bundy case would both begin and shape the career of another powerhouse of true-crime writing, Ann Rule. The oddities of the case allowed Pearson to expound at great length about his countrymen's erroneous and dangerous beliefs that "murderesses," if unfortunate enough to be brought to trial at all, should be handled with kid gloves and nearly always acquitted because of the delicacy of their sex.

Part of this phenomenon was a clear expression of the notion (held by men and women alike) that good-looking, well-bred young women were simply incapable of bloody or depraved acts of violence. Many critics and writers have argued that misguided belief as the single most important reason why Lizzie Borden was acquitted—her jury, middle-aged men from small communities in Massachusetts, could not believe that Sunday-school-teacher Borden committed such an atrocious act. Well-bred women from "good" families were imagined as supremely delicate, liable to faint at the sight, or even the mere mention, of blood or violence. Astute critics of the day saw this belief for what it was, evidence not of regard for sensitive humanity, but of a dismissal of women and contempt for their perceived weakness. Journalist Winifred Black, also known as Annie Laurie, articulated and condemned the prevailing view most eloquently when she wrote that "The man who votes to acquit a woman of murder when he knows that she is a murderess, is usually the sort of man who has deep down in his heart an absolute contempt for women. He thinks of them as little, foolish, emotional, impulsive creatures who can't control themselves anyhow."[8] Interestingly, the view that certain kinds of women—young, beautiful, delicate—were incapable of committing homicide would remain popular for some time, finally being put to rest (with some struggle) many years later in the *Helter Skelter* murder case.

Pearson's work anticipated many later developments in true crime, most notably the reintroduction of a humorous or ironic sensibility about murder that is seen in such television programs as *Till Death Do Us Part*, narrated sardonically by John Waters, and Showtime's *Dexter*, a stylish "serial killer chic" narrative that sympathizes openly with an obscenely violent killer. From the Pearson period until the 1950s, literary true crime consisted of warmed-over collections of old and tired cases, and murder narration outside of the magazines stagnated. In general, 1950s' murder narratives tended toward sensationalism and simply drawn portraits of both the killer and the circumstances of murder, but in some, the percolation of forces and the creation of new techniques of representation that would become hallmarks of 1960s true crime are evident.

Joel Bartlow Martin's 1952 *Why Did They Kill?* attempts to explain the random killing of a nurse by three juvenile delinquents in Ann Arbor, Michigan, in 1951. The structure and focus of this text are crucial for the genre, for it begins with the murder and unfolds by narrating the childhoods of the killers and by exploring the psychosocial forces that shaped their personalities, a format that writers would begin to imitate regularly in the 1970s. The context within which murder occurs is drawn in great detail by focusing on the killers, and the story of murder becomes the story of how killers are made. In the epilogue to *Why Did They Kill?* Martin refers to another of these characteristics in a statement about the type of nonfiction crime writing that he practiced, and that was beginning to emerge as typical:

> Some years back I got the idea that most crime writing of the traditional sort seemed to assume that crime happened in a vacuum. It seemed to me that crimes don't just happen by blind chance—that something causes them. Sometimes the matrix is social, sometimes psychological, most often both. Writing about an individual criminal case, then, offers also an opportunity to write about a whole society: Crime-in-context.[9]

The notion of murder narration as "crime-in-context" is one of the defining characteristics of true crime, and was clearly becoming an important goal for nonfiction crime writers during this period. True crime does much more than simply sketch out the gruesome details of an act of murder—it contextualizes the crime by drawing a "thick description" of the conditions leading up to it.

Lucy Freeman's 1955 *"Before I Kill More..."* narrates the infamous Chicago "lipstick killer," seventeen-year-old William George Heirens, who killed two women and one young girl between June 1945 and January 1946; he was caught and his confession, induced by sodium pentothal, led to life imprisonment. Freeman was an amateur psychoanalyst as well as a journalist, and her text is one of the first instances in nonfiction murder narration of the use of Freudian depth psychology to understand a murderer. Freeman took the title of her book from the note that Heirens scrawled in lipstick on the wall of his second victim's apartment, which read "For heavens sake catch me before I kill more I cannot control myself." *"Before I Kill More..."* is an interesting hybrid of novelistic techniques, contextualization of the murders, psychological study of the murderer, and additional documentary materials, including a transcript of Heirens' full confession, a photograph of the lipstick-scrawled note on the wall, photos of the detectives who apprehended him, Heirens' childhood home, and even a shot of Freeman interviewing Heirens. These elements show an emerging documentary impulse, and they support Freeman's psychoanalytic approach to her subject. Including photographs and evidentiary documents allows Freeman to frame the killer within a subtle and more psychologically sophisticated understanding of madness, for the reader gets to see how essentially "normal-looking" Heirens is, while also viewing his unconscious handiwork in the form of his scrawled plea for help. In Freeman's text, Heirens is portrayed as a mentally ill individual, and the horror of his crimes is subsumed by the representation of the new concept of psychopathy.

This perspective contains within it an understanding of the killer as a sick and troubled person, but a person nonetheless. Throughout the text, Heirens is variously categorized by law enforcement personnel, psychiatrists, and Freeman herself as "emotionally insensitive within," "put together wrong," a "disassociated psychotic schizophrenic," and a "sane psycho."[10] One element of his insanity is noteworthy—for it would have huge implications for true crime—Heirens is characterized as lacking a conscience, that intrinsic ability to empathize with others and feel the wrongness of his crimes. Heirens is questioned by the police about his actions and thoughts in the aftermath of the murders, and they ask him, "How did you feel when you read about it?" [in the papers] Heirens replies "Just like anything else in the paper. It did not bother me." The policeman asks, "Feel any remorse?" and Heirens answers "No." When asked about the murder of the six-year-old girl, Heirens reports that he felt "Nothing at all."[11]

Bill Heirens exhibits the symptoms of what we now recognize as sociopathy, the inability to feel remorse or regret about hurting others. Heirens feels sad and sorry for himself, but not for the people he has so profoundly hurt. Freeman does not dwell on Heirens' lack of conscience, but she writes extensively about his ability, honed since childhood, to repress his own feelings. But instead of characterizing Heirens' lack of feeling as super- or nonhuman, Freeman suggests that this ability is born out of his own pain: "he buried his feelings so no one could know of the resentment unless they penetrated the mask or Bill decided to cast it off for the moment. Those who glimpsed the fury underneath were not allowed to live."[12] Detached from the horror that his pain brought into the world in the form of his ghastly deeds—Heirens dismembered the six-year-old girl's corpse and threw the parts in various sewer grates—Freeman represents Heirens as a frightened child, wracked with psychological anguish and unable to control himself.

Certain time periods are preoccupied with certain types of crimes and killers, and the 1950s was the era of the teenaged "thrill-killer." Martin, Freeman, and Meyer Levin, whose 1956 *Compulsion* narrated the infamous 1924 Leopold and Loeb case, all chose to write about teenaged killers. The crimes treated in these three texts were each stunningly random and meaningless, and were aptly called "thrill-killings," a term that magnified public fears of a generation of depraved youngsters who found pleasure in homicidal destruction. Murder narratives from the 1950s to 1960s would also often focus on two or more killers, enabling the writers to explore from different perspectives the impulse to kill, and simultaneously to suggest more than one way to view a killer. Highlighting pairs or groups of killers also kindled paranoia and panic about groups of teenagers, increasing generational anxiety. The fuller depiction of social contexts, including a more thorough treatment of individual experience, psychology, and daily life, also began to find its way into true crime during the 1950s, as the multilayered, multivalent nature of the true-crime text evolved.

In the 1950s, single case studies of relatively unknown and obscure crimes would begin to appear, such as *Why Did They Kill*, and by the 1960s, such cases would make up the bulk of murder narratives. Of course, sensational crimes would always warrant narrative treatment, and perhaps the most sensational of the period was the assassination of President John F. Kennedy in 1963. The narrative result of that crime, *The Warren Commission Report*, would become one of the best-known murder narratives of all time, as well as one of the most disputed, most rewritten, and most exhaustive. Certainly, the research, depth of detail and structural arrangement of *The Warren Report* reinforced the notion that entire texts could be devoted, very successfully, to a single crime. The combination of these forces culminated in 1966 with the publication of *In Cold Blood* and the lesser-known *The Boston Strangler*.

Truman Capote and *In Cold Blood*

Most scholars and readers consider Truman Capote's *In Cold Blood* (1966) to be the first modern true-crime text, for it brought together the themes and structures that would create the template for the genre that persists to this day. By 1959, Capote was a successful published author of such books as *Other Voices, Other Rooms, Tree of Night and Other Stories, The Grass Harp, The Muses Are Heard*, and *Breakfast at Tiffany's*. As told in two recent films about his life and the events that led to his writing *In Cold Blood* (*Capote*, dir. Bennett Miller, 2005, and *Infamous*, dir. Douglas McGrath, 2006) Capote had been interested in writing nonfiction for many years, and in 1959 he found a suitable topic for a "non-fiction novel" in the rural Kansas shotgun murder of four members of the Clutter family in an apparent botched robbery. Richard Eugene Hickock and Perry Smith were arrested in Las Vegas on January 2, 1960, for the Clutter murders, and they were executed on April 14, 1965. For most of those five intervening years, Capote exchanged letters with the prisoners twice a week, and he lived in Garden City for extended periods of time, becoming close not just to the murderers, but also the detectives involved in the case. The result of all that work was published in *The New Yorker* in four installments in September–October 1965, and published in book form in January 1966. In 1967 the book was made into a film, also a spectacular success, starring the then-unknown Robert Blake as Perry Smith (*In Cold Blood*, dir. Richard Brooks, 1967).

Although it is true that other true-crime texts were published in the 1960s, none of them has generated the lasting literary and popular interest of *In Cold Blood*. Capote brought together and perfected the nascent conventions of what would become true crime, and his basic formula has been copied ever since, to a greater or lesser degree. Such techniques include the shaping of real people into literary characters and the introduction of fiction-writing techniques into nonfiction writing, interweaving the actions of the killers and the victims by juxtaposing and "cross-cutting" scenes, the theme that random violence can easily destroy idyllic American lives, and the representation of the "normal-seeming" killer or sleeper sociopath.

During the five years spent working on the book, Capote became an intimate of the killers, thereby gaining special access to their feelings and memories, and specific experiential knowledge of the judiciary procedures that would become a large part of true-crime narratives. The 1960s and 1970s true crime spent more time narrating the aftermath of murder, not the crime itself, as trials became lengthier, debates about the legality and morality of the death penalty raged, and death-penalty appeals dragged out over years. Because Smith and Hickock were captured quickly, and because they were involved in appealing their sentences for nearly five years, Capote was put in the unique position of having to wait for them to die in order to finish his book, while growing closer to them personally during that time. Capote became very close to Perry Smith; he was also convinced that Smith had killed all four of the Clutters. The simultaneous evocation of compassion for the murderer and horror at his deeds makes *In Cold Blood* a new form of murder narration.

Capote's narrative treatment of his subject would draw the reader into an uneasy and unprecedented relationship with the killers, creating a sense of simultaneous identification and distance between reader and killer. When consuming true crime, the reader experiences the disparity of closeness to the person and distance from the horror of his acts; the writer knows that this tension offers a vicarious thrill, a jolt of fear, and a comforting reassurance that the killer is contained. Perry Smith's most famous statement about Herb Clutter, "I thought he was a very nice gentleman. Soft-spoken. I thought so right up to the moment I cut his throat," was emblematic of the organization of his entire personality: sweet, suave, and fascinatingly fatal.[13] Capote crafted his narrative so that the reader shares his fascination with Smith, who was at once a devious and dangerous loner and a sensitive, wounded man. The ambiguity and intensity of the reader/killer relationship allows the writer to interrogate notions of good and evil, self and other, in his text that writers of previous murder narratives did not and could not do. Capote's closeness to the subjects of his book would set the standard for a different degree of involvement between writer and subject, and would forever change the nature of murder narratives.

Another trope of true crime, the shaping of real people into literary characters and the introduction of fiction-writing techniques into nonfiction writing, is directly attributable to Capote's closeness to Smith and Hickock. Capote was able to use free indirect discourse, which interjects objectivity and intimacy with the subjects, because he knew what the men's most intimate thoughts and feelings were. Another genre-setter was the familiar four-part structure of crime-pursuit-trial-execution, which gives true crime the shape of a classic detective tale; that is, the murders occur in the first chapter, but we don't understand the killers' motives until the third and last chapters. One of the most striking aspects of *In Cold Blood*, and one that would become a major convention in true crime, is the way that Capote structured the sections of each chapter so that the actions of the killers and the victims are interwoven. Particularly in the first chapter, Capote cuts back and forth between scenes that feature either the Clutters or Smith and Hickock, in a technique borrowed from filmmaking. In fact, the book is strangely more filmic than the movie—there seem to be more cuts back and forth between the Clutters and their killers in the book, whereas the movie concentrates more heavily on Dick and Perry.

The puzzle and threat of random violence is one of the defining tropes of true crime, and that theme is important in *In Cold Blood*. The genre always sets "innocence" against "evil," and this convention, combined with the filmic technique of intercutting scenes of victims and killers, suggests the inevitability of violence and the futility of acting against it. The action seems fated, and murder seems destined to occur; the Clutters cannot escape their fate, and Smith and Hickock cannot resist forming their ill-conceived alliance that will ultimately lead them to their deaths as well. This is one of the major themes of true crime, and it is reinforced, of course, by the subject matter—always, when a true-crime book is written, a murder has *already* occurred, and it will occur again within the book. The reader enters a true-crime text knowing the outcome, so that the genre reinforces, and does not allay, the fears and anxieties that knowledge of the presence of brutality engenders. There is no social reform impulse in true crime, just a vast, sometimes sordid and graphic demonstration of the inexorability of evil.

In Cold Blood offers two competing views about what a killer is and about what evil looks like. Richard Hickock is vulgar, ugly, brutal, and shallow; he looks like a murderer, and he wants to rape fifteen-year-old Nancy Clutter before killing her. Perry Smith is sensitive, handsome, artistic, a dreamer; sickened by Hickock's lust, he prevents the rape. Hickock as killer is ultimately less disturbing and threatening—even though, ironically, he plans the crime—because it is clear from the outset that he is capable of violence. He is conventionally frightening, and he is an older representation of what a murderer looks and acts like. Smith, on the other hand, is a more fundamentally disturbing character because he *seems* like a good and harmless soul, even though he agrees to go along with Hickock and rob the Clutters. He tries to stall Hickock on the night of the murders, he gets sick in the gas station restroom, and he almost loses his nerve as they drive up the Clutter's driveway. Smith *can't* go through with it, the reader thinks, and he won't let it happen. But it is Perry Smith who ends up killing all the Clutters, and the revelation of his hidden self is stunning.

Capote reverses the reader's expectations by portraying his most deadly killer as the seemingly kind one, and the one who seemed most threatening and violent as essentially innocent. It is important to remember that these are Capote's designations: in the real case, Smith only confessed to killing all the Clutters as a kind of favor for Hickock, so Dick's parents wouldn't have to live with the idea that their son was a murderer (Smith was estranged from his family). Alvin Dewey, one of the principal detectives on the case, never thought that Smith had killed all four Clutters; he believed that Hickock murdered Nancy Clutter and her mother. Capote shapes his story so that what *seems* most true is that Smith killed them all, for his categorization of Smith and Hickock as two types of killers is a construct that offers a suitably complicated view of murder. But it is a construct that resonated with his readers because it articulated an idea of evil as being hidden, insidious, and mysterious; the killer was becoming a literary character, a complex and masked figure, not the simply conceived and emotionally distant dark figure of some earlier depictions. Contextualizing the crime and exploring the killer's life and psychological makeup in great depth, while allowing the reader to "know" the killer, paradoxically strengthened the emotional distance from the killer.

Capote's use of omniscient narration, another of his innovations, frees the reader to more completely identify with the protagonists. The reader's sense of identification with the killers in true crime is strengthened by the various narrative techniques used, and because the writer doesn't appear in the text. The bonds of sympathy between writer/reader/killer are enhanced when the writer is invisible, because the reader is free to imagine that he is interviewing the killers, asking the questions, that he is inside the killer's head. Just as the writer was becoming more closely identified with his subject, he was becoming more confidante and confessor than reporter, so the reader was able to become closer to the killer. The writer attains credibility not by showing himself with the killer, interviewing and shaping the narrative, but because the reader is allowed more intimate and immediate access to the story. The reader can feel himself interviewing the killer, viewing the action, almost becoming a part of the story. Detached narration also imbues true crime with a sense of timelessness, because events are fixed in the everhappening present moment. Without a strong authorial presence, time and chronology are more fluid and the reader gains an immediacy of experience of the events. The strong reader identification with murderers in true crime is crucial to the new mode of representation that Capote introduced. The detached omniscient style of narration has become one hallmark of true crime, and it became one of the most copied effects in 1970s murder narratives.

The early critical responses to the book were largely positive, as was the popular reception. *In Cold Blood* was an instant bestseller. The novel was published almost simultaneously with an interview in *The New York Times Book Review* in which Capote speaks about his creation of a new literary formula, the "nonfiction novel."[14] Capote really gave the critics something to chew on, for in addition to the book itself being widely acclaimed and worthy of thoughtful criticism, his grand statements about genre creation were taken as a ready-made challenge. Critics argued about the relative merits of this new genre—was it a new genre or simply a rehashing of an old form? Was the novel a "dead" form?—and debates raged about the defining characteristics of fiction and nonfiction, novel and documentary. As a result, many focused in particular on Capote's claims to truthfulness or factuality. Capote himself touted his strict factual accuracy as one of the chief virtues of his book; however, he never denied that he shaped his material. Such debates about strict factual accuracy swirled around early true-crime books, but have lost relevance in the contemporary genre, which assumes authorial power to shape, and sometimes shift, the facts to suit narrative ends.

The Boston Strangler

The Clutter murders, although hideous, pale in comparison to the bloody work of Albert DeSalvo, otherwise known as the Boston Strangler. From June of 1962 until January of 1964, DeSalvo murdered thirteen women in the Boston area; his usual mode of operation was strangulation and sexual assault.[15] In 1966, the same year that saw the publication of *In Cold Blood*, a journalist named Gerold Frank published *The Boston Strangler*, a book about the DeSalvo crimes. Frank's book was well received and was a popular success, winning the 1967 Edgar Award for best "Fact Crime" book; however, *The Boston Strangler* is currently out of print, and it languishes in the twilight world of a now-forgotten sensation, while *In Cold Blood* has been reprinted continually since its publication (and has recently reappeared on *The New York Times* bestseller list).[16] This is both an indication of the significance and lasting relevance of *In Cold Blood*, and of the fleeting popular interest in the real crimes of the Boston Strangler. Capote's literary talent, of course, accounts for some of the success of his book, for he turned plain facts into gripping suspense and pathetic losers into dynamic characters; Gerold Frank was a newspaper journalist, and his portrayal of DeSalvo lacked this power. Most importantly, Frank did not form a friendship with Albert DeSalvo, and his book is weak and uninteresting when compared to the richness of identification and intensity of feeling presented in Capote's.

Just as importantly, *In Cold Blood* remained popular because with it, Capote introduced a new way of narrating and understanding murder.

Frank didn't organize his material or portray the killer in the complex and new ways that Capote did, even though he had the same material as Capote, culturally speaking, to draw on. Working out of the same mid-1960s intellectual, literary, and pop culture climate, Frank did not produce the same innovation in the techniques of murder narration. *The Boston Strangler* doesn't present a new perspective on murder or a different construction of the killer—instead, it offers a picture of the serial killer Albert DeSalvo as a distant, impossibly twisted moral outsider, a fundamentally demented and ultimately mysterious subject. This was the standard 1950s representation of the killer, less intricately drawn, and less responsive to a shifting popular understanding of the epistemology of evil. Although it did introduce a compelling contextualization of the crimes, Frank's book is like a much-lengthened story that would appear in *True Detective*: thorough, but without depth. For this reason, *The Boston Strangler* is a near miss in terms of genre-formation, and it lacks the genre-setting power of *In Cold Blood*.

The 1970s—Formative Years

During the 1970s, certain themes, types of killers, and modes of representation became most prominent within the emerging genre, with the serial and sex killer and feminized victims—women, children, and homosexuals—garnering the greatest interest. The genre was not dominated by any single author, but it was dominated by male writers. Typical examples include William A. Clark's *The Girl on the Volkswagen Floor* (1971), an unsolved murder narrative largely concerned with psychics assisting the police, and John Gurwell's *Mass Murder in Houston* (1974), a small press publication about the Dean Corll homosexual killings of twenty-seven teenaged boys in Houston. Edward Keyes' *The Michigan Murders* (1976) is an early serial killer treatment that wonderfully evokes the culture of a large university community in the late 1960s. *Charlie Simpson's Apocalypse* (1974) is a berserk-Vietnam-vet tale with political and sociological undertones, a miniature *Helter Skelter*. These texts present victims-as-objects, with details about the discovery of fatally wounded bodies, graphic accounts of violence, and means of death taking hideous precedence. Apprehension and description of the psychopathology of the perpetrator is of secondary concern, and in Clark's book, the killer is never caught. Taking a cue from successful articles in the true-crime magazines, forensic science and descriptions of police work also gained prominence within the genre during this period, and the trope of the strong male detective force battling other, deviant men to avenge female victims became commonplace.

In the 1970s, the writer of best-selling true crime would become an agent of law enforcement, evidenced in the work of Joseph Wambaugh and Vincent Bugliosi. From Capote onward, true-crime authors have become involved in their subjects' stories in unprecedented ways: writers have been advocates or adversaries for the killers they have written about (*Fatal Vision, The Defense Never Rests*), they have helped law enforcement agents gather evidence (*The Stranger Beside Me, Murder in Greenwich*), they have acted as confessors (*Dead Man Walking*), befriended and rallied public support for convicted killers (*Dr. Sam—An American Tragedy*), and witnessed the execution of their subjects. Wambaugh's *The Onion Field* (1973) shows certain aspects of the maturing genre, including a more complex narrator/insider, with a different relationship to criminals and crime, and the inclusion of more complicated themes such as guilt, retribution, and the psychology of victims as well as killers. As a police officer, Wambaugh had a unique perspective on murder and undeniable credibility as a witness, a participant, and a commentator. *The Onion Field* further demonstrated that popular true crime could be subtle, sophisticated, and terrifically powerful, and that the genre could support the exploration of serious themes, and was able to transcend displays of graphic violence and sensationalism.

Joseph Wambaugh had been a cop in the Los Angeles Police Department for ten years when in 1970 he began writing novels about policemen and the work they do. His first book, *The New Centurions* (1970), received both critical and popular acclaim. This novel is now understood as one of the first in a genre that would become known as the "police procedural," a form of narrative (either fiction or nonfiction), which details the lives and everyday work experiences of law enforcement agents. Wambaugh is the recognized master of this genre, for he almost single-handedly changed literary representations of policemen from unchallenged heroes into fallible human beings, and crime narratives from simplistic representations of good and evil into complex and ambiguous explorations of modern morality.[17] Wambaugh's work would hugely influence television depictions of police, for he created and consulted for *Police Story*, the 1970s television series, which had a profound and lasting impact on televised representations of police and their work. Wambaugh's cops are fallible human beings, not the cool and stolid investigators of gumshoe fiction or film noir. Wambaugh's best-known work includes *The Blue Knight* (1972), *The Onion Field* (1973), and *The Choirboys* (1975).

Wambaugh's most famous work was *The Onion Field* (1973), a true-crime account of the kidnapping of two LAPD patrolmen by two petty crooks in 1963. On a Saturday night in March of that year, officers Ian Campbell and Karl Hettinger, both relatively new to the job, were disarmed at gunpoint and driven to a remote California onion field by Gregory Powell and Jimmy Smith. Powell and Smith murdered Campbell, and Karl Hettinger narrowly escaped the same fate by running for his life through the field to safety. Hettinger returned to police work immediately, and suffered a nervous breakdown as a consequence of the murder of his colleague and the aftermath of the crime, which included the longest criminal trial in California history. An incredible series of appeals and retrials led to several juries overturning death penalty convictions for the murderers, largely as a result of changing laws and the institution of the Miranda Rights ruling in 1966. Wambaugh was an LAPD officer when the onion field crime took place, and his experiences working alongside cops and apprehending criminals shaped his narratives when he began to write.

In *The Onion Field*, Wambaugh reinforced and further developed the changes that were already underway in murder narratives; because of his unique position as an "insider" in the world of policemen and criminals, Wambaugh brought an intensely intimate perspective to bear on true crime. In both his police fiction and *The Onion Field*, Wambaugh would illustrate the notion that cops and murderers are separated by very thin fibers of moral structure, and that "good" and "evil" are almost inextricably interwoven. Wambaugh's suggestion that cops and criminals are similarly human and driven by forces beyond their control leads the reader into both identification with and distancing from both groups. There are no unambiguous heroes in Wambaugh's writing, because his cops are gritty and flawed, his criminals twisted and damaged people. His work is important to the growth of true crime because—like Capote—he invites the reader to experience a simultaneous attraction and repulsion to his "good" and "bad" characters equally. This distancing/identification underlines "evil" as a moral construct, which was in the 1970s crumbling under the mediation of social forces and new understandings of crime and criminality.

The Onion Field is essentially a story about guilt, but not on the part of the murderers. Just one day after the kidnapping and murder of Ian Campbell, his partner, Karl Hettinger, who had himself almost been murdered, returned to the job; the LAPD offered Hettinger no psychological counseling, for at that time the Department did not recognize that suffering such a traumatic event could have any psychological consequences. Wambaugh himself best describes the story:

> From then on, subtly and not so subtly, the police department and his fellow officers made Hettinger feel responsible for the death of his partner, and he began to deteriorate. Hettinger was condemned by his peers who believed—because of some totally absurd police concept of *machismo*—that he didn't do enough to save his partner. The police department, you see, feels that God kills by thunderbolt, and that you don't let some punk disarm you, kidnap you and kill your partner unless you die trying to prevent it.[18]

Hettinger became so consumed by his unacknowledged, unconscious guilt that he began shoplifting; he then became so obsessed with guilt about stealing that he allowed himself to be caught and fired. The text focuses on Hettinger—it begins and ends with his internal monologue, and the narrative follows his psychological condition into and out of his mental breakdown.

The Onion Field marks another important development in true crime–that of the western setting of most (American) texts in the genre. It is certainly true that the American West, and California in particular, was the site of many spectacularly gruesome murders during this period, and those crimes inspired a great number of popular true-crime texts. But the California of the true-crime imagination would greatly outperform the reality in terms of horror and blood, due to its overrepresentation in the ranks of the genre. California became fixed in true crime as the site of outrageous, rapacious, and stunning violence, an image that was helped along by the likes of Charlie Manson and the Zodiac killer. Because of this, a kind of East Coast/West Coast dualism sprang up, with the Eastern literary establishment metaphorically turning up its nose at the violent and unseemly new genre of true crime.[19] There are very few true-crime texts written between 1965 and 1975 that deal with contemporary murders that occurred in the eastern half of the United States. Most true crime followed the geographical contours that began with Capote—the Clutter murders took place in Kansas—and the early genre is composed of accounts of murders from Santa Cruz, California (*Sacrifice Unto Me*, 1974; *The Co-Ed Killer*, 1976); to Arizona (*The Tucson Murders*, 1970; *The Pied Piper of Tucson*, 1967); to Texas (*The Man with the Candy*, 1974; *Mass Murder in Houston*, 1974). This geographical bias is suggestive of true crime's significant investment in fantasy and unreality, particularly because the most violent region of the United States is and always has been the South, not the West. The western states during this period became a locus of the fear and anxiety that found expression in the pages of true-crime books.

Perhaps it was the influence of Hollywood—after all, during the late 1960s and early 1970s, American cinema became more graphically violent, more bloody, and many times more profitable than ever before. The production site of all this consumable violence being the West, and Hollywood in particular, associating violence with the West would seem natural, and almost preordained by American history as well. The Western frontier has always been viewed as more violent, more primitive, and more unsettled than the rest of the country; perhaps horrific crimes that occurred in the west had more cachet and validity within a genre that focused on unusually brutal crimes. Scholarly work from this period show an interest in violence as part of the American character, in particular Richard Slotkin's 1973 book, *Regeneration through Violence*, which examines the presence and role of violence in American life as a foundational myth. It is also true that the hard-boiled and noir literary tradition set many stories in western and midwestern cities and towns, and the settings of those stories may have had long-lasting implications for the nonfiction portrayals of crime and violence in true crime. In the early 1970s, with the national murder rate rising rapidly, it comes as no surprise that modern violence, emblematized in the figure of the rootless, valueless, psychopathic random killer, would seize the American imagination with such force.

Helter Skelter

The best-known 1970s true-crime text—perhaps the best-selling American true-crime book of all time—is Vincent Bugliosi and Curt Gentry's *Helter Skelter* (1974), which narrates one of the most notorious mass-murders in American history. In August of 1969, followers of Charles Milles Manson slaughtered seven Los Angeles residents in their homes, including the actress Sharon Tate, as a means of bringing on what they called "Helter Skelter," Manson's vision of a futuristic apocalyptic racial revolution. The Manson group also killed at least three other people, and speculations abound about other murders. Several members of the self-styled Manson "family," including Manson himself, are still serving life sentences in California for these crimes. Vincent Bugliosi, the Los Angeles District Attorney at the time, successfully prosecuted and convicted the Manson family killers, and it is his narrative of the crimes in *Helter Skelter* that lives on in the American imagination as the "real" version of those events.

Because of the senseless brutality of the crimes and the social status of the perpetrators—communal-living, long-haired, sexually unrestrained, drug-taking—the Manson slayings came to be viewed as the hideous but not unanticipated end of the joyful, hopeful, and innocent 1960s hippie counterculture. Writers and cultural critics like Joan Didion made such claims at the time, and the middle-class reading public, perhaps eager for such news because they were losing their sons and daughters to the ethos of "tune in, turn on, drop out," ate it up.[20] The Manson killings and ensuing yearlong trial and media circus were the ultimate "I told you so" moment for countless middle-class parents and conservative commentators, as this group of mentally disturbed, deeply aberrant misfits transformed themselves into middle America's supreme nightmare. *Helter Skelter* expressed the fears of the middle class about losing their children to cults, communes, and free love; the book also fascinated those same children, and has been one of the biggest-selling true-crime texts in American history.

No portrayal of Manson has been as wildly popular and well-known as Bugliosi's text; in fact, the very name of his book, *Helter Skelter*, has become synonymous with the entire Manson phenomenon. The cover copy of the 1995 Bantam/Norton edition boasts of its status as "The World's #1 True-Crime Bestseller," and more recent editions report that it has sold more than seven million copies worldwide. One reason for its success, other than its compelling subject, is that *Helter Skelter* brought together all the conventions of the emerging genre into an easily digestible, appealing and endlessly imitable form, with the added feature of ratcheting up the shock-value of the murder narrative. In many ways *Helter Skelter* is the standard-bearer of true crime, a book which, although not itself *sui generis*, bestowed autonomous genre-status upon true crime.

The first reason that *Helter Skelter* is such a crucial text within the formation of true crime is that in it, Bugliosi introduced what would become a standard true-crime ideology about murder and murderers by reinvigorating a rhetoric of evil and applying it to modern murder, and by showing that such evil is, although capable of wreaking deadly and incomprehensible havoc, ultimately containable and subject to the American rule of law. Bugliosi, and much true crime written after *Helter Skelter*, speaks to and for a reading public which neither wants nor accepts ambiguity, reasoned comprehension of murder events and cultural critiques. *Helter Skelter* allows for no moral gray areas, and it began the true-crime technique of juxtaposing the monstrous and the civilized, dangling all that is good and just above the gaping maw of moral chaos and endless murder. Instead of allowing ambiguity by showing that good and evil can exist in one person, each player in the story is designated a set role—the killer-girls are portrayed as inhuman, Vampire-like monsters, Manson is Mephistopheles, and Linda Kasabian (the only Manson "family" member who turned state's witness, who today might be called a "snitch'") is the only relatively good human being in this twisted morality play.

In his summation at the trial, Bugliosi explodes into this bit of sensational invective:

> On the hot summer night of August the eighth, 1969, Charles Manson, the Mephistophelean guru who raped and bastardized the minds of all those who gave themselves so totally to him, sent out from the fires of hell at Spahn Ranch three heartless, bloodthirsty robots and—unfortunately for him—one human being, the little hippie girl Linda Kasabian.[21]

The rhetoric of evil is prominent throughout the book, particularly in the portrayal of Manson family members, because Bugliosi cannot allow any mediation of his moral structure. Bugliosi tells us that a "Mephistophelean" beast reigns over the "fires of hell" in southern California—of all places!—and in such a world, no moral gray areas are allowed to stand. His rhetoric during summation, and throughout *Helter Skelter*, is reminiscent of much older murder narratives. This passage, for example, could have appeared in an issue of the nineteenth-century *Police Gazette*: "What resulted was perhaps the most inhuman, nightmarish, horror-filled hour of savage murder and human slaughter in the recorded annals of crime. As the helpless, defenseless victims begged and screamed out into the night for their lives, their lifeblood gushed out of their bodies, forming rivers of gore."[22] Such inflated rhetoric belongs within an older tradition of murder narration (that of the nineteenth century Gothic horror-inflected murder narrative). Bugliosi resorts to language that places murderers firmly beyond the pale of normal human experience, and renders them ultimately mysterious and unknowable. This gesture would be picked up and copied by other writers, and in true crime, "evil" is an unchallenged, unironic, and unquestionably real force that both motivates and explains certain kinds of behavior. True crime after *Helter Skelter* becomes a monolith, with a tightly structured and undeviatingly formulaic way of narrating and comprehending murder and violent criminality.

To Bugliosi, the architect of *Helter Skelter* lies at the bottom of the slippery slope of moral relativity, which is reflected in his follower's names for him: Manson "family" members referred to Charlie as Jesus Christ, God, Soul, and the Devil. In this leveled morality, "God" and "the Devil" are interchangeable, and there is no separation between the arbitrary categories of "good" and "evil." The language of the family, zen-koan-like phrases such as "no sense makes sense," and "I loved her, and in order for me to kill her I was killing part of myself when I killed her," confirms the reader's worst fears about hippiedom—that it will lead to a moral vacuum that will suck all of Western civilization into a cesspool of violence and annihilation.[23] Manson's followers, those hippie girls/murderous robots, far from being little 1960s California versions of Adolf Eichmann and just following Charlie's orders, are frightening because they're employing familiar words and moral concepts in an entirely new way. The moral relativity of their statements, explanations, and their deeds, is truly threatening, and although they enacted terrible atrocities, the threat contained in their words went beyond murder. They were living an unsustainable, deeply antisocial ethic of no responsibility, no limits, and no rules. Peter Carroll, writing about the 1970s in *It Seemed Like Nothing Happened*, says that "The fascination with evil in popular culture exposed a haunting ambivalence about the rapid social changes of the past decade."[24] This is why Bugliosi must apply a rigid moral structure to his assessment of these events, and deploy the rhetoric of evil. He sees himself as the last and best hope of defending upright, middle American morality from the warped reaches of the counterculture.

Another reason for the importance of *Helter Skelter* within the formulation of true crime is that Bugliosi tapped into rich publishing industry resources in a new way, and his book was one of the first true-crime texts whose enormous sales were propelled by a burgeoning paperback industry. *Helter Skelter* saw separate print runs as a Book-of-the-Month club selection in 1974, and in 1975 it had a *Playboy* Book Club edition, a condensed version in *Book Digest*, and was serialized in *The New York Times*. With *Helter Skelter*, the function of murder narration turns from the impulse to tell a story and better understand the world into the unapologetic creation of a product for consumption. Unlike other books about the Manson crimes, *Helter Skelter* is not a product of culture, a text that grows out of and attempts to explain events, behaviors, and attitudes at a certain time and place; rather, it is a cultural product, a text with the function of transforming a murder story into a product meant for consumption.[25] Like a well-done horror film, *Helter Skelter* is both a phenomenal lowbrow sensation and the popular expression of the cultural concerns of its time, thereby investing sensational material with greater meaning. It brings together all of the conventions that had been laid out before it in nonfiction murder narration, but adds a dimension of contemporaneity and timelessness, making it seem as though the genre had always existed in its present form.

The rise of true crime as a literary genre was helped by the corporatization and consolidation of the publishing industry in the 1960s and 1970s, an economic phenomenon that created the supply of and demand for cheap paperbacks. The huge publishing houses and their divisions, including Pocket Books, Ballantine, Bantam, Vintage, Avon, Random House, and Dell, consolidated their power during this period, and in the late 1970s and early 1980s, many of these houses created their own "true-crime" imprints.[26] The confluence of rising murder rates and a rising paperback book trade helped true crime to grow and mature as an autonomous genre, and *Helter Skelter* was a herald of things to come in the paperback true-crime trade. Its format—photos in the middle of the book, lengthy treatment of one crime or crime event, updated information added as developments in the case occurred, a lurid cover boasting about the book's fearful contents—all would become staples of the genre.

Bugliosi excels at creating the tension between identification with and repulsion for his murderers, another of the important conventions of true crime; indeed, this quality of simultaneously knowing/not knowing the killers, of presenting them as innocent and wayward children and hardened murderers, is a chief strength of *Helter Skelter*. Part of the reason why the American public was both fascinated and horrified with the Manson case was that it offered something for everybody, in that it spoke to and about a multitude of contemporary preoccupations—crazed killer kids for parents frightened by their own children's increasingly strange "lifestyle" choices; a misogynist Svengali hero/villain with supernatural powers over women for the anti-Feminists; radical, if insane, politics for the New Left fringe and Weather Underground freaks; a racial element for disaffected blacks (and whites); a sharp and articulate hero-District Attorney in the figure of Bugliosi for Nixon Republicans. Bugliosi builds on each of these elements in his text, turning the story around himself as the text's moral center and narrative eye. Bugliosi shaped his material to both attract and repel each of these large groups of readers, a shaping so subtle as to be nearly invisible. The seams of the text show when examined closely, however, most clearly in Bugliosi's treatment of the Manson "girls."

At certain points in the text, Bugliosi characterizes the female Manson followers as unfeeling, unthinking children, as when he says that Squeaky Fromme and Sandy Good are "little girls," invoking the identification of the parent-reader. At other points, those same "girls" are portrayed as dangerous criminals—Bugliosi quotes Sandy saying, "Snitches, and other enemies, will be taken care of."[27] But the women who actually killed—Susan Atkins, Paticia Krenwinkel, and Leslie Van Houten—are given superhuman appellations of horror, and Bugliosi portrays them using conventional rhetoric, clichés, and pat phrases. Susan "Sadie" Atkins in particular is written as a murderous, conscienceless brute, atrociously overzealous in carrying out Manson's commands. After her Grand Jury testimony he writes that "The jurors had looked at the heart of Susan Atkins and seen ice."[28] At the penalty phase of the trial, Bugliosi argues forcefully and successfully for the death penalty, proclaiming "These defendants are not human beings, ladies and gentlemen.... These defendants are human monsters, human mutations... There is only one proper ending to the Tate-LaBianca murder trial, verdicts of death for all four defendants."[29] Part of the horror that comes from viewing Atkins' heart, and the minds of the Manson women, is that they are so disarmingly *normal-looking*, so pretty, so quiet. And of course, it is true that these women were simultaneously brutal and loving, killers and mothers, freewheeling love children, and the murderers of mother-to-be Sharon Tate. But Bugliosi underscores this contradiction, and amps up the language of evil in order to further disarm the reader. We are asked to both pity and castigate, love and hate, understand and condemn, the Manson women.

Bugliosi's subtle sexism mimics Manson's much more overt and violent misogyny, and he describes the girls as having "a sameness about them that was much stronger than their individuality... they reminded me less of human beings than Barbie dolls."[30] To Bugliosi, the Manson girls had no autonomy, and did not make the decision to murder on their own. Ignoring the fact that these young women had chosen to live with Manson, had chosen to use him as a father-figure/savior, had chosen the path their lives had taken, Bugliosi instead sees and portrays them simply as murderous Barbie dolls. Of course, the young women were vulnerable and certainly manipulated by Manson, but Bugliosi denies them any agency at all. In this way, Bugliosi acts as the conduit for the reader's uneasy identification with Manson, for Bugliosi saw the girls as Manson did: as little dolls, as objects, present only to be used sexually and to carry out his strange and devious plans. This trope of the "pretty" little girl-killer activates a range of late 1960s and early 1970s American cultural anxieties: the fear of strong women, and of all women becoming stronger with the growing feminist movement, a fear of a loss of control over young adults, and a fear of mind-expanding drugs and open sexuality. Bugliosi never overtly acknowledges or confronts the strength of the Manson women—a destructive, insane strength, to be sure—which would carry each of them through life with Manson, murder, death penalty convictions, and lives in prison.

After the sensation of *Helter Skelter*, Bugliosi continued his writing career, producing many more true-crime and nonfiction texts to the present day.[31] Bugliosi's true crime was popular in the 1980s, although his writing is often thick with overcoverage of minute points of law and extended depictions of courtroom battles. As an attorney, he is preoccupied with the machinations of the criminal justice system, and many readers find his work compellingly interesting. Although he began his career in the true-crime trenches, Bugliosi has steadily moved out of that genre and into straight nonfiction critiques of the American legal system by way of examining specific, sensational cases. His latest book, the well-reviewed and Edgar-award winning *Reclaiming History: The Assassination of President John F. Kennedy* (2007), lays to rest the conspiracies surrounding that event. Bugliosi's true crime is concerned mainly with jurisprudence, systemic failures of justice, and righting the social order. The inheritors of his tradition—writers such as Jack Olsen, Carlton Stowers, and Mark Fuhrman—are prominent within the genre today, and represent one strand of true-crime writing that deals with deviant masculinity, jurisprudential issues, and depictions of sexual-sadistic gore.

During the 1970s, with skyrocketing American crime rates and the appearance of a frightening trend toward social chaos, true-crime texts narrated and helped readers understand such seemingly senseless acts as the Charles Manson crimes and the apparent shocking rise in the sexual murder of young women. The 1970s was also the formative decade of American feminism, and true crime registered the effects of that social movement in a typically paradoxical way: as a deepening interest in the personhood of the murder victim and a threatening commentary on the risks of new freedoms for women. The genre begins to concentrate the graphic performance of male violence against women during this period, and the large number of narratives presenting sexually sadistic murders of young women bespeaks a preoccupation with male power and female powerlessness. Many 1970s true-crime texts are cautionary tales for young single women, warnings against prosaic but new female activities such as hitchhiking and picking up men in bars for casual sex. Throughout the 1970s and 1980s, true crime that was authored primarily by men—and sometimes by women—reflected a fear of more socially, politically, and sexually liberated women.

The Executioner's Song

Since its inception as a genre, more "literary" authors or writers who normally create fiction or work in other literary forms have produced stellar examples of true crime. One such text is Norman Mailer's *The Executioner's Song*, coauthored with Lawrence Schiller in 1979. This text is a significant attempt to narrate and create meaning from murder, although in some ways it defies the definition of true crime. In 1976, longtime convict Gary Gilmore was sentenced to death for the murder of two men in Provo, Utah. At that time, there hadn't been an execution in the United States for ten years, since the 1967 Supreme Court ruling in *Furman v. Georgia*. Gilmore forced the state of Utah to execute him by refusing to appeal, and his case caused a huge national and international sensation. Gilmore's high-profile truculence mushroomed into a media circus like that surrounding the Manson trial. Several months after Gilmore's execution, Mailer collaborated with Larry Schiller, the true-crime media mogul who got his start with the Manson trial, and with whom Mailer had written his biography of Marilyn Monroe, to write *The Executioner's Song*. The book covers the nine months between Gilmore's parole in April 1976 until his execution in January 1977. It quickly became a bestseller and Mailer won the Pulitzer Prize for fiction in 1980.

Mailer uses the conventions of true crime very effectively in *The Executioner's Song*. He skillfully blends fiction with nonfiction, calling his book a "true life novel." Mailer achieves his insider status through his chief researcher, Schiller, who was Gilmore's friend/confessor/publicist during the murderer's final days. Mailer expertly contextualizes the Gilmore crimes and ensuing media phenomenon within the late-1970s Western American social and cultural milieu, and very specifically within the Utah-Mormon context. The book does not strictly follow the formulaic four-part narrative structure, for the narrative does not start with murder; still, *The Executioner's Song* is broken into chronological segments that treat first Gilmore's life and crimes, then his trial and execution. Mailer chose a murderer who fit the usual 1970s' true-crime criteria, for Gilmore's murders are both random stranger-killings. Mailer creates a large and powerful sense of the inevitability of murder and the magnetic pull toward evil, as Gilmore is drawn, seemingly against his will, ever closer to first his crimes, then to his own death. The book is a brilliant murder narrative, at once an insider's view into dysfunctional working-class 1970s American life, and a sweeping portrayal of how that life both creates and sustains violence.

Mailer transforms the most banal and the most dramatic events evenly into a rich everyday fable of the roots of violence, through prose that remains filtered and cool. Mailer's super rational voice narrates everybody's story with equanimity from inside their minds, his eye surveys the landscape and finds scenes such as this, when Gilmore is taken to his last prison: "Outside the prison, night had come, and the ridge of the mountain came down to the Interstate like a big dark animal laying out its paw."[32] Gilmore was the embodiment of Mailer's theoretical notions about the efficacy and importance of violence, and the complicated relationship between Mailer and Gilmore—mediated through Lawrence Schiller, Mailer's researcher—is at the heart of the book. Mailer ultimately valorizes Gilmore by turning him into a mythical, if pitiable, Western outlaw who single-handedly brought the death penalty back into use in American jurisprudence.

The Executioner's Song is as much an exploration of the marketing of murder as it is of the murder itself. The determinism that pulls Gilmore toward murder and execution like a magnet is trumped by the determinism that pulls the American media beast toward his story. Mailer's greatest achievement in this book is how he demonstrates that interpersonal violence in the form of murder sometimes creates and sustains another form of violence, the modern media frenzy. The two halves of *The Executioner's Song* encompass these two great modern American pastimes—murder and its recreation/representation in print and film. The concept of being able to sell one's criminal story was in 1976 as morally dubious as it is now, but the so-called "Son of Sam" laws, which prevent criminals profiting from their crimes, were not enacted until 1978, so Gilmore was able to profit from marketing his story. Schiller, the prototypical murder journalist, is held up for scrutiny just as Gilmore, the prototypical murderer, is. And just as with his portrayal of Gilmore, Mailer valorizes the psychopath, with his treatment of Schiller, Mailer legitimizes the vocation of murder journalist/shill by devoting such loving attention to the story of the story. Schiller's sharp-witted professionalism as a murder-mogul lies in his ability to see the big picture, and to craft an audience as well as a consumable narrative for it from the bare bones of a sordid story.

Many critics have understood Mailer's Gilmore as "an archetype of the displaced American soul of the 1970s," and it's not difficult to understand why.[33] Mailer, often characterized as the archetypal American writer, found Gilmore fascinating because he seemed to embody many of Mailer's themes: violence, why people kill, masculine dignity and self-determination, the life and death of the soul, and the enigma of death itself. David Guest, writing about Mailer in his book *Sentenced to Death: The American Novel and Capital Punishment*, says that "Gilmore's strategy for resisting authority must have seemed familiar to Mailer as it echoed his own writings on crime, art, and the police. Mailer's fascination with hard men and psychopaths dates at least to the time of 'The White Negro.'"[34] In Gary Gilmore, Mailer found a pet psychopath whom he could dissect with his pen in an attempt to understand the hermeneutics of violence. Mailer does this by turning Gilmore into the embodiment of his "white negro," the classic hipster/psychopath, investing

Gilmore with a cool detachment and a personal power that grew mightily as Gilmore resisted prison and state authority. Guest writes that "the narrative tailors Gilmore to fit the hipster model," and "Mailer surrounds Gilmore with mystery and makes him seem menacing."[35] Although a "factual" account of Gilmore's last days, *The Executioner's Song* offers a Gilmore who fit a preconceived mold of the psychopath, a figure recognizable from *In Cold Blood*, *The Onion Field*, and *Helter Skelter*. With this depiction, Mailer turns the sociopath into a recognizably American type.

ANN RULE AND TRUE CRIME IN THE 1980s

In the 1980s, true crime became a consumer-driven publishing industry category, garnering huge profits for mass-market paperback publishing houses in the 1980s and 1990s as the larger publishing houses created their own true-crime imprints during the period. As the fortunes of the true-crime magazines waned, the books grew tremendously in popularity: in the decade of the 1960s, there were approximately thirty-seven texts that treated single cases of contemporary murder and/or the activities of single murderers. In the 1970s, there were seventy-eight examples of the same; in the 1980s, there were 145; and in the 1990s, the number rose to 165.[36] The 1980s true crime focused largely on serial killers, as that threat first appeared on the cultural horizon with the pursuit and conviction of such murderers as Ted Bundy, David Berkowitz, Richard Ramirez, John Wayne Gacy, and Henry Lee Lucas. The 1980s popular culture depictions introduced the figure of the "criminal profiler," as FBI programs such as VICAP (Violent Criminal Apprehension Program) and profiler training captured both federal funding and the popular imagination. Just as the magazines had, true-crime books also educated consumers of pop culture about recent advances in forensic technology and emerging aspects of criminology.

The true-crime worldview and narrative poetics confirms the reading public's shifting and often paranoid fears about violence in America, bringing the reader or viewer into closer relationship with real killers by drawing us "into the minds" of such people, while simultaneously distancing us from the possibility of random violence and death. In true crime, the killers are usually incarcerated or executed at the end of the story, reassuring us with a good old-fashioned reordering of the chaos wrought by crime. The 1980s was a high-water mark for the rhetoric of evil, and the texts are full of descriptions and photographs of gory death scenes and sensational modern monsters. Through representational strategies that posit certain kinds of killers as "monstrous" or outside the realm of human morality, the emergence of the figure of the sociopath/psychopath, the creation of a textual and visual landscape of paranoia and fear of "stranger-danger," and portraying these conditions as reflective of ordinary American reality, the true-crime aesthetic both responded to and helped create fears of crime and violence.

As the threat and hype around serial killers peaked and then faded during the late 1990s, writers turned their attention to domestic murder, by far the most common and varied type of killing in America. Much modern true crime narrates the threats to both men and women of bad romantic choices, and the genre now reflects more anxiety about intimate relationships than the risks of being murdered by a serial killer. Husbands, wives, lovers, in-laws, children, and parents shoot, stab, poison, and incinerate each other with alarming frequency in true crime, and the genre is now dominated by perverse or backward romance narratives. There are many more female writers working in the genre at present, with Ann Rule, Aphrodite Jones, Diane Fanning, and Kathryn Casey most prominent. Ann Rule has shaped the modern genre and popularized the themes of deviant domesticity and explorations of gender expectations and roles, as well as placing greater narrative emphasis on victims' lives and foregrounding mundane details about the environments in which her killers and victims live. She has also enlivened the genre with stories about unforgettable female killers, and a more female-centered strand of true crime has emerged from her pioneering work.

Beginning with her treatment of serial killer Ted Bundy, *The Stranger Beside Me* (1980), Rule has become the premier American true-crime writer, shaping and redefining the genre with her work, and building powerful and lucrative "name-brand" recognition for her product. To date, she has published sixteen single-case texts, thirteen true-crime collections, and one crime-based novel. Ann Rule has a Web site, an annual newsletter, and an enormous fan base; her books are regularly reviewed by publications such as *The New York Times* and *Publishers Weekly*, she has received numerous Edgar Award nominations, and her books appear often on *The New York Times* bestseller list.

After a brief career as a Seattle policewoman, Rule began writing crime stories for true-crime magazines such as *True Detective* in the 1960s, and continued that work throughout the 1970s and 1980s, with special jurisdiction over crime stories in the Northwestern states. Her first book, *The Stranger Beside Me* (1980) was an exploration of deadly and sensational interpersonal betrayal, experienced on a very personal level. In 1971, Rule worked with Ted Bundy at a local suicide-prevention hotline, and during the next decade she and Bundy kept in touch and socialized intermittently. In 1976 Rule was assigned by *True Detective Magazine* to cover a series of abduction-murders of young women throughout the Northwest. Eventually, it became clear that her friend, Ted Bundy, was responsible for the serial murders, for which he was tried and convicted (and executed by the state of Florida in 1989). Ted Bundy would become infamous as one of the most prolific and hideous

American serial killers (one detective who worked on the case estimates that he killed 100 women over his lifetime), and Rule's book became a best-selling blockbuster, the first in a long line.

In addition to giving Rule her first subject, Bundy embodied the notion of the sociopathic personality. The sociopath, antisocial personality, and the psychopath have become familiar figures in the popular media landscape of crime and horror. Bundy and Rule together brought the socio/psychopath into mass or popular consciousness, because Bundy was one of the most devastatingly deceptive serial killers of true crime's formative period, and Rule's book highlighted this aspect of his character. Bundy, as Rule says, has become the "poster boy for serial murder."[37] His ability to mimic human emotions, to appear psychologically "normal," to uphold a façade of ordinariness, has fascinated the public and professionals alike. For many years after the publication of *Stranger*, Rule traveled the country giving slideshow presentations about Bundy to law-enforcement and criminology professionals. Her knowledge about sociopaths has helped to legitimize her work, and she has become a widely respected authority on serial killers. Partly because of her contribution to this body of practical knowledge, Rule is not viewed as a "pulp" writer, nor is her work seen as exploitative or sensational. She is, instead, appreciated by her readers, reviewers, and by criminology professionals as an expert and a professional in her own right; Rule is a female writer who has contributed unique and valuable insights within a male-dominated field of endeavor. That Bundy helped propel her in that direction is one irony among many in her story.

Rule's description of Bundy as sociopath is classic, and the insights she discovered through him form the basis of contemporary understandings about killers:

> Ted could—and did—rub elbows with the governor, travel in circles that most young men could never hope to enter, but he could never feel good about himself. On the surface Ted Bundy was the very epitome of a successful man. Inside, it was all ashes. For Ted has gone through life terribly crippled, like a man who is deaf, or blind, or paralyzed. Ted has no conscience.[38]

In this figuration, the conscience has an almost physical quality, the absence of which cripples like a physical disability. Rule attributes Bundy's murderous core to his lack of a conscience, and this notion has gained great currency in true crime and in popular understandings of what makes people kill. In the contemporary popular discourse about killers, portrayed in the pages of true crime, on TV documentaries, docudramas, and talk shows, and in films, the idea that simply lacking a conscience *in itself* makes one a killer is emphasized to the exclusion of all other theories, and is used to "scientifically" explain behavior that often has no rational explanation. It is clear that Ted Bundy had a woefully undeveloped conscience; it is also clear that many killers lack the ability to empathize with others. But it is equally clear in the psychological literature that not all sociopaths become serial killers. Analogous to the abused-child explanation for such deeply antisocial behavior, one can easily make the argument that not every abused child becomes an abuser, and not every sociopath grows up to become a killer. There remains some other element, some unknown quantity or quality that pushes some over the edge of humanity and into territory formerly explained as that of the Devil.

The Bundy case has shaped the trajectory of Rule's career, and *Stranger* is her best-known and best-liked book, largely because it transcends the simple story of a psychopath and his obscenely destructive acts. The most powerful and interesting storyline in *Stranger* concerns Rule's own relationship to Bundy—her growing realization that he truly is a killer, the painful understanding of his betrayal of her, and the difficult decisions she must make to betray *him*, in a sense, by writing a book about him. After the success of *Stranger*, she penned three quickie serial-killer texts (*The Want-Ad Killer* and *Lust Killer* in 1983 and *The I-5 Killer* in 1984)—using her old pseudonym from magazine writing, "Andy Stack." *Small Sacrifices* (1987), is a story about Oregon child-killer Diane Downs, who shot her three young children in May 1983, killing one and seriously wounding the others. With this book, Rule finds the subject that she would continue to write about for the rest of her career: deviant domesticity, in this case of mothering gone terribly wrong.

Rule's books since *Small Sacrifices* largely concern deviant domestic scenarios, and a survey of her titles shows a preoccupation with the ways in which romance and family life can go wrong: *If You Really Loved Me* (1991), *Everything She Ever Wanted* (1992), *Dead by Sunset* (1995), *Possession* (1996), *Bitter Harvest* (1997), . . . *And Never Let Her Go* (1999), *Every Breath You Take* (2001), and *Heart Full of Lies* (2003). Rule narrated the emotional underside of the 1980s and 1990s, decades of soaring American divorce rates and huge economic losses and gains, of hidden unhappiness amid wealth and fortune. Perhaps in response to the fear-generating stranger-murders of 1960s and 1970s true crime, Rule's texts offer a fearful return to the traditional site of domestic disturbance and violence, the home. In something of a feminist-inspired backlash against the 1970s and 1980s texts, which portrayed women as weak and defenseless victims of powerful men, in the last fifteen years, Rule has brought true crime home and created a unique and sustained critique of patriarchy and domesticity. Now it is the home, rather than the street, which represents the greatest danger to women, physically and emotionally; rather than fear the ruthless predatory stranger, women are now exhorted to fear—and flee from the bondage of—the bad boyfriends, lovers, and husbands, men who should be protecting us. What more fitting response to the grotesque depictions of the horrors waiting outside the home, and the constant warnings against becoming too free?

One interesting aspect of the true-crime phenomenon is that as violent crime rates, and murder rates in particular, have fallen precipitously from the mid-1990s to the mid-2000s, some writers in the genre continue to create the same climate and landscape of fear and paranoia about crime from an earlier era, and such depictions remain popular.[39] It may be the case that as the public appetite for true crime has grown, the genre has outgrown and outlasted itself, and now presents a picture drastically at odds with the reality of American crime. The popularity of depictions of a crime-ridden society supports the notion that true crime is a fantasy genre; one the makes truth claims but is actually depicting a projection of fears and anxieties rather than reflecting a widespread reality. Alternatively, the lasting popularity of depictions of rampant crime and violence as part of American life may reflect an increasing intolerance for violence, and the overcoverage of violent crime may be an indicator of outrage rather than passivity and fatalism in the face of inevitable-seeming violence. In either case, the true-crime literary genre has shown great flexibility by shifting focus onto the domestic sphere and what Laura Browder calls "dystopian romance" stories, responding both to the trends in crime and reader's interests.[40]

That most true-crime fans are women may be surprising, but the long-lasting popularity of textual true crime may rest on the demographics of its readership. Women are overrepresented as responders on Ann Rule's Web site guest book, and Rule has said that she considers her work to be a kind of public service for women, warning them against sociopaths and dangerous romances. Instead of offering answers to the problem of evil, Rule's true crime is a minute examination of lives badly lived and hideously ended; the most she can offer is a warning to men and women alike about the perils of loving the wrong person. For this reason, the shopworn good versus evil, detectives versus killers structure of her stories does not weaken the power and importance of her larger project, which is to write books for and about women. Even the serial-killer treatments reflect a feminist perspective: for example, *Green River, Running Red* (2004) examines the crimes of the so-called "Green River" serial killer, Gary Ridgway, and although the text is conventional in many ways, Rule focuses most of her narrative attention on the victims, instead of the killer, describing the lives and deaths of many of Ridgway's fifty victims. In this way, she continues to challenge the stereotypes of the genre and expand the cultural work that true crime does.

CONTEMPORARY POPULAR WRITERS

Scores of writers have offered their own additions to the genre in the past two decades. The entanglement of Joe McGinniss and his killer-protagonist,

Dr. Jeffrey MacDonald, is a prime example of the kind of vexed relationships that true-crime writers sometimes have with their subjects. McGinniss's *Fatal Vision* (1983) narrates the brutal bludgeoning murder of Jeffrey MacDonald's wife Collette and their two small children in North Carolina in 1970, a crime for which MacDonald was convicted in 1979. McGinniss was later sued by MacDonald for breach of contract because McGinniss portrayed MacDonald as the killer in *Fatal Vision*. In 1990, Janet Malcolm published *The Journalist and the Murderer*, an account of that lawsuit and the peculiar moral difficulties in the journalist/subject interaction, particularly when the subject is an alleged murderer. MacDonald's civil lawsuit against McGinniss went to trial but was eventually settled out of court; MacDonald remains in prison, but new evidence in his case—and a 1995 book, Jerry Allen Potter and Fred Bost's *Fatal Justice*—suggest his innocence. Malcolm maintains that the journalist/killer relationship is always one of seduction on the part of the writer; in his rebuttal to her argument, McGinniss suggests that he was seduced by the psychopathic MacDonald, and when he stopped buying MacDonald's story, the relationship ended in litigation.

The writer/killer relationship is less prominent in some of the genre's recent best-selling works; Carlton Stowers is notable for his "thick description" of social contexts and use of a simplified rhetoric of evil and monstrosity; Jack Olsen has pushed the limits of the genre with innovations like telling the story from the killer's perspective in his book *"I": The Creation of a Serial Killer* (2002). Mark Fuhrman's true crime is detail-laden and, as might be expected of a former detective, narrowly focused on trying to make a case. The work of Harold Schechter is notable for its historic value and well-researched accuracy, and he has written important treatments of long-forgotten killers.[41] *Strange Piece of Paradise* (2006), written by Terri Jentz, is a first-person-victim true-crime book that presents a dramatic and truly innovative turn in the possible relationships between writers and killers. Jentz and a friend were attacked by an axe-wielding stranger on a camping trip in rural Oregon in 1975; both women survived, and the book is a meditation on the aftereffects of violent crime and Jentz's personal search for her near-killer, who was never apprehended. Her unique relationship to her (near) killer adds another voice to the exploration of the ever-fascinating connection between killers and their writers.

As the genre matures and evolves, various narrative possibilities and strategies appear and bear fruit, although the standard, formulaic true-crime texts remain popular. Twenty-first-century true-crime writing continues to respond to murder with both irrational fear and compelling fascination; although laying strong claims to factuality, truthfulness, and realistic representation of actual events, the genre remains driven by and preoccupied with themes of an updated, contemporary gothic horror. American

true-crime writing both responds to and reflects its context and historical circumstance, showing changes and shifts in widespread philosophical
and political understandings about crime, public policy debates, definitions of insanity, and shifting perspectives on the meaning and mystery of
radical evil.

chapter three
FILMS

Look at yourself as a human being; why are you encouraging this violence with your eyes?
—Oliver Stone, in an interview about his film *Natural Born Killers*

True-crime films have a history that spans the last half of the twentieth century, and in their popularity and engagement with larger cultural issues, the films have paralleled the development and trajectory of the true-crime book genre. Film has been an immensely important strand in the evolution of true crime in American popular culture, and has been instrumental in securing a dubious celebrity status for the figure of the psychopath, while documenting a simultaneous decline in the ability of the police to contain deviance. A list of America's most infamous psychopathic killers—Norman Bates, Charles Manson, Ted Bundy, John Wayne Gacy, Jeffrey Dahmer, and Hannibal Lecter—includes both real people and fictional characters who were modeled on real people. Within the heavy fiction/nonfiction crossover milieu of cinema, our modern monsters appear in all their questionable glory for an audience with an ever-increasing tolerance and accompanying desire for blood and gore. At the same time, certain films engage in lively critiques of the true-crime impulse and the tabloidization of crime, posing uncomfortable questions about the viewer's participation in the sanctioning and glorification of violence. In its various forms—straight documentary, docudrama, or truth-based depictions—true-crime film illustrates the process, in place since the 1960s, of the gradual bureaucratization of police agencies and their failure to deal with the social threat posed by the psychopath.

The motion picture Production Code, in effect from 1930 to 1967, severely limited the presentation of crime and violence in films; consequently, the serious development of true-crime films is a post-Code phenomenon. In 1968, the Code was changed, and the new G-PG-R-X ratings system split the audience into different age and taste segments, while allowing for much more graphic depictions of sex and violence. Although film has always narrated crime, the modern murder narrative-as-film is a relatively recent development; unlike the numerous 1930s gangster movies, for example, true-crime film narrates actual murder, posits a psychological understanding of the same, usually includes visceral and graphic depictions of violence, and depicts psychopathy as a way of explaining radical human evil.

As with the magazines and books, true crime on film has gathered a recognizable set of narrative conventions and the genre usually portrays the crime of murder. Specific categories of films—book adaptations, documentaries, docudramas, and fiction films that embellish depictions of real crime and deviance—have emerged as the genre has grown and the representational strategies employed by the filmmakers have evolved and matured. Certain notorious or significant crimes, such as the Manson "family" murders, have warranted multiple treatments and differing perspectives, some art house quality and others solely intended to generate large box-office revenue. As with true-crime books, the films vary in quality, directorial intent, cultural impact, and the critical opinions they generate; unlike books, true-crime films have had to contend with issues of visuality, censorship, and fears about the relationship between filmed and real violence. True-crime film is the vexed place where cinematic violence and real violence collide.

The medium of film, with its strong visual elements, sound and lighting effects, and the shared experience of viewing, has changed the true-crime genre irrevocably, making psychopathic killers and killing an integral part of popular culture. With film, the consumption and enjoyment of true-crime narratives becomes a multisensory experience, one with the potential for immediate social effects—fear of showers, for example, after viewing *Psycho*, or quoting lines and mimicking the qualities of voice or gesture of certain iconic characters. Film is a more social medium than print: films are usually viewed with others in a group situation, subject to the group dynamics that can stir up hysteria or irrational fear; movies are the subject of numberless post-viewing conversations; gripping scenes and characters are imitated, satirized, or built upon in other popular media, completing a continuous feedback loop of viewing-talking-thinking with others about the various elements of a particular film. Film has always produced intense social effects and had unintended consequences on people's behavior, one of which is strong, often irrational fear about the interconnectedness of real and screened violence. The careful control of content, distribution, and ratings is an indication of the power of the medium.

The sheer number of true-crime films is astonishing, perhaps reflective of the well-documented American fascination with violence, and a comprehensive review of every film could fill volumes. With the ever-expanding means of production and distribution—made-for-TV movies (both network and cable), straight-to-video/DVD films, special-interest collections or anthologies, big budget Hollywood movies, Internet content, short films, and independent films—the genre has flourished, creating and satisfying the demand for video violence. Another consideration that complicates any discussion of true-crime films is that, like books, the category itself is flexible and difficult to define: is Alfred Hitchcock's *Psycho* to be considered true crime because it is very loosely based on the deeds of Ed Gein? How about *The Texas Chainsaw Massacre* or *The Silence of the Lambs*, which also springboard from the Gein case? Certain films that depict murder soften the line between fiction and fact (or fact-based fiction); indeed, some of the most significant and popular films of our time have been this type. The medium of film has greatly expanded the cultural work of the true-crime genre in two major ways: first, in popularizing depictions of criminal insanity, which have given rise to the cultural icon of the psychopath, and second, in presenting the murder narrative with a documentary style that highlights the persistence of mystery and ambiguity within a supposedly scientific and objective frame of understanding.

This chapter presents an overview of the major developments and trends within the genre by focusing on a number of key films: *The Naked City* (Jules Dassin, 1948); *Compulsion* (Richard Fleischer, 1959); *In Cold Blood* (Richard Brooks, 1967); *The Boston Strangler* (Richard Fleischer, 1968); *Manson* (Robert Hendrickson and Laurence Merrick, 1973); *Helter Skelter* (Tom Gries, 1976); *Henry: Portrait of a Serial Killer* (John McNaughton, 1986); *The Thin Blue Line* (Errol Morris, 1988); *Paradise Lost: The Child Murders at Robin Hood Hills* (Joe Berlinger and Bruce Sinofsky, 1996); *Aileen Wuornos: The Selling of a Serial Killer* (Nick Broomfield, 1992); *Aileen: Life and Death of a Serial Killer* (Nick Broomfield and Joan Churchill, 2003); *Natural Born Killers* (Oliver Stone, 1994); *Dahmer* (David Jacobson, 2002); *Monster* (Patty Jenkins, 2003); *Capote* (Bennett Miller, 2005); and *Zodiac* (David Fincher, 2007), among others. The major forms include docudrama, documentary, and fact-based fiction. The medium of film has evolved in its true-crime depictions to sustain a variety of perspectives on the murder narrative and to construct the killer in various ways. From quasisympathetic portrayals to delivering the killer as a raging psychopath, from unquestioning devotion to a law-and-order ethos to critiques of the media machinery that turns killers into cultural heroes and thorough examinations of justice-gone-wrong, true-crime films serve up murder and its contexts as thoughtful and challenging entertainment.

THE EARLY, CAUTIOUS YEARS: 1948–1973

> I got you figured for a natural born killer.
> —Dick Hickock to Perry Smith in *In Cold Blood*

The Naked City, its title taken from the book by the pioneering police photographer known as "Weegee," was groundbreaking when released and has provided the prototype for all subsequent police procedural films and television series, from *Dragnet* to *Law & Order*. The police procedural form is itself closely allied to true crime in its reliance on the actual work of police and depictions of crime, and *The Naked City* is relevant to subsequent true-crime films for several reasons. First, it used the city itself (New York) as a backdrop and was not shot in a studio: from the first voice over narration, which opens the film, the viewer is introduced to the city as a character in its own right, filled with different kinds of people doing different kinds of things at all hours of the day and night. As a newspaperman rushes accounts of the day's events into print, a lone woman mops the floor of Grand Central Terminal, fancy wealthy patrons peruse the menus at "Club Trinidad," and a woman is strangled and drowned in her own bathtub. With an unmistakable and seminal emphasis on "reality," this is murder-as-routine-occurrence in a city of "eight million stories," leading to the second innovation in murder narration: the portrayal of real policemen engaged in their plodding, tedious, yet ultimately effective work.

Just as *Dragnet* would do on radio and later television, *The Naked City* portrayed murder as being solved not by the lone Sherlock Holmes-like private detective, popularized in current film noir representations and in the work of classic detective writers from both sides of the Atlantic, but by the group of ordinary men (and women) of the NYPD. The police emerge in this film not as solitary heroes, but as members of a system that ultimately and methodically triumphs over evildoers, mending the social fabric that has been torn by an act of extreme violence. More than that, policemen are depicted as ordinary people, with families, personalities, foibles, senses of humor, and emotional connections to their work. In his efforts to present police most realistically, writer Malvin Wald's research for the story involved spending time with NYPD detectives, taking a course at the Police Academy, reading through police files, and even attending autopsies. The plot of *The Naked City* was cobbled together from several different murders, most prominently the unsolved homicide of model Dorothy King in 1923. Axiomatic tropes in police procedural film and television shows—securing the crime scene, good-cop/bad-cop interrogation techniques, lying suspects, the victim's family viewing the body for identification purposes, investigation of murder as a mundane and workaday endeavor, the police chase through a teeming cityscape—were all introduced with this film, although some first appeared in the gumshoe/hard-boiled detective fiction of the period. Although the film was both a critical and popular success, it is only recently available in DVD form after having been "out of print" for years.

As a variation on film noir, *The Naked City* introduces many of the themes and technical tropes that would inform true crime up to the present day: voyeurism, seriality, the voice over, the menacing but mundane landscape, and violent death as an inevitable fact of modern life. Voyeurism is present in many postwar films, especially film noir, and murders were often seen through windows or doors. Windows figure prominently in *Rope*, also released in 1948, and in Hitchcock's 1954 *Rear Window*. Voyeurism would become a central element in true crime as the impulse to lift the lid on lower-class criminality by depicting lifestyles, places, and illicit activities that seemed foreign and exotic to many viewers and readers. Seriality informs true crime in myriad ways: it is most evident in the late-twentieth-century fascination with serial killers. But it is also present in the idea that although one crime may be solved, there are many others to spring up in its place, and individual murders comprise an inexorable rising tide of violence that threatens civil society. Seriality is a notion inherent to the television true crime or police series, which present new murders every week. The most famous line from *The Naked City*, uttered by the narrator at the end of the film, "There are 8 million stories in the naked city—and this has been one of them," could be the defining statement for every true-crime story that has been told since 1948.

The technique of Mark Hellinger's authoritative voice over narration in the film that guides and contextualizes events for the audience was first copied by the producers of *Dragnet*, but the strong, god-like, omniscient narrator, or host, is heard in countless television and film true-crime documentaries. And finally, the very last scene in the film—a shot of a street cleaner sweeping away a tabloid newspaper cover with the headline "Dexter Murder Solved"—effectively transmits the idea that this murder really is just one among many. Although this particular murder "story" is worthy of extended attention and treatment in a film, there is an overwhelming sense of the numbing meaninglessness that accompanies the huge number of murders that occur in America every day. In this film, we see the hopeful postwar optimism that encouraged public trust in the police as government-sanctioned agents of social control begin to crumble. Such simple-minded confidence could not compete with the feeling of futility that the seemingly multiplying instances of murder and crime engendered, and the result would be an increasingly cynical presentation of both criminals and cops.

Although *The Naked City* proposed that criminal reality was a suitable subject for filmic representation, a different film released the same year took another step in the true crime direction. Alfred Hitchcock's *Rope*, starring Jimmy Stewart and Farley Granger, was a heavily fictionalized treatment of the 1924 Leopold and Loeb murder. This sensational case, wherein two wealthy and intelligent young college friends murdered a fourteen-year-old boy to test ideas about the "perfect crime," contained a frisson of cultural and moral issues of its day: notions about the Nietzschean "superman" theory and philosophical racism, intimations of homosexuality, anti-Semitism, tensions surrounding vast differences in wealth and social class, the media circus around a high-profile trial, and debates about the moral and legal aspects of capital punishment. Hitchcock's film was based on a play that was itself loosely based on the case, so *Rope* concentrated on just a few of the issues raised by the real case and presented the story as a tension-filled psychological thriller. With its character-driven plot (Jimmy Stewart's school teacher character, Rupert Cadell, provides the moral center and focal point of the film) and fictional presentation of the events of the real crime, *Rope* imbued the case with the intensity of psychological drama.

Eight years later, in 1959, another treatment of the Leopold and Loeb case appeared with the film version of Meyer Levin's 1956 best-selling book, *Compulsion.* Directed by Richard Fleischer, who would also direct the film version of *The Boston Strangler, Compulsion* is important as the first film adaptation of a true-crime book with modern contours. A modest financial success, the film was critically well-received; a *New York Times* film critic called it "a tense, forceful and purposeful drama obviously inspired by a purposeless crime that shocked a nation wallowing in prosperity, illicit whisky and vague ideas about abnormal psychology."[1] Unlike the book, which invites the reader to identify with the killers and introduced an important element in the murder narrative formula with the character and role of the narrator, the film emphasizes the psychopathy of the killers (the Richard Loeb-based character in particular) and, perhaps inadvertently, the random nature of the solution of the crime.

This film is also significant because it spurred the real Nathan Leopold to sue Meyer Levin and Richard Zanuck (the film's producer) for violation of privacy. That lawsuit, brought in 1959 after the release of the film, was finally decided against Leopold in 1970 largely on the basis of the first amendment rights of motion picture producers and creators. Beginning with *Compulsion,* lawsuits of varying type would doggedly follow true-crime depictions that the real "protagonists" found slanderous, distasteful, or wrong in some way. In a statement that would echo throughout the lives of "famous" killers and find greater expression as the century wore on, the judge who decided the case also found that because "the plaintiff became and remained a public figure ... No right of privacy attached to matters associated with his participation in that completely publicized crime ... The circumstances of the crime and the prosecution etched a deep public impression which the passing of time did not extinguish. A strong curiosity and social and news interest in the crime, the prosecution, and Leopold remained."[2] This judge's legal recognition of Leopold's status as a public figure carries strong intimations of what was to come with the disturbing celebrity status that attaches to notorious or high profile criminals, particularly killers.

As a murder narrative, *Compulsion* bears the hallmarks of its time period: a teenaged "thrill-kill" perpetrated by smart-alecky kids, the murder isn't shown, and sexuality, homosexual themes, and violence are only hinted at or encoded in language and gesture. The most significant feature of the killers is that they are doubled, which enables the writers to portray a murderous duality; Loeb (Artie Straus) plays the conscienceless and sadistic psychopath, while Leopold (Judd Steiner) is more sensitive, intelligent, and misguided. This figuration would reappear in Capote's *In Cold Blood*, with Dick and Perry playing similar roles as two sides of the same deadly coin. These two-killer depictions suggest that it is the random interplay of two distinct personalities that produces lethal motivation and action. *Compulsion* strongly hints that the murder takes place as a result of the homosexual power games that took place between Judd Steiner and Artie Straus, Steiner pleasing Straus and himself through taking the submissive role and being "ordered" to carry out the crimes that Straus masterminded. In addition to the strongly antihomosexual attitude that such portrayals contained, this iteration of how murder happens is existential and fatalistic, fittingly so for a late-1950s audience that was itself poised on the brink of a purposeless nuclear annihilation. The idea of an accidental convergence of two people who alone would not kill but together generate a spark that blossoms into murderous violence reverberated strongly with the Cold War mentality of mutual assured destruction.

The importance of psychopathy as a cause of murder was another idea presented in *Compulsion* that found considerable cultural traction. Hervey Cleckley's pioneering book that defined and described psychopathy in layman's terms, *The Mask of Sanity*, was continually in print and brought out in several new editions throughout the 1950s, and cinematic psychopaths were finding a wide and receptive audience in film. Artie Straus shows his true psychopathic colors throughout *Compulsion*, as he continually goads Judd into pulling nefarious stunts with him. Artie wants to run down a pedestrian with their car for kicks, and he attempts to incite Judd to rape the girl who agrees to meet him alone in a park because it would be an "intense" experience. Filmmakers were just beginning to discover that psychopaths make the best villains, with or without the psychological explanation for their motives.

The year 1960 saw the release of perhaps the most influential horror film of all time, Alfred Hitchcock's *Psycho*. Norman Bates was created using some of the provocative and ghastly details of the Ed Gein case in 1957, particularly the twisted relationship between mother and son that led to and enhanced Gein's psychopathic tendencies. A purely creepy and unappealing character in Robert Bloch's 1960 book, Norman Bates as interpreted by Alfred Hitchcock and Anthony Perkins would become the prototype for the fascinatingly lethal psychopath. Like Milton's Satan, this character vibrates with energy and engages the twin emotional poles of attraction and repulsion; as viewers, we are fascinated, charmed, and compelled to watch the unraveling of a psychopathic mind.

One defining feature of the cinematic psychopath is his seeming innocuousness, his ability to fit into his environment with a quiet normality. Like Hugh Hefner's iconic "girl next door" who was gracing the covers and centerfolds of *Playboy Magazine* during the same era, *Psycho* introduced the idea of the "killer next door." This notion resonated with Cold War-era Americans who, having come through the 1950s Red Scare, were now on the lookout for a Commie behind every bush. Bloch has said that "I decided to write a novel based on the notion that the man next door may be a monster, unsuspected even in the gossip-ridded microcosm of small-town life."[3] The idea that behind every door, every smiling face, lurked a hidden agent of destruction and violent annihilation, invisible until somehow activated by unwitting deed or gesture, engaged the same kind of duality that anti-Communist rhetoric did. From his earliest incarnation, the figure of the psychopath has symbolized a fear that smooth surfaces can hide inner corruption and the potential for outrageous acts of violence, itself a cipher for the idea that all is not well in American civic, political, and social life, no matter the sunny appearances.

Pop culture psychopaths got an enormous cinematic boost with the release of Truman Capote's *In Cold Blood* in 1967. In his star turn as Perry Smith, the unknown actor Robert Blake personified the creepy/gentle quality that made Capote's Smith so compelling and terrifying. Shot in black-and-white on location in the real Clutter farmhouse, with a tense and atmospheric musical score by Quincy Jones, *In Cold Blood* introduced a gothic sensibility to true-crime film that would inform and influence many subsequent additions to the genre. Many of the film's stylistic innovations were straight from Capote's book, which was itself a cinematic narrative: quick crosscutting between scenes of the killers and victims in the buildup to the murders, delaying the depiction of violence and narrating it from Perry's perspective, and the centrality of the confession scene each debuted in the book and were brought to life in the film. Having two killers handily enabled exploration of two types of murderers and made possible the reversal of audience assumptions as the villainous and lecherous Dick Hickock is unmasked as the softer of the two, while the artistic and emotive Perry emerges as the true psychopath. This idea is central to the film (and the book), for we are encouraged to identify and sympathize with Perry throughout, even as we discover that he is a moral monster.

Another theme introduced with this movie that would have deep cultural reverberations is the overwhelming preoccupation with why and how murder happens. This idea is central to true crime, which very narrowly focuses on crime that has already happened: in this genre, we almost always already know who did it. The question is, *why* did they do it? And more comprehensively, how does murder happen? What confluence of elements, personalities, and events (random or planned), come together to culminate in the gruesome finality of killing? As the psychopath emerged from the pages of Cleckley's book and was fleshed out on screen throughout the 1950s and 1960s, understanding his character seemed to offer some tantalizing hope to answering this question. Exploring his personality, background, experiences, and motivations became the focus of true crime during this period of its formulation into tropes and codified narrative conventions. Perry's explanation of the lead up to murder, which he describes as "like I was readin' a story and I had to know what was gonna happen—how it would end" is provocative, at once an explanation and a renouncement of responsibility or agency. Curiously wrapped in the cloak of necessary narrative closure, the fatalistic, existential sense that certain events and even our own actions are somehow barely out of our control lies beneath such descriptions. Perry goes on to say "It doesn't make sense. I mean what happened or why. It had nothin' to do with the Clutters. They never hurt me, they just happened to be there." This goes beyond randomness and into an existential realm where action, inaction, event or nonevent, all have no meaning whatsoever.

In previous murder narratives from earlier in the century (and in conventional mystery or detective stories), the cynical and nihilistic meaninglessness of crime, when presented at all, is countered by the positivism and teleological actions of the police or detectives. But in the true-crime murder narrative from *In Cold Blood* forward, police work relies just as heavily on the accidental and arbitrary as crime itself does. The cops are highly trained and sensitive to context, delicately and portentously assessing the crime scene and filling the moral vacuum that has been left by brutality, but the solution to murder is as random as the selection of its victims. The cops have no leads or clues until Hickock's former cellmate Floyd Wells decides to call in what would be the tip that broke the case, a chance decision that Wells makes, based not on any kind of moral structure or sense of right and wrong, but to claim the reward money, a substantial and important motive to a imprisoned man. The arbitrary and ad hoc fact of crime is thereby positioned against the equally arbitrary nature of modern police work, as cops and criminals both respond to their chaotic and absurd environment. *In Cold Blood* says that as killers write the book of murder, cops attempt to evoke meaning and coherence from the narrative structure; both impulses are futile and, in modern life, paradoxically overdetermined.

The presentation of violence in the film was discreet and tasteful, somehow made more horrible by inference and the strictures of the Production Code. In August of 1967, Arthur Penn's *Bonnie and Clyde* had broken film taboos of sexuality and graphic violence, along with introducing crosscutting editing techniques that would have a big influence on true-crime film. Released in December of the same year, *In Cold Blood* found ways around overly graphic depictions of violence that made comprehension of the acts more disturbing than their full-on streaming gore could have. Relying on gothic conventions of atmospheric gloom, lingering on the inexorable approach of evil, expressive emotionality of the victims and the camera cutting away at the very last moment, the shootings of the Clutter women are particularly upsetting. It is night, and Perry Smith mounts the stairs in the darkened house, guided by his flashlight and his pounding, mindless desire to annihilate the witnesses. Mrs. Clutter and her daughter Nancy are bound with clothesline and lying on their beds, having just heard the shotgun blasts that killed Mr. Clutter and son Kenyon in the basement; the camera pans to an external shot of Mrs. Clutter's room with door ajar as Perry's shotgun blast briefly illuminates the scene inside. Cut to Nancy's tear-stained face as she hears her mother being murdered and knows that she is next; her eyes shine with terror as she says "No, don't don't don't . . . ". The camera is then outside the darkened house, wind howling as a tumbleweed rolls by and the final shotgun blast roars through the night. A more chilling on-screen murder has never been filmed, especially when the viewer is aware that this is no movie set, but is the exact location where the real murders occurred.

The New York Times film critic in 1967, Bosley Crowther, wrote in his review of *In Cold Blood* that in the reconstruction of the murders "Mr. Brooks exercises his most admirable skill and good taste. For without once actually showing the raw performance and effects of violence, the shooting and the knifing, he builds up a horrifying sense of the slow terror and maniacal momentum of that murderous escapade."[4] That buildup was written into his text by Capote and skillfully brought to the screen by Brooks, whose fidelity to the book was assured by working closely with the writer from conception to finished product. In an essay about the making of the film, Capote wrote that Brooks "was the only director who agreed with—and was willing to risk—my own concept of how the book should be transferred to film."[5] Those conceptual choices included shooting in black and white, using unknown actors for the protagonists, and shooting on location in Kansas and at the Clutter home. Capote loved what Brooks did with *In Cold Blood* and noted that the director had extended his own attempts at the recreation of reality, writing that Brooks had created "reality twice transposed, and all the truer for it." [6] In his distillation of the book, Brooks cut to the chase and eliminated Capote's exploration of context, giving us what we really want to see: the "tensions, the torments, and shabby conceits of the miserable criminals."[7] As an adaptation of a book, this film succeeds because of the prescient and knowing way that Brooks hones in on the real meaning of Capote's work: the recognition of a new kind of evil, of the invisible monster who could be hiding behind the mask of sanity in American society.

The idea of the psychopathic monster hiding in plain sight is in full flower in Richard Fleischer's 1968 film *The Boston Strangler*. Based on Gerold Frank's 1966 best-selling book, the film is a tangle of differing responses to murder: it begins as a standard issue police procedural, with the audience rooting for the cops, and ends as a psychodrama focused on the sympathetically portrayed killer and his battle with inner demons, and is capped off with a reform-oriented statement about dealing with the roots of crime and violence. As one of the first full-bore true-crime films, *The Boston Strangler* offers a preview of things to come, presenting as it does no single perspective on serial killing. Rather than emphasize his monstrosity, the film presents Albert DeSalvo, the "self-confessed" Boston Strangler, as an ordinary working-class family man who cuddles with his daughter as he watches the proceedings of President Kennedy's funeral on television. DeSalvo, portrayed brilliantly by Tony Curtis, is presented as a hapless man who appears to be walking around with a raging case of multiple personality disorder. Given the pro-psychoanalysis context of the late 1960s, this is perhaps forgivable. Statements about DeSalvo by the District Attorney ("He's suffering") and his psychiatrist ("You're looking at a sick animal)" lead the viewer into sympathy as we see DeSalvo squirm while trying to recount his actions for the D.A. He's a poignant strangler—confused, in pain, alone, and isolated with his psychic trauma—who, if we believe this narrative, happens to have murdered eleven women and sexually assaulted countless others.[8] The film ends with this brief typed statement appearing on screen: "This film has ended, but the responsibility of society for the early recognition and treatment of the violent among us has yet to begin," a quaint reminder for the contemporary viewer about the long gone reform discourse in criminal justice, and the 1960s-style optimism that informed some earlier true-crime depictions.

Warts and all, *The Boston Strangler* marks some important developments along the continuum of true crime films. As an early post-Production Code film dealing with a true-crime subject, it led the way in the judicious presentation of sexually sadistic violence, but the makers of *The Boston Strangler* didn't take many risks. The murders in this film are suggested, rather than shown, perhaps because the personal and intimate nature of the mode of death— ligature strangulation with a strong component of sexual deviance—was a taboo that American filmmakers were not yet ready to breach. Apart from one brief, seconds-long view of a dead woman's body that had been violated with a broom handle, Fleischer was conservative in his depiction of violence. The conventions of on-screen violence—aestheticized slow motion shots of bodies being torn, strafed with bullets, mutilated and destroyed in lovingly-rendered detail—would become standard in the following decade, but in 1968 were still uncommon. The denouement of the film occurs when DeSalvo admits that he is the Strangler, an admission that is accompanied by his pantomiming his final murder, that of Mary Sullivan. In a technique borrowed from true-crime writers, the climactic scene shows the way the murder was carried out—but it possesses a strange absence because Curtis is alone on screen, pictured against the white, empty backdrop of the mental hospital chamber where he is confined. No screaming, writhing, dying victim holds our attention, just the sad but fascinating spectacle of a man disintegrating as he reveals his true and hidden self to the world. Such restraint in the portrayal of homicidal violence wouldn't last long, however, and filmmakers were quick to push the boundaries of decorum and taste.

Another important contribution to the genre was the presentation of the contexts of serial killing, an important component of Frank's book that could easily have been lost in the transition from text to screen. The portrayal of context—of the many fears that played on women's minds in Boston during the Strangler period, of the near hysteria the unknown killer bestowed on the city, the multiple press conferences given by the police, bad leads tracked down, kooks brought in for questioning, tips called in that had to be investigated, no matter how outlandish—makes up a large part of the first half of the film. Richard Fleischer used the technique of split-screen presentation, of showing the audience several small scenes at once on the screen, to better depict the teeming and jumbled simultaneity of events. The split-screen effect was also used in place of crosscutting, so that, for instance, we see a woman ironing as the Strangler climbs the stairs to her apartment, see his finger press her apartment buzzer, while she hears it and answers the door. Although intended to convey the rising tension of the action, many viewers found the split-screen technique confusing and distracting; *The New York Times* film critic Renata Adler, in her disparaging comments on the film, said that "the effect is like flipping continuously among TV commercials."[9] This prominent critic hated it, but most audiences responded positively to the film and it was a commercial success.

Apart from these stylistic innovations, *The Boston Strangler*, like the book it was based on, is conservative and traditional in its cinematic language and presentation of violent subject matter. The killer is presented in a sympathetic manner, violence is suggested instead of shown with aesthetic detailing, and the emphasis is on understanding psychological malfunctioning rather than depicting radical and inexplicable evil. Change came slowly to the genre, but the 1970s began with two films that changed certain important conventions in true crime: *The Honeymoon Killers* (Leonard Kastle, 1970) and *Badlands* (Terrence Malick, 1973). The psychological flatness, narration from the killer's perspective, and aestheticized approach to the presentation of violence make these films different and introduce significant changes in the genre. Both films are fictionalized depictions of two "killer couples": *Honeymoon* tells the story of the 1940s "lonely hearts killers" Ray Fernandez and Martha Beck, and *Badlands* poetically narrates the 1958 crime spree of Charles Starkweather and Caril Ann Fugate. Expressive realism is gone, replaced by a world-weary flatness and lack of emotion about murder. The emotional content of the films finds expression in the love stories, but even that is limited, flat, and off-putting rather than compelling.

These films, along with the fact-based cop dramas *The French Connection* (William Friedkin, 1971) and *Serpico* (Sidney Lumet, 1973), also heralded increasing displays of the means of killing, including more realistic presentations of gunshots, stabbings, and other forms of violent death that had been pioneered by such directors as Sam Peckinpah, Arthur Penn, and Stanley Kubrick. The aesthetics of on-screen violence were worked out during this period in experimentation and pushing the boundaries of both Motion Picture Association of America (MPAA) and audience acceptance. Technical conventions such as multicamera filming, montage editing, slow motion, and the use of "squibs" (fake-blood-filled condoms that are wired to explode as the actor is "shot" or "stabbed") combined to make graphic death scenes visually enthralling. Filmmakers have followed these rules of presentation ever since, with the result that, as critic Stephen Prince writes, "Screen violence is made attractive, whether by dressing it up in special effects or by embedding it in scenarios of righteous (i.e., morally justified) aggression. Without these aesthetic pleasures, viewers are unlikely to consent to viewing grossly disturbing violence."[10] Media makers know that "grossly disturbing violence" such as that presented in scenes of actual torture, real death, or film footage of surgery appeals to a very small number of viewers and has limited potential; served with heaps of aesthetic tricks, however, the appeal of visual violence seems endless.

THE MANSON FILMS AS CULTURAL BAROMETER

I'm a reflection of you. I'm what you made me.
—Charles Manson in *Helter Skelter*

The Manson "family" murders in Los Angeles in 1969 have had a deep and lasting impact on popular culture, from the early countercultural embrace of Manson's ethic to the *Helter Skelter* book and movie depictions, to popular Web sites devoted to archiving Manson minutiae. Charles Manson has been heavily imbricated in the formation and dissemination of pop culture depictions of him, and over the years he has become a media-derived/contrived caricature of himself. Since the 1976 made-for-TV movie starring Steve Railsback and the infamous 1989 Geraldo Rivera television interview, Manson the person has become Manson-the-personality, America's favorite psychopath whose ranting and raving performances are self-fulfilling prophecies of the damage caused by overhype (and criminal insanity). The Manson phenomenon has truly been one of the most bizarre collisions of media and murder in American history, and the cultural products that have resulted from that collision magnify issues of celebrity and crime, of violence and entertainment, and misapprehension of the line separating the two. Ranging from the Robert Hendrickson documentary *Manson* (1973) that features real family members spouting their relativist rhetoric of murder to the made-for-TV film version of *Helter Skelter* (1976) to several more recent mytho-revisionist quasidocumentaries, filmmakers have been trying to capture and parse the Manson events since they occurred in 1969. Robert Hendrickson has just released another Manson documentary that uses previously unseen footage; the film was screened in September 2007 at the New York Independent Film Festival, and the interest in Manson continues.

The connections with film and media surrounding the Manson phenomenon boggle the mind: while committing their heinous murders, the Manson family lived on the Spahn movie ranch outside Los Angeles that had been used as a set for countless Hollywood westerns—including *The Lone Ranger* and *Bonanza* television series—a simulacrum for American values that had been emptied of all moral content. The event Manson is most remembered for (even though he didn't actually kill her) was the grisly stabbing of Sharon Tate, a beautiful movie actress who had recently starred in her husband's horror movie spoof (*The Fearless Vampire Killers*, 1967); Tate's husband, Roman Polanski, had directed an influential American horror movie, *Rosemary's Baby*, in 1968; the multifaceted media career of Vincent Bugliosi was launched after his successful prosecution of the Manson family members and his appearance in *Manson*; the iconic film and television footage of the trial and its environs, especially of the Manson "girls" staging noisy public protests on the sidewalks outside the L.A. County Courthouse; the mythic "Manson family movies," a holy grail-like cache of the films that the family allegedly made to document their activities (and the origin of the concept of the "snuff film"); the show business pretensions of Manson himself, who was sporadically pursuing a musical career by attempting to establish contact with celebrities. Finally, during the Manson murders and trial, Ronald Reagan was governor of California, the representative of state power and law and order, who himself was a former film actor. Scratching the surface of the Manson events reveals a weird congruence of elements that manifest the complex enmeshment of murder and media.

The Manson films add fascinating layers to the complexities of the events and the way they have reverberated through pop culture. Since 1970, there have been at least ten feature-length film and television movies made and released in the United States, with many more interviews and pieces about Manson and the "girls" regularly appearing on television newsmagazine programs, Court TV/TruTV specials, and in anthology collections of famous or notorious serial killers (I use the term "girls" to describe the female Manson-followers because that is how they have been remembered, largely due to Vincent Bugliosi's memory-setting book, *Helter Skelter*). The violence presented in the different films varies in intensity, graphic depiction, use of special effects, and "gore factor," but all the films (excluding *Manson*) reenact the murders in some way.

The first film was Frank Howard's 1971 *The Helter Skelter Murders*, a dreadful combination of documentary footage and dramatizations that was based on newspaper accounts of the events. The finest Manson film was a documentary shot between 1969 and 1972 by Robert Hendrickson and Laurence Merrick. This film, *Manson*, was released in January 1973 by Tobann International Films, and it was nominated for an Academy Award for best documentary feature that year, but it did not go into wide release until 1976. The film is singular within the Manson subgenre for the way it takes seriously the political content of the Manson events, its focus on the Manson "family" members rather than on Charles Manson himself, and for its reliance on firsthand documentary footage of the actual people involved. Hendrickson uses a mixture of ethnographic techniques that show the "family" engaged in their everyday activities, both bizarre and mundane, interviews that reveal the radical ideology of the "family" with lyrical intensity, split screen/contrasting color film effects that refer to Andy Warhol-like portraiture, and "kaleidoscopic effects, apparently meant to simulate acid trips recollected in tranquility."[11] Most significantly, and unlike all other Manson films, this film does not reenact the murders, although it does capitalize somewhat on the sensational aspects of the case.

Manson achieves its more balanced and subdued depiction of the events largely because in the years from 1969 to 1972, Charles Manson had not yet become the media icon and cultural signifier of mayhem and subversion that he would in later years, so Hendrickson and Merrick are free to examine the Manson family phenomenon with cooler heads. As a document of the late 1960s and early 1970s counterculture, the film is superb, juxtaposing footage of violent street rebellion, the Vietnam war, and race riots with images of the pretrial family cavorting naked in the desert landscapes surrounding Spahn Ranch, and images of the "girls" staging their own small rebellion on the courthouse sidewalks with the famous "perp-walk" footage of a tiny handcuffed Charlie impishly grinning and staring into the cameras. The solemn voice of the male narrator contains just the right amount of pathos and curiosity, and the voice overs describe even the most nightmarish events without undue emotionality. Quiet, balanced, small; these adjectives in no way describe the Manson family of the popular imagination, because that imagination had not yet been formed by the rash of 1970s and 1980s films that would largely focus on the physical horror of the Manson murders and the evil glee of the "girls" as they plunged knives into their squirming victims.

Manson contains considerable power and interest because the family members are given voice, not simply interviewed and asked questions that would become routine, such as "What was it really like to live with Charlie?" and "Didn't you feel anything for Sharon Tate's unborn baby?" With an ethnographer's eye for the value of self-reporting, Hendrickson lets the family members, mostly young women, describe their own experiences, while spouting their philosophy of half-digested hippie values inflected by drug use and (perhaps) mental imbalance. Apart from a few melodramatic comments (at one point the narrator calls Manson a "Venus flytrap among the flower children"), the filmmakers do not dwell on the sensational and belief-defying elements of Manson's lifestyle and ethic. The women speak for themselves, and the film opens with an iconic sequence of Squeaky Fromme, decked out in a homemade vest/hot pants combo that looks like a taxidermy-enhanced Brownie uniform, fondling a rifle and saying, "Whatever is necessary to do, you do it. When somebody needs to be killed, there's no wrong; you do it. And then you move on. And you pick up a child and you move him to the desert. You pick up as many children as you can, and you kill whoever gets in your way. This is us." The truly haunting soundtrack is composed and performed by Paul Watkins and Brooks Poston, two male Manson followers whose folk songs evoke the era; footage of the family at work at the Spahn Ranch, engaged in communal garbage picking and meal preparation, even the orgy sequences, are presented with an anthropological objectivity.

A final characteristic of *Manson* that the later Manson films gloss over or ignore entirely is the political and sociological content of the events and the antimedia message that the "girls" give voice to. In this film, strong (if unbalanced) women such as Squeaky (Lynette Fromme) and Gypsy (Catherine Share) stare defiantly into the camera as they talk about sexual and social freedom, independence from the moral structure of the "establishment," and their far-out quasifeminist, moral-relativist views on drugs and sex, life and death, and families and children. If not for the fact that these young women were firmly under Charlie Manson's thumb and entirely given over to a patriarchal view of their rights and role in society, they could be seen as radical feminists. The Manson "family" mirrors the family structure of the larger society, with a strong patriarch prescribing and policing traditional female roles of cooking, cleaning, and tending children for all the women, while encouraging subservience. The "girls" seem to exemplify agency and freedom in their rhetoric and action, yet paradoxically, their thoughts are not their own—they belong to "the man," for whom, like Nixon's soldiers, they will do anything.

Hendrickson also raises questions about the society that produced the Manson followers: at one point the narrator says that at Spahn Ranch, "They lived in the ramshackle, broken-down movie sets, panhandled, hustled, stole, shoveled manure and ate garbage. But the obvious discomforts of life with Charlie were far more desirable to these runaways than their parent's comfortable homes," and "the establishment smugly dismisses the Mansons as an oddball phenomenon. These kids came from our own schools, our own neighborhoods, our own homes. By the time the Sadies, the Katies and the Leslies had reached the age of 14, they'd witnessed over 14,000 killings on television." One of the young women elaborates on this notion, saying, "We are what you have made us. We were brought up on your TV. We were brought up on *Gunsmoke, Have Gun Will Travel, FBI, Combat. Combat* was my favorite show." She also notes that Manson is a scapegoat and a distraction from Vietnam, Nixon, and the sinking economy. Unlike the fear-inducing rhetoric of the "sick society," which fatalistically assesses and accepts the status quo, while predicting more degeneracy and decay, Hendrickson's statements critique a concrete aspect of modern American life and suggest that change is possible by including young people into society rather than rejecting them as moral outsiders. In its refusal to sensationalize and its serious assessment of the events, *Manson* is itself a radical and singular film.

Unlike the Hendrickson documentary, the 1976 televised movie adaptation of the book *Helter Skelter* demonizes Manson and is preoccupied with the depravities of the family and their bloody rampages. Directed by Tom Gries, this film solidified Manson's image as a wild-eyed, raving, grinning, singing, howling, and dangerous lunatic, capable of hypnotizing the jury and inducing his followers to carry out murder at his command. This is Bugliosi's version of Manson, and the narrative follows the version of events given in the prosecutor's book in a semidocumentary style, with George DeCenzo portraying Bugliosi as narrator. Performances by Steve Railsback as Manson and Nancy Wolfe as Susan Atkins made the film a television smash hit and helped earn it an Edgar Allan Poe Award for best television feature/miniseries in 1977. Because the book runs nearly 800 pages and the story was so convoluted and complex, *Helter Skelter* is a lengthy movie and was shown over two consecutive nights, skillfully managing to convey the intricacies of the family, the crimes, and their detection. The film was the most popular serialized television movie of all time until it was displaced in popularity by the miniseries *Roots* the next year. Railsback brought a terrifying and convincing Manson into living rooms across the country, and the film (and book) have been instrumental in creating the horror movie myth of Manson that has been the main legacy of those crimes.

The cultural work of *Helter Skelter* was threefold: first, it turned Charlie Manson into a demonic stereotype, a caricature of himself. Second, the film sensationalized the material and standardized the narrative by keying into and reinvigorating horror and mystery archetypes from an earlier period. And third, the movie emphasized certain elements of Bugliosi's book that showed the police as bumbling, incompetent, and incapable of solving the crime because of bureaucratic mishandling. Manson—with his shaggy beard, unkempt appearance, animal magnetism, and supernatural power over the young women—is presented as "the Wolfman." Susan Atkins is a metaphorical and literal vampire who gains power by killing people, encourages other young women to give up their lives by joining the Charlie cult, and relates in a toneless voice how she dipped her fingers into Sharon Tate's blood and tasted it. The other Manson "girls" are zombies, blindly and mindlessly following Charlie's orders and methodically "overkilling" their victims with savagely delivered multiple stab wounds. Bugliosi himself plays Sherlock Holmes, for he solves the mystery of the crimes by putting all the pieces together and even finding key evidence himself, something outside the range of normal behavior for prosecuting attorneys. Through these depictions, *Helter Skelter* engaged the unconscious emotional undertones of the Manson events by correlating the players with a range of familiar horror and mystery-fiction tropes and aligning these incomprehensible modern killers with an older, almost archaic understanding of their actions. Although Bugliosi had presented the Manson killers with the language of horror and as stereotypical monsters in his book, the visual impact of such depictions and the emphasis on elements that fit the mold of the stock characters made the movie version even more powerful and lasting.

Helter Skelter also emphasized that the efforts of the police to solve the crimes were hindered by an unwieldy and overly bureaucratic police system, and although everything presented in the film was factually true, police incompetence is highlighted throughout. An early scene that takes place in LAPD headquarters illustrates this: because of jurisdictional boundaries, two different sets of detectives initially worked the Gary Hinman (a pre-Tate murder) and the Tate slayings, one from the Los Angeles Sheriff's Office, the other LAPD. The Hinman detectives visit LAPD to query the possible connections between the murders, because similar words were left in blood at both crime scenes, but are rebuffed by a detective who says, "The dope angle is the only one that fits here." The Tate killings were at first believed to be drug-related, and this bit of dialogue illustrates the single-minded incompetence of the detectives. After the LaBianca murders, and with the Tate detectives working separately just a few desks away, another cop tries to bring up the rarity of the gun used in Tate as a possible way to crack the case. A detective tells him, "That's not the way you break cases, Hank. You do it by filling out forms . . . in triplicate." And yet another scene demonstrates bureaucratic interference (and how mightily it is resented) by prominently showing a sign that hangs on the wall at headquarters that reads, "To err is human. To forgive is against departmental policy." Valuable evidence—the bloody clothes worn by the Tate killers, the gun with a broken handgrip that was thrown down a ravine by the same—is found by, respectively, a television news crew and a nine-year-old boy. And Bugliosi is shown tracking down key evidence, including magazines about Hitler and a door covered in "Helter Skelter" graffiti, at locations the police couldn't or wouldn't search.

Such depictions of police are not surprising in the era of *Serpico* and *The French Connection*, films that dramatized a police culture of corruption, incompetence, and absurd directives from above that combined to leave the individual cop alone in his fight to apprehend criminals. The notion of effective police work as a struggle against a nameless, faceless, and uncaring "system" was beginning to emerge out of society-wide distrust of "the establishment" that was articulated by 1960s youth movements and culture. Specific issues within law enforcement, such as the struggles with implementing the Miranda rulings and a shift away from brutality and "third degree" tactics as a result of increasing pressure from the liberal courts also contributed to a perception that the cops were no longer able to do their jobs effectively. In addition, rapidly rising rates of violent crime during the period did little to help the public image of the police. The combination of these pressures resulted in the valorization of the rogue cop as the only agent of real justice, as in *Dirty Harry* (1971), arguably "the first film to face straightforwardly the strain that the criminal psychopath puts on the law enforcement system."[12] In *Helter Skelter*, the rogue-cop role is filled by Bugliosi, for he is a kind of "super-DA" who ignores jurisdictions, steps on toes, and angers his superiors. But he solves the crime, and successfully prosecutes it.

The Manson films since 1976 offer a glimpse into how the national psyche has processed and filtered the Manson cultural phenomenon. In 1984, director John Aes-Nihil offered his *Manson Family Movies*, an arty-weird Super-8 film with the premise in the title: that this was a collection of the family's fabled films of their murderous deeds and secret sexual rituals. As a film, it is nearly unwatchable; as an exercise in fetishizing Manson and the "girls," it is exquisite. Nikolas Schreck released *Charles Manson: Superstar* in 1989, a conventional documentary (still photos, voice overs, interviews) that purports to tell the "truth" about Manson after two decades of media hype. The film manages to articulate and examine the myth of Manson, although it is uncomfortably sympathetic to his "ideology" and cause. Church of Satan founder Anton LaVey stepped into the conversation with his *Death Scenes: Manson* (1989), where he posits the interesting theory that the real killer, Tex Watson, has been ignored, usurped by the media-generated focus on Manson. This is actually true, for Watson—Charlie's right-hand man and the only male presence at all the murder scenes—quite literally orchestrated the killings but has been curiously absent from media representations of the Manson events.

In 2004, another film version of *Helter Skelter* appeared on television, less powerful than the original because the ground has been covered so thoroughly. Referring to the fact that Linda Kasabian, the prosecution's star witness against Manson and company, had started her life over after the trial and is now a grandmother, *New York Times* television critic Alessandra Stanley wrote, "How someone so closely involved in those murders could start over and create a placid new life might be more intriguing at this point than reliving the crimes themselves."[13] Perhaps because of the ongoing power of the Manson mystique, *that* movie has yet to be made, although the forthcoming *The Manson Girls* (Matthew Bright, release date unknown) holds some promise. Finally, Jim Van Bebber's *The Manson Family* (2003), frames the original events within a competingly weird storyline that follows a group of punk-junkie oddballs as they enact their own exceptionally bloody murder spree, bashing in the brains of a television producer who was making yet another Manson documentary. A surprisingly good film, this one manages to critique media-inspired Manson worship and senseless violence, while offering a fresh and coherent perspective on the murders— that each murder episode was a schizo-paranoid response to Manson's failed interactions with the world outside his "family."

It seems that the sociological phenomenon of Manson is here to stay, for, as he has famously said, "I am whoever you make me . . . you want a sadistic fiend because that is what you are. You only reflect on me what you are inside of yourselves."[14] Manson does have a point: he *is* the monster we have made him, regardless of his actual behavior. Charles Manson the person has come to represent so many things that he has crumbled under the symbolic weight and morphed into his media-projected image. Nearly forty years of Manson films illustrate a trajectory of true-crime meaning: from earnest shock and outrage about an LSD murder cult in our midst through tangled levels of fetishizing the same, to a world-weary postmodern acceptance of the mindless savagery he represents and an accompanying critique of media-created mythology, the meanings of Manson list the various ways American culture has understood psychopathic and irrational violence.

TRUE-CRIME AND THE DOCUMENTARY IMPULSE

> Why did I meet this kid? I don't know. Why did I run out of gas at that time? I don't know. But it happened. It happened.
> —Randall Adams, explaining how he met David Harris in *The Thin Blue Line*

> Heard of the proverbial scapegoat?
> —David Harris on Randall Adams in *The Thin Blue Line*

One of the most compelling and influential documentary films of the late twentieth century is a true-crime masterpiece: Errol Morris's *The Thin Blue Line* (1988). Although *The Thin Blue Line* (*TBL*) did not invent the reenactment as a way of narrating criminal events, Morris's use of the technique brought into true crime a register of timelessness and inexorability, amping up the graphic sense of murder as "always already happening." With its strong noir-inflected mood, dark lightning, hypnotic and repetitive musical score, presentation of quirky characters, and the seedy, often invisible lives of the American underclass, and mixing elements of fact and fiction, the film echoes *In Cold Blood* (both book and film versions) and advances the true-crime trope of a fatalistic, voyeuristic sense that murder is inevitable. *TBL* has been called a "non-fiction film noir," a "nightmarish meditation on the difference between truth and fiction," and "an eccentric investigative documentary that's a cross between '60 Minutes' and a Laurie Anderson performance."[15]

Like *Rashomon*, Akira Kurosawa's 1950 masterpiece about the evasiveness of truth, *TBL* presents multiple perspectives on the murder event through the statements of different interviewees, calling into question the boundary between the "factual" and the "true," which true-crime texts had been blurring for years. However, the film makes very clear that its chief subject, Randall Adams, has been framed and wrongly imprisoned by a corrupt criminal justice system, insisting on the truth of Adams' innocence. *TBL* also blurred the boundaries between reality and representation by actually changing a criminal justice outcome: partly because of the serious questions Morris raised in the movie about his guilt, Randall Adams, the convicted cop-killer whose story is told, was set free on appeal.

The cultural work of *The Thin Blue Line* is multifaceted, as it has impacted murder narration, filmmaking, and public trust in the efficacy and soundness of our criminal justice system. The film introduced a strong critical and investigative impulse into true-crime filmmaking and altered the stylistic and thematic direction of the genre. Morris used heavily stylized reenactments to demonstrate ambiguity rather than to arrive at a single visual truth about past events, a technique that is widely seen now in the contemporary *CSI* television series. Because of its focus on trying to right a wrong, the film is not an exploration of the "how" and "why" of a crime, but rather the "how" and "why" of the aftermath: What went wrong and who was to blame for the miscarriage of justice? With a kind of split focus, Morris investigates the tangled knot of "crimes" that follow the murder of Dallas police officer Robert Wood and led to the victimization and false imprisonment of Randall Adams: the lies of David Harris, the sociopath who implicated Adams in the murder; the corruption of the Dallas prosecutor who withheld evidence and "bought" witnesses; and the malfeasance of the judge who presided over the faulty trial that convicted Adams. Indeed, the movie functions as the trial that Adams should have had, with its interviewees "speaking into the void" (Morris's characterization of his interview technique) and the viewer positioned as interrogator, the presentation of evidence in the form of documents, drawings, and reenactments, and the final "confession" of David Harris that is bestowed on the audience through the distancing mechanism of a tape recorder (a fortunate accident of filmmaking; Morris's camera broke on that day and he used his tape recorder instead).

Morris rectifies a gross injustice with his film, but still leaves the viewer with questions and doesn't offer a tidy conclusion. Instead, the unraveling of one mystery—the death of policeman Robert Wood and how Randall Adams came to be blamed for it—leads to many others, as we wonder, along with Morris, "To what extent were the people involved in this case aware of what they were doing?" and "If you could make a pie graph of lying, which part would be self-deception, which part greed, which part self-aggrandizement, and so on?"[16] These are the deeper questions that lie at the center of this case, and they are never answered by the film. The mystery of human misbehavior remains, even as the mystery of murder is "solved." *TBL* bestows on its audience an "awareness of the final inaccessibility of a moment of crime, violence, trauma, irretrievably located in the past."[17] No matter how many times the crime is reenacted, Morris demonstrates that truth—even a truth that seems etched in stone and therefore discoverable, as in "David Harris pulled the trigger"—is evasive, elusive, and impossible to attain. Randall Adams may have been exonerated by the system that imprisoned him for twelve years, but the "truth" of the situation remains officially unknown, because David Harris was never charged with the crime. Morris's film is unique in that it presents a murder narrative that moves the audience further away from certainty and knowingness and deeper into the unexplored and frighteningly postmodern territory of contingency and the malleability of memory and truth.

The Thin Blue Line helped shape public awareness about the terrifying ease with which an innocent person can be framed, convicted, and sometimes even executed. In the 1970s and 1980s, widespread and increasing public fears about violent crime and random victimization led to draconian sentencing laws and an enormous number of incarcerated people, and Morris's film introduced the possibility that in more cases than previously suspected, the system had failed. In that pre-DNA era, "scientific" certainty was arrived at through forensic methods now recognized as deeply subjective and flawed: polygraph tests, hair analysis, coerced confessions, and eyewitness testimony have each been discredited as reliable and accurate ways of finding the truth of a crime event, but they continue to be used in murder cases. As "the first movie that has solved a major murder mystery and led to a reversal of a decision at trial," *TBL* opened new possibilities for true-crime filmmakers to engage in more investigative techniques and to develop a critical, rather than just exploratory or explanatory, sensibility.[18] *TBL* has had a major impact on television murder narratives in particular, and has led to the kind of investigative journalism seen in such programs as *20/20, 48 Hours,* and *Dateline: NBC.* The growth of such television fare exploded during the late 1980s with the television shows *Cops* and *Unsolved Mysteries,* and *TBL* catalyzed the creation of a true-crime subgenre: that of "justice-gone-wrong."

Although *TBL* remains the only major documentary film in the genre to have led directly to the exoneration of an innocent man in a murder case, other filmmakers have challenged convictions and advocated for their misapprehended subjects. One such case is explored in two HBO-produced documentary films, *Paradise Lost: The Child Murders at Robin Hood Hills* (1996) and *Paradise Lost 2: Revelations* (2000), both directed by Joe Berlinger and Bruce Sinofsky. The films together present a study in how cultural bias, police incompetence, ignorance, and fear can result in the wrongful conviction of innocent people by investigating the mutilation murder of three eight-year-old boys in West Memphis, Arkansas, in May 1993. Through a combination of police inexperience with unusual violent crime and the influence of the "satanic panic" of the late 1980s and early 1990s (the widespread irrational and hysterical belief that many ordinary individuals were engaged in secret satanic cult rituals and responsible for the murder and sexual abuse of children, among other crimes), three unconventional and hapless teenagers were convicted of these terrible murders, based largely on the coerced and false confession of a subject with an IQ of 72.

Both films are straight documentaries rather than "docudramas," eschewing such technical elements of fiction as reenactment, voice over, or narrator intrusion. Instead, the story is told through interviews of the primary subjects (victims' parents, the accused killers and their families, police, prosecutors, defense attorneys, and the judge involved in the case), actuality filming of the trial, the clever use of network news footage of the case, and disturbing scenes that show the stepfather of one of the dead children acting out his grief and anger, and exorcising his own possible guilt. The result is a forceful and terrifying portrait of ignorance, fear, and the inexorable forward momentum of an unwieldy legal system that, once set onto the wrong track, is nearly impossible to set right. Unlike Randall Adams in *TBL*, the wrongly convicted killers have not been exonerated and are still working on their appeals, but the films (especially the first one) have publicized the case and helped gather support for the "West Memphis Three."

The *Paradise Lost* films feel unfinished and leave the viewer with uncomfortable ambiguity, as the gruesome and tragic murders are never solved; in *TBL*, the real killer is known to the viewer and is satisfyingly incarcerated. In fact, a turning point occurs two-thirds of the way into *TBL*, when David Harris, dressed in a bright orange jumpsuit and talking into the camera, suddenly brings his hands up to scratch the back of his head. For the first time, we see that his hands are manacled, an image that powerfully relates the danger and violence that lurks beneath his chatty and amiable exterior. *Paradise Lost* offers no such reassuring images; instead, we are drawn to the (perhaps erroneous) conclusion that the ultrareligious, gun-wielding, vindictive, and mentally unstable stepfather of one victim is the killer of all three boys, but he is never regarded as such by the police. Sinofsky and Berlinger also show the dead bodies of the three children in crime scene video footage and in autopsy photos, whereas Morris implies mortal violence through the reenactments, distancing the viewer from the full-on graphic horror of death and mutilation. Images of the stiffened, nude, mud-and-blood-streaked children's bodies stay with the viewer and are mute testimonials that inspire disgust and outrage, emotions that Morris elicits much more subtly.

Since *The Thin Blue Line* was made, crime documentarians and fiction filmmakers alike have made murder narratives with more varied and critical postmodern themes and narrative styles. Like true-crime books, true-crime films are generally conservative, as the narrative tropes and conventions engage strong emotions of outrage, anger, and pity and posit a law-and-order ideology and an after-the-fact retelling of events, which allows little room for differing interpretations of or response to the crime event. But some films—and books—offer a different understanding of the specific nature of some crimes and criminal behavior. The "justice-gone-wrong" subgenre is one such response; other films in this category include *Brother's Keeper* (Berlinger and Sinofsky, 1992), *Murder on a Sunday Morning* (Jean-Xavier de Lestrade, 2002), *Unreasonable Doubt: The Joe Amrine Case* (John McHale, 2002), *After Innocence* (Jessica Sanders, 2004), *Picture This: A Fight to Save Joe* (John McHale, 2005, a follow-up to *Unreasonable Doubt*), and *The Trials of Darryl Hunt* (Ricki Stern and Anne Sundberg, 2006). These documentaries explore murder narratives that engage larger issues of community and race-based standards of justice and injustice, plead specific cases (the subjects of both *Unreasonable Doubt* and *The Trials of Darryl Hunt* have since been exonerated), and examine the difficult circumstances that face exonerees. Another nexus of understanding murder has, since the mid-1990s, grown out of the work of legal-affairs organizations that use DNA analysis to revisit contested or questionable violent crime convictions. The work of attorneys and Innocence Project founders Barry Scheck and Peter Neufeld appears in some of the recent documentaries, as they advocate for the wrongly accused and assist with high-tech and often prohibitively expensive DNA testing of evidence that has sometimes been mishandled or not tested at all. A different murder narrative emerges from these exonerations, one that focuses not on the originating crime but on its devastating consequences for the wrongfully accused and on the fascinating and troubling belief, held by most jurors and lawyers, in the sanctity of eyewitness testimony and confessions.

The two Nick Broomfield films that detail the life story, criminal behavior, trial, and execution of Aileen Wuornos, although not strictly of the "justice-gone-wrong" type, are serious examinations of the cultural issues and media hype that surrounded the Wuornos case. In the first film, *Aileen Wuornos: The Selling of a Serial Killer* (1992), Broomfield narrates the way that Wuornos—a confessed killer of seven men—was betrayed, sold out, and manipulated by both her lover and the mercenary policemen and attorneys who surrounded her as the media storm erupted around "America's first female serial killer." The film has an unfinished feeling and it leaves many questions unanswered, partly because it documents a liminal moment during the Wuornos events: the time between her confession and her execution by the state of Florida. Much of the film shows Broomfield on his visits to Wuornos's representative, a born-again Christian woman who "adopted" thirty-five-year-old Wuornos, and the pot-smoking, self-aggrandizing and narcissistic attorney who encourages Wuornos to plead guilty to the murders. In cinema verité style, the camera follows Broomfield in his thwarted attempts to interview Wuornos where she is being held in a maximum-security Florida prison, and the much-anticipated interview appears at the very end of the film. Broomfield's flat, drawn-out British-accented voice adds layers of pathos and irony to the sordid events and desperate characters who make up the narrative; consistent with the subjects of the justice-gone-wrong subgenre, Aileen Wuornos appears more authentic, honest, and likeable than any of the other characters, even though her status as murderer is never in doubt.

In the second film, *Aileen: Life and Death of a Serial Killer* (2003), our sympathy for Wuornos grows as Broomfield documents her paranoid delusions that have only increased and gained prominence in her psyche during twelve years on death row. This film covers the last few months of her life and the preparation for her execution, and it delves into Wuornos' childhood and past. Most interesting are the interviews with Wuornos that show her seesawing between protestations of innocence and guilt; she had always maintained that her "serial" killings were all in self-defense, although at the very end she admitted to a robbery motive, which may have been a tactic calculated to avoid any further delays and appeals. *Aileen: Life and Death* is more finished, more mature, and less pedantic than the first film, although Broomfield slightly overstates his major point: that the death penalty is barbarous and inspired solely by the desire for vengeance. Broomfield's numerous on-camera appearances, although they somewhat needlessly showcase his own wry humor and witty repartee with the players in this drama, lend a palpable "you are there" feel to the footage and guide the viewer into an understanding that Wuornos is mentally ill and also caught in a deeply irrational system of punishment and retribution. As murder narratives, these two documentaries introduce badly needed rationality and balance into a deeply wrenching, reactionary, and emotionally fraught area of human experience. The *Aileen* films prove that the murder narrative doesn't have to play only in the registers of pathos and pity.

EVOLUTION: TRUE-CRIME FILMS AND THE SELF-REFLEXIVE HABIT

The true-crime documentaries raise an interesting question: where does entertainment end, and action—or activism—begin? Each of the major true-crime documentaries questions one of the "systems" that shape and govern modern American life, systems of law enforcement, criminal justice, and the workings of major media. In these films, murder as entertainment and spectacle is the catalyst for action and activism, through political advocacy, greater awareness of the issues involved, or simply the questioning of authoritative power structures. The conventional murder narrative is in these instances replaced with a narrative of outrage and the desire for reform. As true-crime film has developed, matured, and interacted with other mediums, it began to more frequently challenge and question itself, in some cases profiting from the very appetites it reprimanded the viewer for having. Beginning in the 1980s, writers and directors, perhaps taking a cue from Mailer's work in *The Executioner's Song*, started to interrogate the construction of serial killing as a subject of pop culture preoccupation, along with the larger issue of the American infatuation with aestheticized representations of violence.

The 1986 fiction film, *Henry: Portrait of a Serial Killer*, was very loosely based on the criminal lives of the real serial murderers Henry Lee Lucas and Ottis Toole, and it is significant within the genre for its critique of the viewer's implication in and consumption of outrageous and explicit displays of violence. *Henry* is an act of self-reflection, for in it the writer and director John McNaughton questions the viewer's participation in the portrayal of acts of brutal violence, giving us a serial killer who metaphorically gazes out and indicts the viewer for voyeuristic pleasure in watching his heretofore private acts of murder. By 1986, serial killer hysteria was in full flower, and *Henry* caused a sensation because filmgoers were not quite ready for a sophisticated critique of the media-induced phenomenon. Instead of more of the same—uncritical and titillating film representations of sadism, gratuitous sex, and violence of the Freddie and Jason horror variety—McNaughton presents serial killing from the perspective of the killer, and the visual texture of the film is unremittingly dark, dreary, and nihilistic. We are encouraged to sympathize with Henry's motivations and desires, as one of the most disturbing murder events is first videotaped, then enjoyed in later home-screenings by Henry and his crime partner Otis—and us. As Laurent Bouzereau writes, "It's almost as if he [the filmmaker] dared you to sympathize with him or to become fascinated with the nuts and bolts of serial killing."[19] Both a critical and underground/cult success, *Henry* changed the rules of the game by introducing the viewer as a third and willing participant in the killer-victim relationship, and exposing the latent voyeurism inherent in the film-going experience.

The development of a critical sensibility around public consumption of murder narratives continued with such films as *The Positively True Adventures of the Alleged Texas Cheerleader-Murdering Mom* (Michael Ritchie, 1993), a "mockumentary" that narrates the underside of media exploitation and public fascination with depravity and criminally narcissistic behavior. This infamous tabloidesque case involves the mother of a pre-teenage girl in Texas who contracted to have her daughter's cheerleading rival and the girl's mother killed, although the murder was never carried out. The outrageous Belgian-made satire *Man Bites Dog* (Rémy Belvaux and André Bonzel, 1993) extends the self-mockery of the serial-killer genre, as it narrates the increasingly perverse interdependence of two young filmmakers who follow, document, and eventually participate in the over-the-top murders of a gregarious and friendly serial killer. Although not an American film, *Man Bites Dog* found an audience who appreciated the witty lambasting of American-type excesses of media entanglement with murder and murderers.

Serial killing presents a strange chicken-or-egg conundrum when considered within popular culture: as a unique type of murder, it seems to have become more prevalent in the past few decades than it was prior to the 1960s, but the interest that heightened during the 1980s and 1990s, along with the recognition and official classification of serial killing by the FBI during the same period, make it impossible to determine which came first—the increase in serial killing or the public and pop culture preoccupation with it. As defined by the FBI, a serial killer has murdered three or more victims with a varying time lapse between each, and often with a psychosexual component. Because of the extreme deviance, sexual motivation, repetition, and complete objectification of the victim that this type of violence contains and signifies, serial killing fascinates on many levels, and the serial killer has become a mythic monster who activates a range of meanings about the human condition, some new and some very old. Serial killers have been interpreted in various ways by criminologists, sociologists, cultural critics, and feminist theorists: as symbolic arch capitalists acting out Marxist labor theory of the pathological separation of the worker from his product, as expressions of entrenched misogynistic patriarchal values, as atavistic superconsumers whose deeds are documented and sold to other consumers, and as good old-fashioned devils, evil incarnate that fits our modern world and lifestyles. In the 1980s and early 1990s, serial killers were still emerging in pop culture as icons of real splatter-gore violence and representatives of an apocalyptic kind of murder that was a cipher for alienation, anomie, economic unease, and fear-based perceptions about the effects of violent entertainment on young people. *Henry* seemed to make a case for the serial killer as just another member of such a "sick" society, neither endorsing nor condemning his actions.

In an essay about *The Honeymoon Killers* and the flattened-out morality of killing that is presented in films like it, film studies professor Martin Rubin references another impulse, writing that "These bleak, nasty little films have preferred not to join in our current version of the 'era of good feeling,' serving instead to keep alive an endangered spirit of negation."[20] Such a "spirit of negation" is an often overlooked or misinterpreted force that, like Edgar Allan Poe's "Imp of the Perverse," insists on the importance of a countervailing drive of nihilism and depravity; such a spirit enlivened the serial killer craze of the 1980s and 1990s and made films like *Henry* both possible and popular. True-crime films that document and display the crimes of serial killers partake of the kind of depravity and dark insistence on the negative that has always had a place in artistic representation; that our modern explorations of decadence, perversity, and murder are also objectively "real" illustrates the same shift toward the confessional and self-exploratory mode that accounts for the popularity of such art forms as the memoir, the documentary film, the television talk show, and reality television. Murder narratives reflect the same desire to touch "the real" and to gain vicarious experience that is evident throughout American culture at the present time.

Oliver Stone's *Natural Born Killers* (1994) is a fiction film that both embraces and rejects this spirit of depravity as it engages many of the themes present in late twentieth-century true crime: video voyeurism and the titillation experienced by the watcher, the allure of sex and violence, the media-created cult of personality that forms around the most outrageously brutal and selfish murderers, the American appetite for both real and unreal violence, and the celebration of the outlaw in his modern incarnation as the psychopath. As happens with other directors who attempt sophisticated critiques of violence while depicting it—Sam Peckinpah, Stanley Kubrick, and Michael Haneke all come to mind—the attraction to and repulsion from the violence produces too much tension, distracts from the meaning of the film, and ultimately undermines and undoes the satire.

Stone's intent is to unmask violence and our base interest in it, and to disarm the mesmerizing power of splatter imagery. To that end, *Natural Born Killers* (*NBK*) offers a range of exceedingly graphic death scenes and intense depictions of sadism, but Stone's project outgrows his ability to control it. The violence is too beautiful—it can't be otherwise, or viewers wouldn't watch—and the irony loses its teeth as his absurd and cartoonish characters win the viewers over, and the film ends up glorifying and endorsing rather than challenging the romantic myth of the outlaw killer. As feminist critic Jane Caputi writes, "All of *Natural Born Killer*'s energy, beauty, and poetry is invested in the pair of killers, themselves figures of ready identification: young lovers with an intense lifelong commitment."[21] Mickey and Mallory Knox are, in the end, simply too irresistibly sexy and attractive, and the audience ends up mindlessly and unconsciously rooting for them rather than questioning that impulse and the underdog status the pair maintains throughout the film.

Other worthy entries in the serial killer genre include the 1992 made-for-TV movie, *To Catch a Killer* (Eric Till) which stars a gravid and frightening Brian Dennehy as John Wayne Gacy, and *Ed Gein* (Chuck Parello, 2000), a strikingly straightforward and tasteful narrative version of one of America's most infamous psychopaths, portrayed by Steve Railsback (whose forté appears to be brilliant depictions of psychopaths—see *Helter Skelter*). *The Silence of the Lambs* (Jonathan Demme, 1991), although not technically true crime, contains two culturally significant serial killers, with the purely fictional Hannibal Lecter taking precedence and popularity away from Jame Gumb, who is very loosely based on the real Ed Gein. As Martin Rubin says, "Like most films on the subject, *The Silence of the Lambs* cultivates the exotic orchids of psychokillerdom; *The Honeymoon Killers et al.* confine themselves to the weeds," and the "exotic orchid" Hannibal Lecter has amassed a fortune in cultural capital as America's favorite cannibal.[22] In the documentary genre, Dark Sky Film's 2005 3-DVD set, *The Serial Killers: The Sick Minds behind the Most Gruesome Murders in America*, offers low production values but remarkable, rarely seen footage of the killers; Ted Bundy and Michael Bruce Ross stand out as spectacularly awful cases that received sensational media coverage but in this anthology collection are simply narrated and allowed to tell their own stories, a rare occurrence within true crime (for excellent moral reasons—allowing the killer to "have his say" foregrounds his legitimacy as a subject of inquiry and further "silences" the victim).

As the serial killer mythology has lost prominence in the first few years of the twenty-first century, more thoughtful criticism and deeper characterizations have, in certain films, replaced knee-jerk, stereotypical depictions and rhetorical demonization of sensational killers. Two important true-crime films of this type include *Dahmer* (David Jacobson, 2002) and *Monster* (Patty Jenkins, 2004). *Dahmer* is a sensitive and intelligent portrayal of Jeffrey Dahmer, one of the most sensational and gruesome American killers of the late twentieth century. In the film, Dahmer emerges as a pathetic and unbelievably tortured soul, but a soul nonetheless. Unlike most Dahmer stories that make simple monstrosity of his cannibalism and necrophilia, *Dahmer* explores the singular psychological disturbance that fueled his intense desire to possess another person in such ways. *Monster* explores the human counternarrative to the "official" tabloid version of the Aileen Wuornos story, rejecting the "female serial killer" designation and instead allowing the viewer to see the interrelated social and cultural structures of violence and power that produced such a failed human being. These films each present a new conception of the murderer as a deeply flawed person, and not simply as a moral monster whose personality is defined by a lack of conscience.

It may be significant that both *Dahmer* and *Monster* deal with homosexual killers who murder men instead of women, a twist that may help explain the narrative and emotional differences that mark both films. As homosexuals, both Dahmer and Wuornos were social outsiders whose stories could be lifted more easily from the web of myth and meaning that both inheres within and produces serial killer narratives. Already considered freaks by a homophobic culture, there was no reason to further demonize and distance Dahmer and Wuornos from normative morality, so their stories could paradoxically present more understandable and sympathetic depictions of serial killers. In his second *Aileen* film, Nick Broomfield says that "The idea of a woman killing men, a man-hating lesbian prostitute who tarnished the reputation of all her victims brought Aileen Wuornos a special kind of hatred." This is undoubtedly true; it may also have freed her (for some people) from more conventional representations as a psychopath. For if, as Wayne Douglass observes, the psychopath is the "symbol of what we want to be and what we are afraid we may become," both Dahmer and Wuornos alter that formula with their homosexual status.[23] In American culture, homosexuals are not heroic outsiders, nor are they admired and identified with in the usual manner as protagonists. Instead, they are almost uniformly vilified, demonized, and cast out, both metaphorically and sometimes literally.

Capote (Bennett Miller, 2005), *Infamous* (Douglas McGrath, 2006), and *Zodiac* (David Fincher, 2007) represent the further development—and perhaps the future—of true-crime films, for each are book adaptations that focus not on the details of murder or killers biographies, but on the writers' obsession with the killers and the backstory of the creation of the books. These films present a different kind of murder narrative, one that explores the effects of murder on the living and suggests that "meta-nonfiction" is an artistic category that can succeed. Both films trade the standard psychopath-fixation for character studies of the writers who shape the psychopaths' stories and stake a claim for the interests of a more media-savvy and crime-oversaturated audience in how murder stories are constructed. *Zodiac* in particular resists the true-crime conventions in its focus on the writer instead of the killer, who remains free, its unresolved, ambiguous ending, and its close-range, non-aesthetic depiction of homicidal violence.

Having exhausted the fascination with psychopaths, true crime may now be heading in a meta-nonfiction direction with filmmakers who are interested in pursuing the story behind the murder story. Another long-neglected area of narrative exploration could be the aftermath of real murder and its psychological and social effects on individuals and communities. More balanced and "realistic" representation of the American social and racial underclass that experiences murder in the greatest numbers is unlikely, for stories about everyday, inner-city tragedies, and mundane, quickly forgotten dramas usually don't contain the base, symbolic or mythic possibilities that serial killing offers. The richly sensory medium of film may resist such new directions and anti-aesthetic presentation of violence; splatter, after all, still sells. The direction of true-crime film remains to be seen, but television and the Internet hold out some tantalizing possibilities for new directions and themes.

TELEVISION

The crime genre obscures its penchant for order and control behind a style so realistic that its ideology seems natural and appropriate.
—Gray Cavender, "In 'The Shadow of Shadows,' Television Reality Crime Programming"

The more 'realistic' a programme is thought to be, the more trusted, enjoyable—and therefore the more popular—it becomes. Yet realism too is an artificial construct. Its 'naturalness' arises not from nature itself but from the fact that realism is the mode in which our particular culture prefers its ritual condensations to be cast. There is nothing natural about realism, but it does correspond to the way we currently perceive the world.
—John Fiske and John Hartley, *Reading Television*

Remember: you *can* make a difference.
—John Walsh, host of *America's Most Wanted*

Television and true crime sustain a prolific relationship: from the hand-held you-are-there drama of *Cops* to the measured sensationalism of *Forensic Files*, the genre has flourished on the small screen and offers something for nearly everyone. Within the smaller subgenre of murder narratives, television true crime appears in three major forms or types: the crime documentary or reenactment programs, the forensics-driven detective fiction programs, and the crime drama that makes use of real stories for plot. The documentary/reenactment format includes such shows as *Unsolved Mysteries* (1987–2002), *48 Hours*, and *48 Hours Mystery* (1988–present), *America's Most Wanted* (1988–present), *Cops* (1989–present), *City Confidential* (1999–2005), *Cold Case Files* (1999–present), *Forensic Files* (2000–present), *The First 48* (2004–present), and the Court TV network (1991–2007). Forensics-driven fictional detective dramas include *Quincy M.E.* (1976–1983) and the entire *CSI* phenomenon (2000–present). Both series runs of *Dragnet* (1951–1959, then 1967–1970) used real events and inspired or influenced many subsequent fact and fiction crime programs. Many other series fit into these basic categories or use some of the conventions, and the fiction or nonfiction crime genre shares popularity and ubiquity with such other major forms as sitcoms, soap operas, standard dramas, and reality programs. Televised true crime serves multiple functions, and each show blends different impulses and emphases: from reinforcing a law-and-order ideology and encouraging viewer participation, to informing and educating the viewer and using real crimes as entertainment, true crime on television has been surpassingly popular and lucrative for television networks. Crime "infotainment" has been an early and strong part of the trend toward reality-based programming, and the conventions, boundaries, and definitions of true crime continue to expand with each new program.

Televised true crime does different kinds of cultural work: it has helped create a nation of crime pseudoexperts, ordinary viewers who feel they have some knowledge about real-life criminalistics practices based on what the programs present; true-crime TV feeds the desire for arcane knowledge by making tedious forensics techniques interesting and "sexy" to the viewer; like all true crime, the television programs both present and then solve mystery, offering that deeply satisfying diversion as entertainment; and the TV shows both perpetuate and assuage anxiety and fear about crime, presenting multitudes of murder scenarios, almost superhuman killers, and an insider's view of the pain that people inflict on each other. Like true-crime books, true-crime TV allows a glimpse into the lives of others, both reflecting back middle-class mores and lifestyles and holding a flashlight into more darkened corners of American life, including the criminal, working-class, hidden or secret lives of the middle- or upper-class, and geographically or culturally isolated spaces.

Unlike magazines, books, or films, true crime on the small screen affords visual intimacy, as murder is literally brought into the home. The experience of watching television, with its many commercial interruptions and myriad environmental distractions, domesticates true crime and makes it prosaic and commonplace. When viewed in context with other types of programs—news, dramas, game shows, reality programs, comedies, or sitcoms—true crime becomes just another form of entertainment, just as real, or unreal, as the others. Because it offers an endless parade of killers but brings them closer than ever by projecting them directly into the viewer's living room, television true crime reinforces the paradox, already a major aspect of the genre, which offers both closeness to and distance from murder. In addition, as true crime has blossomed and flourished on television, the genre has expanded its audience and a nation of TV addicts has been given another drug—real murder and its detection.

Beginning with the renowned "police procedural" series *Dragnet*, television dramas that use real crimes in their storylines and production advice from actual cops have educated viewers about law enforcement procedures, policies, and constraints. The various versions of *Law & Order*, with some of its plots "ripped from today's headlines," give the viewer detailed knowledge about how the criminal justice system operates, highlighting both the fissures and connections between the law enforcement and judicial systems. *Quincy, M.E.* introduced another type of true-crime television with a forensic technician-detective protagonist who shoulders the Sherlock Holmes tradition and presages contemporary forensics television such as *CSI*, a program that continues the tradition of educating and entertaining with crime, the stranger and more complex the better.

America's Most Wanted (AMW) brings the viewer into closer relationship with murder (and other crimes) by asking for direct viewer intervention to help apprehend criminals. The saturation coverage on both network and cable television of serial killer cases such as Ted Bundy, Jeffrey Dahmer, and Aileen Wuornos and the growing fascination with heroic FBI agents and criminal profilers in the 1980s and 1990s led to the creation of many more true-crime programs, and consequently educated the consumer/viewer about the value of both physical and psychological forensic evidence. By the mid-1990s, courtroom procedures, rules of evidence, and the relative merits of expert witnesses describing DNA evidence (puts the jury to sleep vs. provides important scientific credibility), brought to life most famously by the O. J. Simpson case, became standard American dinner table conversation. True detective programs that explicate complex forensics procedures have proliferated since the late 1980s, and a seemingly endless array of murder narrative vignettes airs nightly on cable and network channels.

Television has taken the place of magazines and books in the genre, particularly in the docudrama type programs and in weekly newsmagazine shows such as *48 Hours Mystery*, which airs true-crime vignettes and offers up-to-date weekly accounts of contemporary crimes. The introduction and growth of cable television changed true crime dramatically, for today the major programs in the genre appear on cable stations. Since the early 2000s, both Court TV (renamed "TruTV" in January 2008) and the Arts and Entertainment (A&E) cable network have added more true-crime programming to their schedule in response to high ratings and the popularity of forensic science. In late January 2008, a Discovery Channel subsidiary, Investigation Discovery, began broadcasting a largely true-crime format. Whether the impulse behind "crimeophilia" is self-defensive, lurid, and voyeuristic, driven by an out of proportion fear of crime, or is part of an ironic and cool desire to transcend such fears, what remains clear is that the American mass media consumer has grown increasingly savvy and sophisticated about murder and how various institutions deal with it. As the saying goes, "a little knowledge is a dangerous thing," and this has proven true with the intense but narrow education that crime infotainment offers.

An irrational fear of crime has paralleled the growth of knowledge about criminalistics, forensics, and courtroom procedures, as if knowledge, instead of bringing light, has brought darkness. In addition, many studies have shown that such programs reinforce existing attitudes that contribute to social problems such as racism.[1] Particular types of crimes—sadistic or brutal sex-murders of young, attractive women or the victimization of children—are overrepresented in true crime, a phenomenon that can distort public perceptions about the homicide problem in America and negatively impact public-policy decisions and debates about appropriate responses to crime in the courts and prisons. Such depictions marginalize the most commonly victimized through ignoring other kinds of murder, such as those linked to gang activity or the illicit drug trade in urban environments. Constant and repeated depictions of "real" human depravity on television creates an environment of anger, outrage, and a sense of futility that may translate into voters backing such draconian punishment measures as the "three-strikes" legislation and unreasonable mandatory minimum sentencing requirements.[2]

The so-called "CSI effect" is a consequence of the popularity of true-crime television that causes viewers to misjudge the limitations of the knowledge they glean from portrayals of detective work on television. The CSI effect is a phenomenon that has been documented by jury consultants and trial lawyers as influencing or conditioning jurors to expect all serious criminal cases (such as rape or homicide) to contain some forensic evidence; the more *CSI* potential jurors watch, the more they come to expect forensic science to be a prominent part of any trials they may adjudicate. Because of the power of the medium and the invisible shaping of "reality" that such programs engage in, true crime on television has cultural, social, and political effects that are still evolving and not clearly understood, but are certainly far-reaching and profound.

THE PROGRAMS: PRIME TIME FOR TRUE CRIME

Televised true crime as a genre got its start in the 1950s with *Dragnet*, the pioneering program that depicted police work by using stories taken directly from the files of the Los Angeles police department (LAPD). *Dragnet* started as a radio program in 1949, and had two very successful television series runs, the first from 1951–1959, and another from 1967–1970. The radio program continued on-air until 1957, and many of the radio stories were subsequently produced for the television series as well.[3] Itself deeply influenced by the 1948 movie *The Naked City* (dir. Jules Dassin), *Dragnet* is an important progenitor of the police procedural television show form, and has been copied, spoofed, and embedded in American popular consciousness for decades. The 1950s episodes are like *True Detective* articles sprung to life in black-and-white animation: the flat, clipped, staccato dialogue, documentary-style narration and voice over placing time and date, and setting the context and scene at the opening of the show mimic the style and form of the magazine articles. Here's a typical opening monologue by Sergeant Joe Friday (played by Jack Webb), from "The Big September Man," which aired on May 8, 1952:

> This is the city. From one night to the next it's never the same. They make it that way. Counting the suburbs, there's four million of 'em. Most of the people have something they add. A few of 'em are out to take it away. In my job, they're the ones who keep you on the move. I'm a cop. It was Wednesday, September 28th. We were working the night watch out of homicide detail, my partner's Ed Jacobs, the boss is Thad Brown, chief of detectives, my name's Friday.

Each episode began with a monologue like this, delivered in Webb's deadpan, machine gun rhetorical style. This hard-boiled style of narration that objectifies the citizens of Los Angeles and paints criminals and law abiders with the same brush mimics that in the true-crime magazines of the same period, a style that had deep roots in crime fiction. The major difference is in the emotionless description of the crime in the television show, as opposed to the hyped and sensational rhetoric appearing in the magazine articles (a comparison of titles illustrates this point: a story about juvenile delinquency is "Jerry the Wildcat" in *True Detective* versus "The Big Seventeen" in *Dragnet*). But in most other respects, 1950s episodes of *Dragnet* are like televised versions of their magazine counterparts, and the magazines did not fail to notice. The March 1950 edition of *True Detective* contained a story about the production of the radio show, suggesting that the magazine's readers were also viewers and fans of *Dragnet*.

The idea of using true police stories for *Dragnet* plots originated with Jack Webb's desire to portray real policemen and the techniques they used, to counter the prevailing images in books, radio, television, and films that depicted cops as incompetent, corrupt, or idiotic, criminals as brilliant masterminds of deception, and gumshoe private eyes as bulletproof Sherlock Holmes-like super sleuths. In an instance of supreme good fortune, Webb met police detective Marty Wynn on the set of *He Walked by Night* (1948), a film-noir depiction of the pursuit of a Los Angeles cop killer. Wynn had a casual conversation with Webb, telling him that cops were depicted all wrong in the movies, and that "It rankles every damn cop in the country when they hear those far-fetched stories about crime . . . They're all jazzed up, and the detectives are all supermen, and they do it with mirrors. *Real* cops don't work like that! . . . I can arrange for you to have access to cases in the police files. Maybe you could do something with them."[4] Webb took Wynn up on his offer, pitched the radio program to CBS and NBC, and began his successful decades-long relationship with the LAPD and law enforcement generally.

The desire to portray "real" cops working real cases resulted in a meticulous attention to the details of that work. *Dragnet* was produced and written in close collaboration with the LAPD, and was advised by Los Angeles police chief William A. Parker; writers spent time visiting the cops and riding in the prowl cars, and stories came directly from case files. Eventually, stories were solicited from patrolmen and detectives and then given professional script-writing treatment, so episodes were "based" on real events and cases but were written with plenty of "poetic license." The cop who submitted the story would receive a small honorarium and also act as technical consultant on the set of that episode. Realism and authenticity were extremely important to Webb, who was actor, director, and producer of the series, and his conservative law-and-order personal politics and beliefs created a desire to present cops as tenders of civic order, patiently and relentlessly righting wrongs and restoring social equilibrium.

As the series went on, Webb's character became more preachy and judgmental, and his even-keeled, low-key approach to crime gradually changed. Eventually, "Friday was perceived by many as law enforcement's moral conscience," and that perception stuck. By the second run of the series, from 1967 to 1970, Webb's goals for the show were different: he told the press "There's been a breakdown in our mores . . . a total disregard for constituted authority. I hope a series like *Dragnet* can do something to help restore respect for the law."[5] By 1967, the social order had begun to be shaken by the civil rights and youth movements of the period, and the "moral conscience of law enforcement" responded with tirades against drugs and hippies. The 1967 inaugural episode, "The Big LSD," tracks the illegalization of LSD by following a dealer called "Blue Boy," and the episode is now a cult classic for its dated depiction of drug-culture and hippies. The portrayal of such social problems as drug abuse and juvenile delinquency may look like caricatures to a twenty-first-century viewer, but the show was responding immediately, sometimes awkwardly, to the new and pressing challenges of its time.

Another such challenge was the presentation of the difficult and evolving issues surrounding the rights of the accused, particularly in police custody. Because it depicted actual police procedures, *Dragnet* was an important site for a public appraisal of new U.S. Supreme Court rulings intended to protect the rights of both accused and imprisoned subjects. The prominent reading of the so-called "Miranda" rights to suspects before they are arrested on the show, now a standard and unquestioned convention of the police procedural genre, emphasized the new strictures under which cops were operating in the mid-1960s. *Escobedo v. Illinois* (1964), *People v. Dorado* (1965), and *Miranda v. Arizona* (1966) were instrumental legal rulings that together led to the national Miranda Rights Law, which holds that arrested individuals must be made aware of certain rights when they are initially detained. The "Miranda Warning" was widely criticized when first introduced: many in law enforcement felt that it would hamper interrogations, and many people felt it was an unjust and misplaced protection of the criminal to the detriment of the victim. On *Dragnet*, Miranda was criticized by angry crime victims, as in the following speech from an irate father in a 1970 episode about drug dealing: "'Who in his right mind would give drugs like that to a twelve-year-old boy? . . . And when you catch 'em, what happens? A bunch of over-aged, ingrate judges turn 'em loose because you don't kiss 'em before you run 'em in! Never mind the kid's rights; the rights belong to the crumbs!'"[6] But reading the Miranda rights was also smoothly integrated into the arrest procedure on the show, and people could see that it did not interfere with cops' abilities to function. Public education about so-called "criminals' rights," has largely been received through television cop dramas, and Miranda is now an expected part of the arrest procedure.

Just as in the true-crime magazine stories, the crime on both runs of *Dragnet* was always neatly solved and successfully prosecuted, beginning a long tradition of reality-based crime-TV programming that dramatizes the reordering of society after the disruption and disorder introduced by criminal events. Sgt. Joe Friday always got his man because the writers, at the request of the LAPD, based their stories exclusively on real crimes that had been solved and successfully prosecuted. Since *Dragnet*, with few exceptions television true crime has presented a relentless and monolithic view of crime as solvable and knowable, and human deviance as frightening and destabilizing, but ultimately containable. Competing strands of meaning vibrate through television true crime, keeping tension alive and the viewer riveted: cops and detectives are the "thin blue line" that separates the innocent and good citizen from the chaos and terror of random violence, but cops are also fallible and corruptible human beings. Criminals are devious, dangerous psychopaths, but they are also our neighbors, friends, relatives, and companions. Crime is random and soul-shattering, safety an impossible chimera, but in the end all the loose ends are tied up and the guilty are punished. An imagined community of good and well-meaning citizens ("us") is at war with an equally powerful community of depraved and indifferent underminers ("them"), but we CAN fight back, with the help of heroic and honest cops, detectives, and prosecutors.

When Jack Webb decided to end the series in 1971 and concentrate on his new police show, *Adam-12*, *Dragnet* found even greater success in syndication. Like much true-crime television, the series did as well in reruns as in its original runs. True crime on television had a slow start; in addition to

Dragnet, an early reality-based series was *Police Story* (1952), which dramatized real crimes from national police department files. *The FBI* (1965–1974) starring Efrem Zimbalist Jr., was supervised and checked for accuracy by J. Edgar Hoover, who tightly controlled the agency's media image, beginning with his columns penned for *True Detective* magazine in the 1940s. But the 1970s and 1980s were the first golden age of fictional cop dramas, with a corollary dearth of televised true crime. *Police Story* (1973–1977) was a fiction police procedural series that was advised and produced by Joseph Wambaugh; as in his books, the focus was on portraying the human and personal realities of police work. *Police Story* was groundbreaking in its depiction of cops as multidimensional and fully realized characters with histories, character flaws, and messy personal lives. The encyclopedia of 1970s and 1980s cop shows is full and rich, and many series based their plots on real stories, used real cops and detectives for their models, and portrayed police work in an increasingly realistic fashion. One such program that would have lasting importance in true crime was *Quincy, M.E.*, which began to air regularly in 1976. Although it did not portray real cases, *Quincy* would have a major impact on true-crime television because it helped popularize a little-known facet of detection and law enforcement: forensic science.

Jack Klugman was the personality that drove the popularity of *Quincy*: his character was a middle-aged Los Angeles medical examiner who doubled as a detective when presented with strange or mysterious deaths, and the character was purportedly based on the real LA County Medical Examiner, Dr. Thomas Noguchi. Klugman played the role with gusto and enthusiasm, and the aggressively workaholic Dr. Quincy tempered his sarcastic anger at "the system" (personified by his skeptical and disapproving supervisor) with kind-hearted and heroic detective work. The *Quincy* formula, familiar to fans of both police procedurals and later true-crime programs, is as follows: a "typical" death crosses Quincy's autopsy table, usually one classified as a suicide or accident; Quincy suspects foul play; Quincy battles his superiors in the Coroner's office and the LAPD to pursue the murderer; Quincy solves the crime with forensic science. The series had a very successful eight-year run and did well in syndication.

Because it is a fiction series, *Quincy* contains a range of narrative devices that move it out of the realm of conventional true crime: for example, Klugman's character is a heroic protagonist who regularly crosses disciplinary and jurisdictional boundaries that would never be tolerated in real police work, and his personality is a focal point of interest for viewers. In later years, the series became polemical and overly focused on the portrayal of social problems or issues, and the forensic science matters are often unrealistic (such as Quincy's theory that killer's fingerprints can be lifted from the skin of murder victims). Quincy's relationships with other characters are highlighted throughout the series, especially with his female love interests, his younger coworker Sam and his antagonistic boss. But the program has value as the first televised series that focused on forensics as a crucial component of the murder narrative, an important development in both the real work of detectives and in fashioning stories of how homicides are solved. The forensic science in *Quincy* looks dated and quaint to a twenty-first-century viewer, indicating how far the field (and its televised form) has evolved in the last quarter century.

After *Quincy, M.E.,* true-crime television moved into documentary and reenactment forms. The first true-crime documentary series, *Unsolved Mysteries,* created the conventions for this genre and was a popular hit, on air weekly from 1988–1997, and sporadically from 1997 until 2002. This was the first reality crime series to make use of the reenactment/interview montage format, and to ask for direct viewer participation, setting the template for much of the crime-reality television programming that would become popular in the following decades. The show's formulaic mix of such documentary techniques as dramatic reenactments, voice overs, simulations, interviews, still photographs, and "actuality" filming of detectives and forensics experts at work have been copied by numerous true-crime television series, and the same narrative conventions are also used on the weekly newsmagazine programs that depict crime. *Unsolved Mysteries* used a striking and authoritative narrator, Robert Stack, an actor who had portrayed Eliot Ness in another popular series about the FBI, *The Untouchables* (1959–1963).

Because the documentary true-crime programs don't have reappearing characters and protagonists, and each episode contains new people, the narrator or host becomes the recurring character that viewers can identify with and associate with the program. His—or her—role is to guide the viewer's perceptions about the various characters and to metaphorically hold back the curtain on the murder-drama, making visible that which had been hidden. During its most popular decade, Robert Stack *was* the voice of true crime and real mystery, and his look—always sporting his signature trench coat and stepping into or out of a wall of fog—contributed to his appeal. Although the series also portrayed other kinds of "mysteries" such as UFO sightings, adoption or lost children narratives, missing persons accounts, and paranormal phenomena, it became best-known for its pleas to the public for help solving difficult murder cases, capturing fugitives, and reuniting long lost relatives.

Unsolved Mysteries represented a major departure from the standard true-crime trope of narrating only cases that had been solved, relying instead on viewer interactivity and interest in a "mystery" formulation. In a review of contemporary true-crime television programs for MSNBC, Gael Fashingbauer Cooper suggests that "true-crime shows are a much purer form of mystery than their fictional counterparts," largely because of the absence of complex characters, messy and intricate relationships, and the labyrinthine twists of plot that characterize modern crime drama.[7] In true-crime television, every image, every interview, every bit of narration or monologue is focused on the solution of mystery. This obsession with closure and certainty offers a way to channel the feelings of outrage and sadness produced by the crime, but it is not always rewarded with a neat conclusion. As a pioneer of the genre, *Unsolved Mysteries* perfected that mix of satisfying formula and tantalizing ambiguity that keeps viewers coming back. Regular updates became part of the show as cases were solved, adding a delayed sense of closure and the enactment of justice, and upping the ante for viewer involvement in solving cases and calling in clues and information. Even though most cases were never closed, the fact that some were actually solved held promise and sustained viewers' interest in the series.

The visual iconography of documentary-style murder narration in true-crime television started with *Unsolved Mysteries*, which began the year after Errol Morris' 1987 film *The Thin Blue Line* was released. Morris's film used the reenactment and simulation in innovative ways to tell a murder story, and television very quickly copied the techniques, if not the effect, which *The Thin Blue Line* made famous. The reenactment, either shot with professional actors or the actual victims or survivors involved in the case, is the most common and informative narrative technique in this genre. The reenactment has strong reality claims, as it seems to portray "what actually happened," but is in fact a constructed and carefully orchestrated portrayal that resembles the free indirect discourse, or imagined dialogue, employed by true-crime writers. After all, nobody but the victim and killer are privy to the actual movements, behavior, sounds, and words of a murder event; in attempting to recreate the act, television producers may work closely with police investigators, profilers, surviving victims, or family members and friends, but they can never portray exactly what happened. A close resemblance may be enough for the viewer, but it blurs the line, continually contested in true crime, between fact and probable act, and advances misconceptions about crime and its circumstances.

Of course, the genre of nonfiction by definition presents possible versions or interpretations of reality, not reality itself. But true crime representations masquerade as reality, not interpretation: as crime infotainment, they claim journalistic authority while creating fictional, hyperreal landscapes, events, and characters. True-crime television depictions take on weight and meaning that can have unintended and serious consequences. In an essay about reality crime television, Gray Cavender writes that reenactments

> have virtually displaced the spectacle of public punishment as a vehicle for symbolically affirming moral sentiments and reproving their violation. The crime genre renders moralistic plots in which criminals,

whose villainy symbolizes social malaise and disorder, threaten the established order. Their defeat resolves the plot's tension, reaffirming moral boundaries.[8]

Thus the sexual predator who rapes and kills children becomes a symbolic villain who bears the condemnation of the entire society and provides a focal point for outrage at a range of social ills, some unrelated to the issue at hand; the home-invasion killer symbolizes the disappearance of an idealized and quasipastoral America (that was never a reality for all) where "people didn't lock their doors at night," replaced with a greedy and rapacious nation of sociopaths; the con man killer who bilks lonely women of their savings channels the sadness and disillusionment accompanying a mistrust of strangers, which is a mundane fact of life in a large modern society. The symbolic criminal acts out his violent impulses on the decontextualized stage of reenactment, where he is known only as the frightening, evil outsider and the victim is the completely innocent and good "insider" attached to the threatened community.

The symbolic value of such televised acts of violence and community betrayal replaces meaningful comprehension of the roots of crime, and reinforces an ideology of clichéd faux-safety. The notion that "it couldn't happen here" competes with the equally powerful idea that "it could happen anywhere," a complex emotional interaction that ultimately produces both apathy and inaction. On television, "here" is always "elsewhere," reenacted, real-but-unreal, next-door but not behind "my" door. The reenactment offers a modern form of catharsis, for it allows the viewer to visually participate in the crime, experiencing the horror and fear the victim felt, while then (usually) presenting the capture and punishment of the perpetrator that is the only satisfying conclusion to such tragedy. Through the interviews, which are interspersed within the vignettes, police officials and law enforcement agents guide the viewer and offer a symbolic reassurance of closure, capture, and the reestablishment of order. The power of enacting closure and capture in the reenactment would be deployed more regularly in the programs that followed *Unsolved Mysteries*, beginning with *AMW*.

Apprehension of criminals on a public stage followed by swift and sure punishment is the raison d'etre of one of the most popular and enduring television reality crime series, *America's Most Wanted*, a pioneering program in the field of interactive television. The series first aired in 1988, and has been an unstoppable television phenomenon ever since. Produced in conjunction with the FBI's Public Affairs Office, *AMW* continues the partnership of law enforcement and media that began with "The Line-Up" feature in *True Detective Magazine* and continued with *Dragnet* and *The FBI* in the 1950s and 1960s. The program was conceived as an entertaining and helpful response to the high rates of violent crime in the late 1980s, and it was modeled on two shows from Europe: Germany's *Case XY . . . Unsolved* (1967– present) and Britain's *Crimewatch UK* (1984–present). *AMW* was also influenced by the *Crimestoppers* phenomenon, which began in Albuqurque, New Mexico, in 1976, with the first recorded broadcast of a crime reenactment aimed at soliciting the help of viewers to identify a murderer. Although it has never gained huge market-share according to the Nielsen television rating system, the program has a reliable core audience and maintains a high-profile presence on the Fox Network. In 1996, *AMW* was briefly cancelled and replaced by two sitcoms; public and law enforcement community outcry was so great that the network brought the show back immediately, and it has become the longest-running series on the Fox Network, along with *Cops*, which began airing in 1989. The programs have aired back-to-back on Saturday nights since 1989, and the reality-crime-TV combination produces steady ratings and a pro-law enforcement reputation for Fox.

The host of *AMW* is John Walsh, whose six-year-old son Adam was abducted and murdered in 1981. In the years since that crime, John Walsh has become a well-known crime victims' and children's advocate, cofounding the National Center for Missing and Exploited Children and working steadily on victims' rights legislation. He was recruited to host *AMW* because of his authenticity as a victim and his status as crusader against crime. Here was a victim who "made a difference," a catchphrase that has become synonymous with the sense of empowerment and sanctioned vigilantism that *AMW* espouses. As a survivor/victim of violent crime, Walsh has unimpeachable credentials and is immune to criticism: any claims by detractors or critics that he endorses a narrow-minded, sanctimonious, and ultimately ineffective good-vs.-evil approach to crime is squelched by equally strong claims to his rights as the parent of a murdered child who is helping others overcome tragedy by "putting the creeps behind bars where they belong." The tabloid sensibility of *AMW* is often overlooked because the program does actually help catch fugitives and find missing children. As of May 2008, the show's Web site claims that it has "captured" 1,000 fugitives to date, an average of four per month.[9] Some of the captures are coincidental, and would have happened without intervention by *AMW*, but many are based on tips called in by viewers.

AMW has made the "perp-walk," where the captured, handcuffed suspect is paraded in slow motion across the television screen, escorted by triumphant police officers, a part of the national vocabulary. One early criticism of the show was that it undermined the principle of "innocent before proven guilty" by profiling suspects and people wanted for questioning, as well as convicted criminals who have escaped from prison. Even potentially innocent people are made to look guilty when given the *AMW* treatment, so the program now tends to concentrate its efforts on the already convicted, usually prison escapees or bail jumpers. Another criticism aimed at *AMW* is that because of its obsessive focus on serious and violent offenses, it gives a skewed picture of American crime, and it almost entirely ignores the problem of white-collar or nonviolent crime. The show also contributes to the widespread belief that the American murder problem is limited to white, middle-class sexual predators or domestic violence-related attacks, ignoring the more "mundane" reality that young, urban African American and Hispanic men kill and are killed in much greater numbers than middle-class whites. *AMW* relies on the same true-crime formula of reenactment/interview/simulation/still photos for its vignettes, but it also includes shots of call center workers in the background of the set "standing by to take your calls" if the viewer recognizes a fugitive. Every episode features follow up footage of captures from previous televised segments, many highlighting the perp-walk that offers the loyal viewer a sense of righteous closure and justice served.

AMW portrays crime as a symbol of unraveling social order and the collapse of civic good, and uses it as a stand-in for anxieties about a growing focus on the individual's wants and needs and away from community or communal concerns. This is particularly apparent in the *AMW* rhetorical style: its subtitle since 1996, "America Fights Back," is shorthand for proclaiming a community defensively posed in anxious solidarity against threats presented by dangerous criminal "others," a televised projection of a circle-the-wagons mentality. *AMW* promulgates a deeply negative and nonproductive ideology of fear and containment that focuses the anger of crime victims (and potential victims) onto certain individuals, encouraging viewers to ignore the murky root causes of crime and instead concentrate on those who have transgressed, those whose bodies can be tangibly caught, contained, and displayed. *AMW* encourages distrust and surveillance of community, family, neighbors, and friends, while creating a sense of "televised intimacy" as "the audience sees families struggle to maintain composure during an emotional interview."[10] The creation of, on the one hand, a community brought together by outrage and grief, alongside the encouragement of suspicion and paranoia about others, is a paradox that works for *AMW* and that its viewers find both captivating and satisfying.

The passive viewer involvement that reenactments offer works particularly well in the interactive milieu of *Unsolved Mysteries* and *AMW*. In an article about how *AMW* and other programs in the genre reinforce a law-and-order ideology, sociologist Pam Donovan identifies nine separate but related "realities" of reality crime TV: among others, she says that these programs reestablish the moral authority of police; they "pitch" law enforcement to a disillusioned public that is sometimes hostile to police; they allow viewers to feel empowered to "make a difference"; posit punishment as the "primary solution to crime"; they present a transparent and knowable world, allowing viewers to see how the "other half" (the poor, disenfranchised, lower class, transgressive, law breaking) lives; and they offer a model for involved and responsible citizenship, one that lets "viewers become partners by doing what they are already doing: sitting there."[11] The programs ultimately counter the paralyzing sense of futility and anonymity that many people feel by personalizing overwhelming crime statistics and presenting individual cases that can be—and sometimes are—solved by ordinary viewers. The cultural work that the interactive programs do is multilayered and complex, laden with paradox and encouraging a kind of passive activism.

In 1989, the year after *AMW* began regular weekly broadcasts, another innovative true-crime television series was introduced: *Cops*. Born of a combination of new and emerging videotape and handheld camera technology, the popularity of Geraldo Rivera-style guerrilla journalism, and the needs of local police agencies to burnish their public image, *Cops* has generated consistently high Nielsen ratings since its inception. Although *Cops* is a live-action police procedural, and therefore outside the boundaries of the usual true-crime television genre (it doesn't present murder narratives and instead focuses on the pursuit and apprehension of all types of suspects and lawbreakers), the program is a significant addition to reality crime-TV. Its "video-verité" look, camera positions that allow the viewer to vicariously accompany police officers on their calls, and unscripted format have been parodied, copied, and emulated, leading directly to the production of other shows with more of a true-crime focus.

Cops has been widely criticized for many reasons, including racist portrayals and overrepresentation of black perpetrators and suspects and its uncritical presentation of police. The uniformly positive depictions of police can be explained by the fact that without the cooperation of police agencies, the show could not exist, so *Cops* heavily edits its segments and refuses to air video footage that can be construed as damaging to or critical of law enforcement. In addition, to ensure viewer interest, *Cops* focuses on dramatic encounters, particularly those involving violence, drugs, and danger. The resulting construction of a criminal reality pushes the viewer into the same hyperreality that *AMW* does, and positions the cops as countering a deeply violent and dangerous American criminal landscape. The result is a program that entertains with a simple "us vs. them" ideology and an unquestioning acceptance of containment and punishment as a solution to the "crime problem"; ultimately, in the words of critic Aaron Doyle, *Cops* "is about hyperreality but, more importantly, is about a brute reality: the punitive politics of law and order."[12] The reactionary politics of both *AMW* and *Cops* conveyed a sense of growing threat at a time of peaking violent crime rates, in the late 1980s and early 1990s, but the shows have not eased their emphasis on menace with the decreasing violent crime rates over the past decade. In the face of drastically reduced rates of violent crime in America,

the "reality" portrayed on these programs presents a more carefully constructed vision than ever.

The popularity of coverage of real crimes and law enforcement in real
time led to the creation of the Courtroom Television Network (Court TV)
on cable in 1991. Steven Brill, an attorney and founder of the monthly
law magazine *The American Lawyer*, began the network with the idea of providing gavel-to-gavel television coverage of important or sensational trials,
with the larger goal of countering public ignorance about real courtroom
proceedings. At the time of its inception, skeptics thought such a channel
could not sustain audience interest, but Brill believed that the combination of education and entertainment would work. In an interview about
the network's origins, he said "frankly, Court TV's goal is to substitute real
law for *L. A. Law*. We want to teach people that constitutional rights aren't
technicalities used by soft judges and slick lawyers, but are the bedrock of
a system of rule of law that is the envy of the world."[13] Brill was referring
to prevailing pop culture images (*L. A. Law* was a television lawyer drama)
that at the time gave a skewed picture of the judicial system and fostered
false perceptions that defendants had more constitutional protections than
crime victims. While its original goal of education has often collided with
more pressing needs for advertising revenue by presenting sensational or
tabloidesque content and biased or controversial commentators, until recently Court TV was the only television venue to offer complete coverage of
major American criminal trials. It remains to be seen, with its January 2008
name and format change to "TruTV," whether the network will remain true
to its original goals or give in to the pressure to provide sensational "real"
content.

Court TV's role in producing and broadcasting true crime became significant during the late 1990s, as the network moved beyond trial coverage
into presenting both fiction and nonfiction series in an attempt to boost
ratings. After its mid-1990s popularity surge, which was largely due to its
complete coverage of such lurid cases as the Lorena Bobbitt affair and
the Menendez brothers parent murders, serial killer Jeffrey Dahmer, and
O. J. Simpson murders, Court TV's Nielsen ratings sagged and the executives
took the network in a new direction. In 1998, under the direction of then
new Chairman-CEO Henry Schleiff, Court TV implemented a branding
strategy that included adding more high-profile lawyer-commentators and
creating stronger daytime, current events, and true-crime programming.
Since the early 2000s, the network has been producing such programs as
Forensic Files that have boosted their ratings, and in 2003 a new advertising campaign branded the network as "The Investigation Channel." Now
owned by Time Warner broadcasting, the network is aggressively pursuing a reality-TV agenda, and the format shift away from crime coverage
and into sensational reality-type programming has already started with such

programs as *Court TV RED (Real. Exciting. Dramatic.)*, which presents video footage of accidents, car crashes, explosions, and so forth shot by amateur or coincidental videographers, and *Bounty Girls*, a program that follows the life and work of female bounty hunters.

Court TV/TruTV airs a large variety of documentary-type true-crime programs that present murder narratives with an array of themes and perspectives: *Psychic Detectives, Haunting Evidence, Dominick Dunne's Power, Privilege and Justice, 'Til Death Do Us Part, Body of Evidence, Murder by the Book, L. A. Forensics, North Mission Road*, and *Arrest & Trial*, each provide a slightly different take on the act of murder. The various themes include an antiscientific emphasis on paranormal or psychic powers to illuminate mystery, pointed critiques of the privileges available to the wealthy, the use of dark humor to lighten the heavy load of murder and satirize social norms, and conventional quasidocumentary treatments that portray criminal profilers or satisfy the recent viewer interest in forensic science. By far, the most popular are the programs that highlight or feature some aspect of forensic science and add a liberal dash of suspense and mystery. With Court TV's format and name change, The Discovery Channel will launch another network called Investigation Discovery that will focus on true-crime programming, and on its Web site, the network "promises to deliver remarkable insight into the real life world of investigation, exploration of the latest forensic analysis and dramatic true stories that piece together puzzles of human nature."[14]

Court TV/TruTV and the Arts and Entertainment (A & E) cable channel, which also airs many true-crime documentary forensics programs, have found that such programs have an enormously successful "retention rate," the lucrative ability to retain viewers through commercial breaks. According to a 2004 article in *Advertising Age*, "the complexity of the programming draws a unique type of viewer, who networks say has higher attention and retention levels than viewers of other cable programming" and "Court TV research shows that its 18-to-49-year-old prime-time viewers have a retention rate of 95% through commercial breaks, which is No. 1 among ad-supported basic cable networks."[15] In a dramatic reversal of position from that of the 1940s librarians and English teachers who worried about the deleterious effects of reading true crime, commentators are now citing the superior intelligence and focus of true-crime fans. Of course, producers of true crime always made such claims, and much of the retention is simply the power of a good old-fashioned murder mystery.

But viewers have learned much about forensic science—and such previously obscure types of forensics such as pathology, entomology, toxicology, and odontology—because of recent true-crime trends; at least one pop culture critic, Stephen Johnson, believes that instead of deadening the intellect, contemporary television programming actually makes viewers smarter. In his book, *Everything Bad Is Good for You: How Today's Popular Culture Is Actually*

Making Us Smarter, Johnson connects rising American IQ scores over the past few decades to (among other things) the gradual increase in narrative complexity, structure, and technical information contained in some of the most popular television series. In his introduction, Johnson writes "popular culture has, on average, grown more complex and intellectually challenging over the past thirty years. Where most commentators assume a race to the bottom and a dumbing down—'an increasingly infantilized society,' in George Will's words—I see a progressive story: mass culture growing more sophisticated, demanding more cognitive engagement with each passing year."[16] Certainly, true-crime TV has been a part of that "progressive story," as viewers have been increasingly exposed to detailed depictions of the criminal justice system and how it works, information about very specific laws and procedures, and minute facts about forensic science and psychology.

In the late 1980s, when *Quincy, M.E.* was on-air, forensic science had recently evolved from the standard and somewhat rudimentary ballistics-fingerprints-and-blood type analysis into more sophisticated and careful gathering of microscopic evidence, use of powerful laboratory tools such as electron microscopes, and the emergence of DNA gathering and testing technology. The 1994 O. J. Simpson trial proved that television audiences could both stomach and follow extraordinarily complicated scientific details, if explained in layman's terms and layered with suspense and drama. Television producers took note of these developments and launched what has become a runaway hit subgenre with the documentary forensics programs. Two early cable series, HBO's *The Autopsy Files* (1994–1995) and The Learning Channel's *Medical Detectives* (1995–2000), were important forerunners of such later series as *Forensic Files* and *Cold Case Files*, as both highlighted the way that forensic pathologists can sometimes solve intractable and mysterious cases with science. Standard and conventional in most respects, comprised of a mix of interviews, reenactments, voice over narration and actuality filming, the first forensics-based programs positioned the scientist as a modern priest or oracle, a figuration that later programs would follow; in the words of the narrator of *The Autopsy Files*, the medical examiner or forensic pathologist is the "interpreter of the voices of the dead" who "reveals their secrets to the living." Although very scientific and serious-minded, the focus is on communication with the dead and the suggestion that although the body dies, it can still tell truths and in that sense, transcend death. Forensic science as portrayed in the true-crime programs blends the practical and the spiritual, science and faith, detachment with deepest emotion.

Many of the documentary-style programs include forensic elements, but all rely on various combinations of reenactment, detection, and contextualization. There is a surprising amount of variety in the reenactment/documentary shows, with each one slightly augmenting the standard formula, adding its own perspective, and pushing the boundaries of the conventions.[17] A & E's *Cold Case Files* depicts the die-hard and passionate persistence of detectives who follow dead-end leads and resuscitate seemingly impossible-to-solve cases. A & E's *City Confidential*, narrated by the velvet-gravel voiced Paul Winfield until his death in 2004, catalogues American murder according to place: each episode presents one story from a different American city, creating a kind of "murder map," while offering a mini-history, culture, and geography lesson at the same time. Court TV's *Forensic Files* portrays murder cases whose solution rests on physical forensic evidence, and it depicts forensic scientists unraveling bizarre or especially difficult crime circumstances using both standard and innovative techniques. A & E's *The First 48* follows real detectives as they try to solve a murder (or at least generate good leads) within the crucial first forty-eight hours following the crime, after which the chances of solving the crime decrease by 50 percent. This program does not use reenactments, instead relying only on the "live-action" quality of filming detectives at their work, echoing the video-verité camera work in *Cops*. The Oxygen Network's *Snapped* profiles female murderers and has been criticized for making murder an equal-opportunity endeavor and engaging in victim-blaming in its domestic violence cases; A & E's *American Justice*, narrated by the authoritative Bill Kurtis, presents various crimes, not always homicide, which challenge or complicate the law, and examines the legal, social, and moral issues involved. Court TV's *Arrest & Trial*, produced by Dick Wolf (the creator/producer of *Law & Order*) and narrated by Brian Dennehy, is the nonfiction counterpart to *Law & Order*, even sharing a visual style and similar graphics.

The documentary crime shows rely on similar visual and production techniques: dramatic reenactments, voice overs, simulations, interviews, still photographs, and actuality filming of detectives and forensics experts at work. The mixture of these elements varies in the different programs (*City Confidential* relies on more contextual information, *Forensic Files* focuses on the work of scientific criminalists), but the conventions remain solidly in place. Audiences have come to expect a formulaic murder narrative from these programs and to accept the presentation of "truth" that they construct. *Psychic Detectives* presents reenactments not just of the crime, but also of the events that take place during the investigation, and *L. A. Forensics* reenacts the entire sequence of events from crime to solution in an annoying jump cut music-video style. Both series are heavily stylized and presented with unusual and various camera angles, posed shots, and computer effects added to the footage and vignettes.

One program that does not use reenactments is the weekly CBS newsmagazine, *48 Hours Mystery*. Because it is a "news" program, journalistic standards preclude the use of actors to depict events, and reenactments are forbidden by the networks Standards code. The program began life as a single 1986 journalistic exposé called *48 Hours on Crack Street*, which was serialized in 1988 as an in-depth portrayal of two days spent on each subject. The program's various names—*48 Hours, 48 Hours Investigates*, and finally *48 Hours Mystery*—reflect the changing focus of the show throughout the 1990s, as it moved through investigative journalism topics such as those covered by *60 Minutes* or *20/20*, then began to focus exclusively on true-crime material. The "*Mystery*" title appeared in the early 2000s, with the surprise success of the CBS-produced *CSI* franchise, and its producers imagine the show as a "true life" counterpart to *CSI*, with the presentation of one murder narrative each week analyzed through various perspectives, but usually solved at the end of the hour. The majority of its narratives portray murder among middle-class or affluent whites, with an overrepresentation of domestic homicides, and their narratives always include a major element of mystery or surprise plot twists. Like much other true-crime material, *48 Hours Mystery* has a largely female audience, and the ads that support it—a preponderance of pitches for household cleaning products, allergy medicines and cold remedies—reinforce the Nielsen reports on viewership.

The reenactment sanctions and encourages voyeurism, but for specific ends: for *Unsolved Mysteries* or *AMW*, the stated aim is to catch the perpetrator. The reenactments that *Unsolved Mysteries* presents rely on the actors and play like conventional story vignettes: standard camera angles (as if you are a third person viewing the events), natural lighting, no computer-visual effects, certain shots from the perpetrator's perspective for creepy effect. *Unsolved Mysteries* uses standard fiction-TV techniques that narrate events chronologically and with a simple focus on narrative and characters, unlike the later shows that often present their vignettes and reenactments with blurred faces and layered computer effects that distance the viewer from the events being portrayed. *UM* concentrates its attention on presenting the actions of the victim and suspects, while later shows sometimes also reenact the investigation.

For other programs, the goals may be different: some use the reenactment to build suspense, revealing the hidden and mysterious details of the exact means of death of the subject only after the capture or confession of the murderer. In this way, the reenactment provides narrative resolution, because it often delays the revelation of the exact rendering of death. The structure of *Forensic Files* finesses this point, as each episode shows the full reenactment of the crime only at the very end of the program, after the crime has been solved. A recent episode illustrates this strategy: a five-year-old girl was abducted from a Christmas party, with her mother standing just a few feet away. At the beginning of the program, abduction and murder is suggested as the child steps away from a stationary camera that then captures the space where she had just been as the voice over relates the mystery and horror of her disappearance. Not until the abductor is caught do we get the full picture: the girl had wandered into a hallway to get a drink from a water fountain, and the janitor snatched her away and escaped, dragging her through a broom closet window to his waiting vehicle and later killing her. Although the janitor never confessed the precise details of the abduction and murder, only after he was caught are we shown the entire scenario of abduction. Delaying the reenactment of the abduction titillates the viewer by gratifying the desire to see what was hidden and unknown, allowing a glimpse into an act that was carried out with great care and secrecy.

Reenactments also obey certain rules of decorum and usually avoid graphic depictions of gore and bloodshed. When reenacting serious and culturally taboo crimes like murder, abduction, and molestation, true-crime television uses a visual rhetoric of techniques like slow motion, unconventional or jarring camera angles, blurred faces, lighting that obscures, and suggestion and euphemism rather than overt details of physical violation. After all, the shows have to make it past the censors, even on cable; reenactments are notoriously tame and gestural, especially when compared to the live-action crime reality programming seen on *Cops* or *The First 48*. The former doesn't hesitate to depict real violence, and the latter shows the actual aftermath of violent crime, including bloodstains and spatters, bodies (usually draped with sheets or in body bags, although glimpses of the dead are shown), and the detritus of rescue left behind after the Emergency Medical Personnel and police leave. Reenactments allow the shows to both sanitize murder and to have more careful control over the reality they present.

That reality reflects audience expectations and desires for murder to contain such elements as mystery, intrigue, profound aberrance, the discovery of hidden or "secret" elements to a person's life, psychosexual drama, and the unvarnished portrayal of such human failings as greed, envy, or lust. The documentary/reenactment programs choose stories with some or all of these elements, always amplifying the more dramatic emotional tensions and forces that direct both the killer's and the victim's actions. The result is to make murder—which is often sordid and enacted for petty reasons by pathetic, stupid, or essentially boring people—"interesting" in some way. *48 Hours Mystery* or *Forensic Files* can transform a sad and dismayingly common domestic murder into a thrilling narrative that pulses with suspense and tension, handing the viewer a perfectly crafted tale of a devious and greedy husband whose pernicious desires are thwarted by a steadfast and observant forensic scientist. The writers and producers of these programs are charged with the task of crafting the suspense, surprise, plot twists, and incredible coincidences that make murder worth watching, and they deliver, night after night and week after week.

The large number of these programs adds a layer of paradox to the formulation of murder that posits mystery or singularity as its most important element. The presentation of so *many* murderers (several separate cases are televised every single night!) in so *many* mundane and ordinary contexts—in the subdivision, at the dentist's office, in the city park—impresses the viewer with the frequency and prevalence of murder, so that regular viewing erases the "mystery" of monstrous murder. In this way, the uncommon becomes very common, challenging the notion (present in so much true crime) that killers are aberrant monsters. The true-crime programs must maintain a delicate balancing act between presenting the "monster-next-door" as both strange and mundane to retain viewer interest in its serially same subjects. In its attempt to present the strange and outrageous in a drama-rich context, true-crime television paradoxically makes murder among the middle-class familiar and almost prosaic.

The First 48 offers a different perspective on murder, one that further erases its strangeness and advances the idea that most murder is commonplace, uncomplicated, and devastatingly routine. The program presents murder as it occurs most often in America: between people of color, in urban high-crime neighborhoods, and caused by seemingly petty disputes, missteps in drug-buying and selling, and absurd or tragic "accidents." This program, like *Cops* does with patrolmen, follows actual working detectives in real time as they respond to and investigate homicide, and it has a necessarily pro-law enforcement bent; unlike *Cops*, *The First 48* complicates a straightforward "us vs. them" ideology of threat and containment by examining context and humanizing both victims and perpetrators. The major forensics-based reenactment programs almost uniformly portray white middle-class victims and perpetrators, making such murder circumstances seemingly normative; in fact, they are not the norm, and *The First 48* (like the *LA Times* journalist Jill Levoy's Web log *The Homicide Report*) counters this erroneous idea. This program undermines its audience's preconceptions about what American murder is and shows the seams of the standard murder narrative in mainstream media by presenting victims whose lives aren't shattered by mystery or serial killers, but by stray bullets, poverty, limited opportunities, and enormous challenges to dignity, prosperity, and life itself. *The First 48* offers a different reality than the other true-crime documentary series, one that demystifies both the murder narrative and the murderer.

In contrast, the wildly popular *CSI* franchise (*CSI-Las Vegas, CSI-Miami, CSI-New York*) remystifies murder, while paradoxically making it transparent and knowable. Like *Forensic Files*, the various versions of *CSI* focus on bodies as the location of mystery and truth, the hidden and the known/knowable. In the words of Anita Biressi in her study of true crime in Great Britain, these programs present an "emphasis upon the dead and decaying body of the murder victim as both spectacle and clue."[18] In *CSI*, occult knowledge—of past actions, of bullet trajectories, of body-mysteries, of monstrous but "real" deeds—is revealed through science, and just as in the original forensics-documentaries, the forensic scientist is a priest who finds and speaks truths offered by the dead. In addition, and taking a cue from *Quincy*, the *CSI* investigators are also detectives, fulfilling dual roles in a way that doesn't ordinarily happen in real police work, therefore embodying the archetype of the Holmesian super-scientist-cop. These heroic figures on *CSI* regularly "resurrect" the dead and perform magic with the microscope, with DNA, and with a range of other fictional and actual technologies. In an article in *The New Republic* about the popularity of such programs, critic Lee Siegel says:

> If ever there was a show that expressed our solitary, computer-riveted sense of being there but not being there, of being mysteriously injured or depressed yet feeling healthy and optimistic, of being helpless to influence events but feeling strangely that we are powerful enough to do so, it is these raw, entertaining, gripping, utterly delusive fantasies of transparency and control.[19]

On *CSI*, the murder is always solved and complete closure attained, although sometimes there are lingering ambiguities about motive or specific details of the crime. The imagined reenactments—like those deployed in *The Thin Blue Line*—show possible realities, versions of events or ideas about what *might* have happened. Additionally, the *CSI* reenactments allow the viewer to transcend ordinary physical boundaries, as the ultra-closeup camera follows a bullet fracturing into bone or traces the microscopic elements of a drug making its way from drink to throat to receptor cells in a victim's stomach. Nothing is hidden or mysterious here, and the secret ways of violence and bodily harm are laid bare for the viewer to see and to know.

In the *CSI* world, the ultimate injustice (murder) is always rectified through science and solution, and presented as a perfect mixture of the ultra-real and the truly fantastic—crime, technology, and tedious dirty police work alongside great beauty, style, and instantaneous results. *CSI* is murder as music video, juiced up by sexy and attractive characters and a musical soundtrack perfectly attuned to pop sensibilities. Theme songs by rock supergroup The Who—*CSI*'s "Who Are You," and "Won't Get Fooled Again" for *CSI: Miami*—highlight the mystery of criminal identity and the pure excitement of pursuit and capture. A hybrid cop drama, *CSI* fits into the genre that now presents the ambiguity, drudgery, uncertainty, and moral doubts that accompany real police work, but gives them the shine and luster of assured competence and certain, usually quick solution. Categories of the known and the unknowable blur together as murder is first remystified, then uncovered and traced by beautiful characters who are armed with the outrageously powerful weaponry of microscopic science.

With most reality crime-TV shows, except for the pioneering *Unsolved Mysteries*, everything is always solved and certain: *Forensic Files*, *American Justice*, *Cold Case Files*, and *City Confidential* each present a neat package of facts satisfyingly tied with a bow of solution. The drama unfolds with suspense and uncertainty, but in the end the murder is (nearly) always cleared. *48 Hours Mystery* attempts to leave the viewer with some lingering questions by presenting cases that contain some unexpected "twist" or surprise element, but the murders are usually solved by the end of the hour. The programs offer both mystery and reassurance, for we are assured that we'll be given a killer, a motive, and justice in every episode. Good guys and bad guys are identified, and ambiguities, if they persist, are minor. On the true-crime programs, certainty and closure are assured, continuing the creation of fantasy and control, of order and solution rather than chaos and dissolution. *CSI* offers an antidote to the postmodern terror of ambiguity and injustice presented by Errol Morris in his film *The Thin Blue Line*, which, although in some ways predictive of the style of the modern forensic/cold-case television genre, is thematically opposite.

That tidy presentation of facts began with *Dragnet*, where this chapter started. Jack Webb's signature phrase, "All we want are the facts, ma'am," describes the quest of the entire true-crime television genre. As a hybrid true-crime/fiction series, *Dragnet* shares some common elements with *CSI*, but it has also informed the other types of true-crime television. Because its focus was on presenting the realities of police work, the murder narrative on *Dragnet* was unremarkable. Murder was presented as simply another form of crime, no different from the robbery, drug pushing and abuse, fraud, kidnapping, burglary, and rape that also appeared in the series. Friday and his partners were less interested in the "why" than the "who" of murder, and the stories left unanswered the larger questions of motive and psychology. The show gave the viewer responsibility for piecing together the justification for the killer's actions. In the 1952 episode *The Big Cast*, Lee Marvin plays a psychopathic killer of twelve men who confesses after a long night of talk with the detectives. He keeps emphasizing that murder isn't as big a deal as the "mystery detective writers" have it. People murder for mundane, small reasons, not for what he calls "the big buildup." As the killer confesses over a health food dinner, Friday eventually asks him if he's ever seen a psychiatrist. Marvin's character answers with "No, why?" giving the viewer the idea that there's something disordered about this man's mind, something not quite right. This illustrates an older idea of the psychopath: he's not yet the moral monster of later depictions, but still just a man, mentally ill but not incomprehensible. The important part, for Friday and his police force, is simply that the killer is apprehended and stopped; he doesn't have to be understood.

The murder narrative in the documentary forensics programs is focused on showing how the killer has done the deed, an explanation always arrived at through both old-fashioned detective work and high-tech scientific forensic analysis. The questions that drive these programs revolve around pragmatic and logistic circumstances of murder and on putting together the minute scraps of evidence that killers leave behind: is that one tiny blood stain on the car door handle enough to prove guilt? Can the pulp in the teeth of a burned corpse be used for DNA identification? *Forensic Files* excels at this kind of presentation of murder, with each episode exploring an intriguing and perplexing murder that is always solved and successfully prosecuted. The great popularity of forensics owes much to an old and powerful idea, one used in murder stories since the creation of Sherlock Holmes: that science can conquer the irrational and extract order from chaos. With each newly invented crime-solving technology, the power of science is updated and tested anew, and this is borne out by the latest forensics-TV craze: since the arrival of advanced DNA testing and the compilation of the CODIS database (the FBI's Combined DNA Index System, a computer database that makes it possible to identify unknown perpetrators through DNA left at crime scenes), forensics-based true-crime television has flourished.

Knowing and attempting an accurate presentation of "just the facts" is much trickier than it appears, and the demands of nonfiction compel the makers of murder narratives to shade seamlessly into fictional depictions of reality. The excerpt at the head of this chapter speaks to the conundrum of reality television: that "realism is an artificial construct" and "there is nothing natural about realism." As it shapes the reality of murder, true-crime television largely fulfills the same expectations that murder mysteries do: that murder is sexy, interesting, and mysterious, a spectacle, but somehow always *elsewhere*. Titillation and excitement accompany the viewer's experience of fear, dread, and anxiety: like riding a roller coaster, we get to look danger and death in the eye and walk away. Only with such critical distance is the extreme closeup possible, for television is not interested in overwhelming its audience with horror. As the genre expands and continues to draw viewers, new formulations appear: Showtime's serial killer drama *Dexter* first aired in 2006 and presents murderous perversity as chic, hip, and fastidious while collapsing the psychopath and the detective into one character, suggesting the ideological and moral closeness of those two figures. In the summer of 2007, the cable station Spike TV debuted their new series *Murder*, taking the genre to its next possible step with the morally dubious presentation of real murder as a kind of game show. On each program, contestants try to solve a real murder—one that, thankfully, has already been solved and prosecuted—using forensics and their powers of detection. The vast emotional distance between the players and the reality they are playing with makes the game possible, a distance that true-crime television has honed to perfection.

chapter five

THE INTERNET

Crimeblog: NOUN: A personal Web site that may provide regularly-
updated links to news articles about crime. A CRIMEBLOG may also
include additional independent research, commentary, and speculation by the author about the news story.
—Steve Huff, http://truecrimeblogroll.blogspot.com/

True crime appears on the Internet in great abundance and in various forms
and categories. Unlike the other media forms—magazines, books, films, and
television programs—Internet true crime offers opportunities for audience-
producer interactivity that changes the relationship between the consumer
and the content, opening possibilities that have expanded the cultural work
of true crime and the genre itself, including greater access to previously unavailable information, the creation of communities of true-crime fans and
critics, documentation of open cases that are sometimes solved or resolved
because of direct participation by viewers, and the development of a critical
sensibility around true crime that eschews tabloidism and favors productive analytical thought about murder and crime. Alternately, the Internet
has also opened up more public space for tabloidism, exploitation, and
sensationalism, most prominently in the "serial killer chic" category with
its arch murder-is-entertaining sensibility and fun-house horror aesthetic.
True-crime blogging, while opening new opportunities for talented writers
to explore different kinds of cases and address some of the representational disparities in mainstream media crime coverage, ultimately upholds
the true crime status quo. Neither all bad nor all good, the Internet revolution has impacted true crime as profoundly as it has other aspects of
modern existence, most prominently in the realms of entertainment, news
and information, and communication.

Internet true crime encompasses all other media forms covered in this
book in the form of television program, magazine, and film Web sites and

databases that offer additional information and interactive features, and author Web logs or book Web sites. The Internet also offers historical databases and scholarly archives, official government documents and statistics about homicide and other types of crime, and an immense variety of true-crime Web logs. The Internet is now another prime location for crime "infotainment," with its global reach, both targeted and broad audiences, lack of stringent centralized regulation, and twenty-four-hour continuous news cycle. The true-crime aficionado now has unprecedented access to formerly unavailable materials, from a trove of twentieth-century true-crime magazines to the nearly impossible-to-find Robert Hendrickson documentary film about Charles Manson, intelligently written accounts of historical true-crime stories, official and up-to-date FBI or Department of Justice homicide statistics, or witty commentary about the latest headline-grabbing murder. Without the Internet, I would have spent many more hours in museums, archives, and libraries researching this book; instead, almost everything I needed was available on my own computer. The combination of availability, instant easy access, and very little regulation has changed true crime and the behavior and thoughts of those who research, write, and read it; this chapter explores the landscape of Internet true crime in its present form, its peaks and valleys, and the personalities who inhabit and create it.

LIFE IN THE TRUE-CRIME BLOGOSPHERE

The most interesting and innovative Internet true crime appears in the form of "blogs," the diary-style Web sites or virtual bulletin boards that include a "comments" function, making reader interaction a crucial component of the medium. The scope and variety of the true-crime blogs hints at the immensity and diversity of interest in the genre: the gamut of ideological, political, and lifestyle beliefs represented on the blogs encompasses liberal/conservative, outsider/insider, amateur/professional, freak/straight, and even criminal/noncriminal. Because crime and transgression can be such an emotionally charged area of interest and communication, the emotional register of the blogs is also quite broad, from shrill and castigating to low-key and objective. True-crime blogging began in earnest in the early twenty-first century, with the development of "Web 2.0," the second generation of Internet activity and presence that includes blogs, wikis, social networking sites, podcasts, and RSS feeds.

In his book *The Rise of the Blogosphere*, Aaron Barlow writes that blogging as a form of public journalism and communication with a diverse audience grew out of early computer bulletin board systems or discussion boards that were created and inhabited by individuals involved in computers and (often) progressive politics in the 1980s and 1990s. The first bulletin or discussion boards were mainly local or regional, but the formation of online communities soon outgrew any geographical boundaries as the World Wide Web coalesced into its present form in the mid-1990s. Barlow identifies the post-9/11 failure of mainstream media and cable and network news agencies to adequately cover world events as the catalyst for the surge in the number and kind of political blogs in the early 2000s, which coincided with the availability of user-friendly blogging software.[1] Blogging has reinvigorated and democratized journalism and is challenging conventional beliefs in the special powers and privileges of the journalist to find, sort, and report the news. As reported on Technorati.com in late 2007, there are currently 112 million blogs worldwide, with no signs of subsidence or falling-off, and "there are over 175,000 new blogs (that's just blogs) every day."[2] The medium is changing so rapidly that by the time this book goes to press, much of this information will already be outdated, and the blog-list will certainly be longer and more complex.

True-crime blogs offer a multilayered response to a monolithic and deadening mainstream media oversaturation with formulaic presentations of murder. In their finest form, the true-crime blogs present reasoned, well researched, and fully documented opinions and information about past and current crimes, with an overwhelming focus on murder-events. In a recent post about the True Crime Blogroll, a Web site that presents a regularly updated compendium of the best of the true-crime blogs, a Canadian blogger known as "Harding" says that

> The true crime bloggers of the TCB [True Crime Blogroll] provide a vital public service. . . . It is clear to me now, more than ever, that mainstream media have a very particular, almost narrow focus of the crimes they cover. The editorial choices that go into reporting are limited to a very small, virtually unnoticeable number of criminal cases. True crime bloggers bring an infinite number of them to the surface, and focus on details that the popular dailies tend to miss, or skim over.[3]

The critical urge of many true-crime bloggers is implicit, as they work against a tide of oversensationalized, superficial, and dumbed-down depictions of murder in such mainstream news organizations as CNN and Court TV, one that is relentlessly focused on the murder or disappearance of young, attractive, middle- or upper-middle-class and (usually) white women or girls. Bloggers report on a fuller range of murder and crime events, often with a self-conscious political agenda to examine and document a range of under-reported cases.

At the same time, some of the most prominent true-crime bloggers are following the well-worn path that their predecessors, the print and television journalists, have already trudged. Because the ironclad conventions of the true-crime genre are so rigid, breaking out of the traditional rhetorical styles, patterns of narration, and choice of topics is extremely difficult for the true-crime writer and blogger. The bloggers may cover their stories with greater depth and thoroughness, but the murder of vulnerable victims—attractive young women and children—remains a topic of choice, sexual crimes and missing persons cases receive great amounts of coverage, and the purple prose that expresses maudlin emotionality or simplistic fear-based retrogression is unfortunately abundant. Steve Huff, a well-regarded true-crime blogger, is one such example. Although his True Crime Weblog (http://www.truecrimeweblog.com/) is serious in tone and meticulously researched, the cases that he covers stay within a narrow range: usually white, suburban/exurban, middle class, or extremely deviant working/lower class victims and perps. The standard true-crime preoccupation with mystery, whether it is the puzzle of a missing young person or the unknowable enigma of "evil," is prominent on this blog as well; the "missing-white-woman-of-the-week" is a big hit on the Internet, where she is endlessly pictured, commented on, psychologically dissected, and publicly mourned. In a *Rolling Stone* review of Internet true crime, Huff says about his blog that "A big part is to keep a focus on unsolved crimes...crimes that are neglected by the mainstream media"[4] Intelligently done, decently written and entertaining, Huff's true crime is the best example of a worn-out formula that has been resuscitated rather than reinvigorated on the Internet. His criticism of major media true crime is shallow and does not extend to creating an alternative to the rhetoric or framing devices that trivialize homicide by turning it into entertainment and keep most of its victims unknown and unnarrated.

One reason for the lack of imagination in true-crime blogging is that the true-crime sensibility meshes harmoniously with the impulse to blog, for the amateur journalism and political activism enacted in the blogs can counter the feelings of futility engendered by true crime. As suggested by David Kline, blogging is an antidote to the "alienation, powerlessness, and crushing anonymity that seem to be such overpowering features of modern life," features that true-crime narratives tend to reinforce.[5] Most true crime emphasizes depravity, perversity, sexually motivated crimes, serial killing, and the abduction-murder of children, thereby reinforcing an erroneous impression that all American neighborhoods—whether rural, urban, exurban, or suburban—are patently unsafe, and that we are each alone in the fight against the sexual predators and murdering monsters who inhabit our environment in ever-greater numbers. The true-crime worldview fosters anger and a sense of futility about specific aspects of American crime: the seeming ubiquity and increasing number of pedophiles, the rapists and killers who are regularly paroled or given sentences that don't seem to fit their crimes, the serial killers who stalk and prey upon young and vulnerable women, all are regular entrants in the true-crime parade.

Those who produce works in the genre are as susceptible as its readers and viewers to the anxiety and paranoia engendered by true crime, even as the act of blogging can create a sense of community and of having a powerful positive impact on the world. The bloggers' work spreads awareness about local or regional crimes, those perversions, abuses, and murders that don't make it to the national stage and that the larger press outlets have no time or space to cover in any depth. But this awareness creates a double-edged sword for the reader: on the one hand, reading the true-crime blogs may increase a reader's consciousness of latent danger and hidden threats in a particular environment, amping up the anxiety by bringing on even more crime, potentially in the reader's own backyard. Simultaneously, by following the murder narratives and the comments on a blog, the reader can get a comforting sense that he or she isn't alone, anonymous, or separate in individual comprehension of and reactions to crime, and that other ordinary people share the outrage and horror. The bulletin board and communal nature of the blogs counters the alienation and anonymity that can accompany more solitary consumption of true-crime narratives.

True-crime blogging can also empower both the blogger and the reader by creating communal outrage that can be, and sometimes is, channeled into productive and meaningful action. It gives authors and audiences an unprecedented opportunity to voice their responses to death and violence and show their desire for justice in a public and instantaneous manner. Blogs provide a kind of social space that is at once public and private, inside the home or office yet also within the larger public sphere, both intimate and distancing. Reading and commenting on a blog means joining a community of anonymous strangers who share a common interest or goal; when that goal is the dispersal of accurate and timely information or the creation of a support community around a local criminal event, the Internet can be a very powerful positive tool. One such case is the Yahoo discussion group that formed in 2003 in response to the Baton Rouge, Louisiana, serial killings perpetrated by Derrick Todd Lee, which is documented in the book *In Search of Derrick Todd Lee: The Internet Social Movement That Made a Difference.*[6] Although not technically a blog, the group worked in a similar message board way and was started by "criminal profiler" Maurice Godwin to encourage information sharing about the case. It quickly and spontaneously became a support and information center for women and girls in the Baton Rouge region who were beset with misinformation while coping with the fear and panic created by the knowledge that an unknown man was targeting and killing local women.

The Yahoo group served a range of functions, and by logging on and following various threads, users could engage with each other for positive and productive ends. Perhaps most importantly, the discussion group helped people to sift through the contradictory and confusing accounts about the case that were given in the mainstream media, as group users with valid information would respond quickly to media reports that were often erroneous. This instance of online community satisfied the desire to find alternatives to the "official" news and realities about the case within a media-saturated culture that deems only televised events as "real." In a postmodern paradox, blogs can empower by countering the simulacra generated by intense television coverage of events and environments with the formation of face-to-face community involvement and the sharing of personal, anecdotal experience of reality. Members used the group to strategize and plan activities and protests designed to call attention to the murders. Some used the group to critique the Baton Rouge Serial Killer Task Force, and many people expressed and worked through difficult feelings in the discussions. The closeness of this particular group to the crimes, both in physical proximity and through the interaction of victim's families and friends with their posts to the group, made it uniquely effective as a grass-roots public forum for community empowerment. The women in this group weren't reacting to a serial killer many miles or states away, but to one in their midst.

Because the true-crime bloggers have the luxury of time and space to explore complicated cases that print and television journalists often do not, they are freer to uncover details, add regular updates, and include comprehensive contextual accounts; the use of web links greatly facilitates the creation of richer, more nuanced and informative narratives. Links are often embedded in the story, as in a recent blog entry on The True Crime Web log for November 18, 2007: this account carried a story from North Carolina entitled "'Blood and Gore Fanatic'—Andrea Maxwell and Joe Lee Coleman II Accused of Murder" that included links to the alleged perpetrator's myspace page, local newspaper accounts of both the murder and an earlier shoplifting arrest, and a wikipedia entry defining an arcane religious term used by Andrea Maxwell as part of her online identity on myspace.[7] Links to an individual's personal web pages on social networking sites such as myspace or facebook are an increasingly common feature on the true-crime blogs and are especially relevant when young people, who are more likely to craft elaborate identities on such Web sites, are involved. The notion that an alleged killer can be "known" somehow from his or her myspace page, although problematic and even misleading, allows the reader to have a more direct and personal experience of the killer's personality, thus adding another layer of mystery and meaning to the murder narrative. Links that appear in the margins of the true-crime blog pages always include lists of like-minded blogs, and are often suggestive of the blogger's political bent: for example, the conservative web-author of Lost in Lima, Ohio, gives links on her blog to *America's Most Wanted* and The Anti-MOVE/Mumia Blogspot; When a Child Goes Missing offers a link to arch-conservative Bill O'Reilly's Web site.[8] Other bloggers link to historical documents and newspaper databases, most notably Laura James on her blog, Clews.

Each of the true-crime blogs has a slightly different focus or theme, according to the writers' interests and abilities. Laura James' blog Clews is "devoted to the discovery and dissemination of the fascinating stories to be found where murder, history, and journalism overlap."[9] Clews is a comprehensive and exhaustive historical true-crime blog, and James exhibits an encyclopedic knowledge of the genre in its past and present forms as she explores little known, older, or forgotten cases. Her links are arranged into such categories as "True Crime Author Sites, Recent Comments, City Crime Reports, Out-of-Print True Crime Booksellers, Crime Encyclopedias, True Crime Bloggers, Death Penalty Links, On the True Crime Genre, Interesting Sites and Blogs, and Laura's Favorite Stories," and Clews is representative of the personality-driven type of blog, shaped by the unique and recognizable voice, interests, and intentions of its author. James is a former attorney and journalist whose polished and personable writing style invites readers to share an aesthetic appreciation of true crime and its writers, particularly for older cases and forgotten practitioners of the genre.

One recent post on Clews entitled "Old clipping of the week" presents a scanned 1958 newspaper account of Kansas family killer Lowell Lee Andrews with the following comments, which illustrate James' writing style: "This story comes from the files of the venerated *Kansas City Star*. Unfortunately the digitized archive for the Star is no longer online (sniffle) but someone was kind enough to send me a page containing the most remarkable story of family annihilator Lowell Lee Andrews, who makes a minor appearance in *In Cold Blood* as he awaits his execution."[10] Clews is a favorite in the online true-crime world because James reinvigorates the tradition of witty and sardonic true-crime writing, of which the best American exemplar is Edmund Pearson, a style that has been crushed by the weight of the post-Capote true-crime conventions. Historical distance from atrocity allows for a liberal dose of black humor that modern sensibilities find offensive when mixed with murder narratives. Because she reports largely on murders whose victims, perpetrators, and survivors have long since passed away, James has the freedom to be playful with her narratives, and her readers respond with enthusiasm.

Steve Huff, arguably the first and most famous true-crime blogger, writes about contemporary or unfolding cases on his True Crime Weblog. An able reporter and investigator, Huff is known and respected for his exhaustive coverage of cases that are given "drive-by" or superficial treatment in mainstream media outlets, as well as in depth coverage of the more sensational and high-profile murders that grace the covers of the tabloids and saturate cable television. Other notable true-crime blogs include The Malefactor's Register, maintained by Mark Gribben, which presents lengthy narratives of individual cases. The 1947 Project attempts to reconstruct noir-era Los Angeles by posting newspaper crime accounts from that year and others (they are now posting stories from 1927). In Cold Blog guest-features "the leading voices in the genre" in a compilation form, drawing on the large pool of true-crime writers, journalists, law enforcement professionals, and other bloggers whose comments and current projects always interest their peers and readers, and Crime Rant is authored by Gregg Olsen and M. William Phelps, both well-published true-crime writers. Black and Missing But Not Forgotten was created by a black female blogger (who remains anonymous) as a response to the underrepresentation of missing and murdered women of color in mainstream media outlets, and offers a compilation of news accounts and public information rather than crafting narrative treatments of the cases.[11]

Much Internet true crime keys into the paranoia and panic surrounding sexual predation and child molestation, playing on the well-founded fears that accompany the popularity of social networking sites where anonymity seems to offer an open door to (mostly) men seeking sex with children and teenagers. In addition to fragmenting the true-crime audience and creating "niche-markets" for various kinds of true crime, the Internet has quite literally created a new class of criminal behavior that engages the most volatile parental emotions—the "cyber-predator." "Trench Reynolds" is the pseudonymous author of MyCrimeSpace, a blog devoted to covering crimes related to the Internet, with a specific focus on the "dangers and myths" of the social networking sites. Parents Behaving Badly, Missing and Murdered Children, and When a Child Goes Missing, each tackle the subjects of child abuse, abduction, and murder, with a focus on dissemination of public information, crime prevention, and the passage of legislation designed to address these crimes in various ways. Teachers Behaving Badly is "A Collection of Teachers and Other Educational Staff Behaving Rather Badly," which reports mostly on sexual misconduct. The somewhat reactionary blog, Michelle Says So, covers "True Crime, Missing Persons, Sex Predators, Women's Issues and the Latest Controversial News," including stories that feature children as victims.[12]

The "comments" section of any blog is crucial to its identity and tenor; there one can observe the reactions of the audience, gauge their interests and motivations, and glean clues about the identities of a blog's readers (or at least, those who comment openly. "Lurkers," those readers who rarely or never post to blogs, are notoriously hard to pin down). The true-crime online community appears to be small, passionate, and quite close-knit, with comments posted by the same people at numerous sites and frequent references to other bloggers and posters. Because of the open and public nature of blogs and their true-crime content, comments are usually monitored closely by their authors for offensive or inappropriate material. Perhaps not surprisingly, Laura James says that "many true crime bloggers report that their blogs are trawled by creeps looking for weird content, like naked autopsy photos and stories of women being hanged."[13] "Weird content" is the true-crime writers' stock-in-trade, and moderated comments are a necessary evil on the blogs. On the well-traversed and serious true-crime blogs, the comments tend toward honest engagement with the issues at hand, with a generous sprinkling of compliments to the authors; animosity is rare and balanced commentary is the norm.

Although the blogs offer multiple perspectives on crime and murder, there is an unwritten and probably unconscious consensus of style, rhetoric, and tone embraced by most writers. Their major contributions to the true-crime genre are the depth and breadth of story coverage and the opportunity for reader engagement offered with the comments function. For the most part, the blogs are an interesting addition to true crime, but they do not comprise a new direction for the genre in terms of the subject matter and the way writers shape the raw material of murder and its circumstances. One notable exception is *Los Angeles Times* reporter Jill Leovy's blog, The Homicide Report, which chronicles every homicide that occurs in Los Angeles on a weekly basis and notes the race, age, gender, and circumstances of death of each. The Homicide Report started as a yearlong project in 2007, but has been continued (with the addition of another contributor) into 2008, perhaps because of its popularity and impact. The blog receives about 300,000 hits per month, and the *LA Times* deputy innovation editor Aaron Curtiss says that it's one of the paper's most popular blogs; in addition, "people spend a lot more time on it than they do on most other sites—about six and a half minutes, average. That tells us they're really digging down into it."[14] In a personal e-mail to this author on November 27, 2007, Leovy wrote that

> I am very deliberate in trying to counter a true-crime tradition in homicide coverage. I strongly dislike true-crime style stories. Some crit-lit doctoral student could have a field day writing all about the fetishes and freakshow sensibilities embedded in the true-crime tradition, and the way they conspire to keep the marginalized marginal (and therefore likely homicide victims). For me, I can only say that I find the prevalence and staying power of this tradition is remarkable, and it has done a great deal of harm to the way we talk about the homicide problem in this country. Homicide is too serious for that style of reporting, yet it endures and endures.

Leovy is attempting to rewrite true crime, quite literally and with conscious political goals: to make visible those homicides that the true-crime genre has rendered invisible through selection and marginalization.

The Homicide Report is rooted in a vastly unrepresented and unreported reality rather than in the murky and formulaic waters of crime "infotainment"; as such, it indicates a positive and newly emerging direction for true crime. The Homicide Report echoes the cultural work done by the television program *The First 48* in that it deals squarely with the fact that much homicide in America occurs within and impacts communities of color (mostly African American and Hispanic populations), and is a result of gun violence between young men. As Leovy explains in the blog's "FAQ" section, "Race and ethnicity, like age and gender, are stark predictors of homicide risk. Blacks are vastly more likely to die from homicide than whites, and Latinos somewhat more likely. Black men, in particular, are extraordinarily vulnerable: They are 4% of this country's population, but, according to the Centers for Disease Control, they represented 35% of homicide victims nationally in 2004."[15]

As a genre, true crime has generally ignored the intersection of race and poverty in its formulation of the dominant murder narrative, largely because true crime is a quasifantasy genre, one invested in entertainment, escapism, and most recently in the tragic reversal of the romance narrative. The magazines, books, films, and television programs that cover black victims frame the murder using the same rhetorical techniques that narrate serial killings or sex crimes, perhaps illustrating an ethical color-blind sensibility, but ignoring the actuality of most homicide. The true-crime aesthetic finds interest and drama only in the extraordinary, the monstrous, the incomprehensible, and not in the everyday drive-by shootings and war zone depravities of life in some neighborhoods of contemporary Los Angeles and other large cities. The Homicide Report is undoing and redefining the genre itself in its insistence on actuality instead of hyperreality.

Instead of projecting fears of violent crime, anxieties about security and safety, and desires for social control onto the demonized other in the figure of the serial killer or sociopath, as standard true-crime narratives do, Leovy deals with the fears (of violent crime), anxieties (the government can't control violent crime, police are the enemy) and desires (to live without the threat of street violence) of that segment of the American population that experiences homicide most regularly. The poor, the powerless, African American and Hispanic communities—this is where homicide devastates individuals and neighborhoods, and where true crime has very infrequently gone. It is hopeful and exciting to imagine a true crime that, instead of trading in the spectacle and sensation that generates impotent emotional responses directed at a small number of depraved individuals, could actually weave a narrative that attempts to understand the social causes of crime, violence, and abuse. This would require an understanding of homicide as a public health problem such as AIDS or drug abuse, rather than as the outrageous and bizarre actions of the occasional—and statistically rare—psychopath.[16]

In a section of the site that explains the focus of the blog, Leovy writes that "The report seeks to reverse an age-old paradox of big-city crime reporting, which dictates that only the most unusual and statistically marginal homicide cases receive press coverage, while those cases at the very eye of the storm—those which best expose the true statistical dimensions of the problem of deadly violence—remain hidden."[17] Newspapers respond to a variety of forces that limit crime coverage, including the dictates of audience, advertisers, and political concerns, as well as the very significant limitations of space in a daily paper. Such limitations reinforce media stereotypes about race and class in crime reporting that use of the Internet, with its unlimited space and different deadline schedule, circumvents. In The Homicide Report, every murder is covered equally, given the same size font (no screaming headlines or high-profile tactics here), and described in similar tones. Race, age, circumstances of death, and some details are always reported in a bare-bones style that is unexpectedly compelling, resulting in "an austere elegance to the daily listing of victims and the numbing litany of ways in which they died."[18] One truism of true crime is that some deaths "matter" more than others, and that some killers "matter" more than others. This blog is radical in its refusal to reiterate true-crime tropes and in its insistence that every death matters equally.

It is in the comments section of The Homicide Report that the most radical work of this blog takes place—that of giving voice to the usually voiceless, ignored, or stereotyped survivors, witnesses, and victims of inner city homicide. The self-selection which shapes the comments section—it is, after all, limited to those with Internet and computer access, basic language and computer literacy, and knowledge about the site itself—renders it not entirely representative of the community, but it is nonetheless a spontaneous and unique public forum. Without the clichéd, codified, and regulated pathos that appears in normative print and televised true-crime narratives, victims are remembered, mourned, and above all, humanized. These two entries refer to a man named Rudolph Smith who was killed on November 9, 2007:

> I HOPE THE PERSON WHO DID THIS TO COWBOY IS FOUND AND PUT AWAY. I WILL ALWAYS LOOK BACK AT ALL THE TIMES IN THE BACK HOUSE. COWBOY YOU WILL BE MISSED. IT JUST WONT BE THE SAME WITHOUT YOU. YOUR LONG BEACH FRIENDS HAD MUCH LOVE FOR THE MAN WE ALL KNEW AS COWBOY RIP . . . MUCH LOVE SHAWN, MOMI, DEE DEE, BRINA. . . . [sic]

> Cowboy brought joy, and laughter to all that knew him. There was never a doll [sic] moment when you were in the presence of Cowboy!

He was a comedian, and he could dance his behind off . . . Thank you Cowboy for all the laughs, because it was good for our hearts! Thank you for taking out the time to encourage the children. My nephew cherishes the football patch you gave him. You are missed, but your laughter lives on in our hearts!"[19]

Far from noting just another dead black man, another numbing statistic, or another clichéd expression of sadness and loss, these comments help the reader understand that a real person has died—one who had friends, family, acquaintances, neighbors, a community, a personality, and a real life. The poignancy of some comments testifies to the way that murder affects entire communities, such as these two on the death of twenty-four-year-old Jonah Alexander on December 15, 2007: "I was a volunteer at the hospital and watched him die. If the family gets this e-mail please respond to my e-mail. I am sorry for your lost [sic]. I think about him a lot and will be praying for you" and "i now have known 3 people that are dead and reported on this homicide blog (TWO in december) jacklyn villanueva (stabbed in lincoln park) and NOW jonah alexander from junior high (32nd st magnet) . . . this is just too much."[20] The frequency of such spare and touching expressions of loss, coupled with the whittled-down reporting style that views each death in equal terms, makes the standard true-crime iteration of the "mystery" of homicide laughable. There are no intriguing and entertaining mysteries here, just poignant and sincere expressions of emotional pain.

The comments section of The Homicide Report opens up and makes public the way that social fabric is torn by homicide, deconstructing the shopworn stock character of the "innocent murder victim," which typifies the more formulaic true-crime stories. True crime in print, television, or film shapes actuality to fit the contours of the expectations and assumptions of its consumers, seldom straying from use of the codes, symbolic associations, and iconography of the genre. One such icon is that of the "innocent" victim, usually a woman beset by either random or domestic violence. Comments on The Homicide Report counter the default-position image of innocent victimhood as various friends, acquaintances, and family members offer sometimes-competing or negative accounts and remembrances of the murder victim. The shooting death of thirty-seven-year-old Timothy Johnson on November 25, 2007, generated a voluminous and volatile mixture of comments, ranging from an outpouring of outrage and sadness from Johnson's family and friends to this expression of angry satisfaction: "TIMOTHY JOHNSON, A.K.A. 'SINISTER' LIVED BY THE GUN AND HIS ASS DIED BY THE GUN. 'STREET JUSTICE HAS BEEN SERVED.'"[21] Apparently, Johnson was a former gang member and accused killer whose street name—"Sinister"—and all it implied followed him beyond his reformation and death, and many of the commenters remark that he was a murderer as well as an eventual victim. A later poster writes "I am a mother who has losted [sic] her Son to death with sinister as the trigger man. He took my son's life, Nov.12, 2004."[22] This comment opened a dialogue that led from the death of this specific person into a conversation about the possibilities of redemption, the meaning of gang affiliation and membership, and the myriad social problems that both lead to and are caused by the gang phenomenon. The Homicide Report creates public space for the expression and documentation of responses and emotions that break the boundaries that are normally imposed by true crime, and the comments sections are organic memorial sites that are added to and continue to grow as the months pass, and an authentic public forum where people can air their grievances, educate each other, and get schooled by others.

Gang violence accounts for most of the homicides that show up on The Homicide Report, and the commenters display various perspectives on gang membership and the violent, chaotic lifestyle it entails. Most comments convey the anger, sadness, frustration, and sense of powerlessness of those who are affected by gang violence, but some are gang-positive, expressing the poster's desire for vengeance or reassurances that a friend or relative's death will not be forgotten or in vain. Occasionally, a poster relates his own gang affiliation, like this one on the Johnson murder who speaks of the realities of gang life and "street justice":

> It's like enlisting in the army—you got to be prepared to die for what you represent. Sin understood that. How do I know? I knew him. [Jr. High (Drew) high school (Fremont)—jail] He understood what street justice meant. One of my homies got killed by a busta from the hood—that busta is in jail when he SHOULD be in the ground. Some say it's wrong, some say its street justice, Malcolm X said it's a case of chickens comin' home to roost. To my family and my homies: If I get taken by the streets, leave my killer alone if you can't place him in the earth . . . Peace be unto Sins family. From his neighboring set (The BOPS,) 'K—DOUBLE—O—L.'"[23]

True crime doesn't usually accommodate such voices and sentiments because they overstep the genre's normative values of belief in the law and in a codified channeling of vengeance through judicial prosecution and, sometimes, the death penalty. The street gang ideology of outlawry and sincere belief in a violent code of honor and behavior subverts social control and in this case is also marginalized and inflected by race and social class. It's hard to feel remorse for a remorseless killer, but this poster expresses his respect for "Sin," which may be an accolade the victim would have preferred.

The huge number of comments (140 as of January 18, 2008) and the multiple differing responses to Johnson's death highlights the significance of the issues that his life and death brought into the open, and together they comprise an organic and valuable dialogue about life in South Central L.A. Many posters relate sentiments such as these, signed by "Worried": "yes racism and prejudice still exist, however now Black mother's don't worry that their son's will be killed [b]y the Klan. Now they worry that they might be killed by someone who looks exactly like them and many times over NOTHING [sic]." One of Johnson's female relatives writes, "Tim Johnson was not the first Family of mine that has been lost to the streets of senseless violence; the feeling isn't unique, by no means and I fear that he will not be the last, brother, son, uncle, father, cousin, lover," and a responder writes, "Understand the meaning of what people are saying. You know as well as I do what type of person Sinister was. He might have been loving and gentle with his family, but not with the rest of the tribe."[24] These comments offer intricate insider's rundowns of the social relations that led to the moment of murder and pain-filled descriptions about the lived realities of "black-on-black" crime and how it feels to be a member of the underreported but overrepresented-in-homicide-stats population, a population that is constantly blamed for its own problems, stereotyped, and subject to low expectations compared to other "minority" groups within the United States.

Racial politics, gang dynamics, biased media coverage, "ghetto" economics, and moving out versus staying in the "hood," are all volatile topics in The Homicide Report's comments section. One particularly explosive subject that generates heated debate is the "stop snitching" policy, the unwritten code of "street" behavior that dictates total and absolute noncooperation with the police. Born from a historically justified suspicion of the police and fear about the real dangers of testifying against murder defendants in open court, the "stop snitching" code stymies murder investigations but is an integral and necessary part of survival in some urban neighborhoods, and comments on The Homicide Report show how deep emotions run on this subject. Some posters endorse a no-snitching ideology, but most abhor and speak out against it, proclaiming that "no-snitching" means living in terrified silence among murderers and gangsters.

In the November 27 e-mail to this writer about her goals and motivation for creating the blog, Leovy wrote that "Trying to give the homicide problem a new language—a new set of terms, a new kind of narrative—is the most difficult thing I have ever undertaken as a journalist." Unfortunately, The Homicide Report is an anomaly among the true-crime blogs in its murder coverage, exemplified by the evolving rhetorical techniques that comprise Leovy's attempt to break out of the confines of a genre that presents a very narrow depiction of murder in America. True crime remains rooted in a poetics borrowed from fiction, including the use of speculation about thoughts and events, the building of "characters" from the known elements of the major player's personalities, and the creation of mystery, drama, and suspense through a vocabulary of stock phrases and such techniques as withholding information and rearranging the structure of events to fit a recognized pattern. The effect—part intentional, part unconsciously shaped by the writer who cannot help but be influenced by the true-crime atmosphere—is the portrayal of the murder as dramatically important and the projection of a worn and feeble set of emotional waves that reverberate with the audience. The terms of the genre are pity, sadness, a sense of futility, sympathy with the victim and the victim's family, suspicion, instability, fear, and disengagement and alienation from others, all directed and focused on the alleged killer rather than at the system that creates and sustains fatal violence.

In fact, most true-crime bloggers still use the old language of their genre, even as they attempt to illuminate different kinds of lower-profile murder cases, advocate more strongly for victims, and write eloquently about old cases or the interface of newer technologies and murder. Most of the bloggers appear to be middle class, white, and invested in the status quo of homicide narration and reportage; after all, true crime is a conservative genre, one that has staked out its boundaries and regulates itself through the powerful engines of book sales and television ratings. True-crime blogging is part of the larger phenomenon of a widening of material and content available on the Internet but with no real changes in perspective, focus, goals, or political motivation. As David Kline speculates about the progressive political potential of blogging, "are we in danger of replacing one narrow coterie of opinions and interests in the national discourse (i.e., the establishment's) with an admittedly broader but still dangerously unrepresentative one?"[25] Excepting The Homicide Report, which attempts to undermine true crime as a rhetorical structure that sustains disinterest in homicide as a problem and the marginalization of most of its victims, the answer to that question as it pertains to true crime blogging is, unfortunately, "yes." Another exception, Paul LaRosa's newly implemented blog called The Murder Book that attempts to track media coverage of every murder in New York City during 2008, holds promise to direct the interest of true crime in a more sustained and focused critical direction.[26]

Maintenance of the status quo of murder narration and journalism within the new technological medium of blogging can be seen in other big-city newspapers that are now producing their own "homicide blogs," which mimic the form of The Homicide Report but lack its critical focus, instead reconstituting the usual true crime fare in a different web-based format. Examples include The Orlando Crime Report and Baltimore's Murder Ink, blogs that track and report daily crime in those cities, but use the same old rhetorical style and appeals to emotion that are present in much standard true crime. Such headlines as "Daytona PD Chief: 'We'll search for serial killer into the ends of the earth,'" typical of The Orlando Crime Report, display a business-as-usual approach to murder narration.[27] Many city police departments and newspapers run blogs that give brief accounts of all recent crime in their locales, including Kansas City, Boston, Los Angeles, Miami, Charlotte, and Baltimore; independent web operators run sites that cover Reno, Houston, Chicago, and Richmond. In an effort to implement human-geography mapping, and perhaps in imitation of The Homicide Report, which posts a map of Los Angeles that pinpoints all the homicides in the year, most of the crime-log sites offer a map feature that plots recent crime. Many have links to local police departments, and one, Crime in Charlotte, North Carolina, posts mug shots of arrestees and gives links to the local police department that show the criminal records of each person.[28] These sites trade in the usual sensationalism, generation and projection of fear, and reactionary gestures that have become typical in true crime; it's the same old thing in a new and different form.

TRUE-CRIME WEB MISCELLANY

Other forms of true crime on the Internet extend and deepen the type of material available elsewhere, with a strong emphasis on the lurid and controversial. One excellent source of information about high-profile crime cases and murderers is the Court TV-sponsored Crime Library at http://www.crimelibrary.com, an encyclopedia of criminal bi-ographies and case histories. Court TV also maintains The Smoking Gun at http://www.thesmokinggun.com/, a site that displays government and court documents, mug shots, and autopsy photographs relating to celebrity or high profile crime. The future of these sites is unknown, as "TruTV" takes over and many Crime Library writers have been informed that no new content will be added to that site. Because of the anonymity and the personal intensity of Internet use, web authors are free to highlight and indulge in the latent voyeurism and fanaticism inherent to the genre. Some sites consciously admit their sexual or titillating motives, such as http://www.detective-magazine.com/, a site devoted to 1960s and 1970s true-crime magazine covers depicting "women tightly bound and gagged in inescapable rope bondage." CharlieManson.com offers any and every-thing related to Charles Manson, with a focus on both arcane and up-to-date information pertaining to the Manson phenomenon. The so-called "serial killer chic" Web sites are numerous, including SerialKiller.com (http://www.skcentral.com/main.php), a compendium for all things re-lated to that topic, with an off-putting pro-murder tone.

With its lack of official government or institutional regulation and wide-open public accessibility, the Internet may seem like a perfect place for the market forces that propel true crime to go into overdrive and foster all kinds of excesses. Indeed, it seems like anything goes with Internet true crime, from the availability of extremely graphic official crime scene photos to disturbing, uncensored rants from actual killers. However, there are some limits: one interesting instance of moral self-regulation has occurred around the trade in "murderabilia," or the buying and selling of items associated with high-profile crimes and perpetrators. The popular online auction site e-Bay has a no-murderabilia policy: that is, e-Bay administrators remove any listing for an item that is advertised as having some association with a crime, because they believe that "The sale of items closely associated with individuals who are notorious for committing murderous acts is deeply offensive to the families of victims."[29] The trade in murderabilia continues unabated on other Web sites, however, including murderauction.com, supernaught.com and daisyseven.com, indicating an ongoing interest in buying, selling, and owning items associated with murder. Internet true crime offers an interesting mix of old and new rhetorical styles, goals both noble and scurrilous, and a range of different voices saying some of the same old things. True crime on the Internet flourishes, and is one expression of the ever-present pop culture interest in murder.

CONCLUSION

Evil is not an abstraction. It is always a story. It proliferates in systems of stories—lies and truth interwoven, myths, cultures.
  —Lance Morrow in *Evil: An Investigation* (New York: Basic Books, 2003), 94

The elision between crime and its narration leads the journalist to ask rhetorically whether serial killers should be viewed as evidence of a culture in decline or as its clearest metaphor.
  —Anita Biressi in *Crime, Fear, and the Law in True Crime Stories* (New York: Palgrave-Macmillan, 2001), 169

At the end of this survey of the vast and varied landscape of modern American murder narration, some key questions remain: why does true crime appeal so strongly to women? Why do depictions of psychopaths resonate so deeply with readers and viewers? Does true crime have a moral center, or is it simply a degraded popular form that traffics in lurid appeals to base interests in sex and violence? And finally, what can the popularity of true crime tell us about ourselves? I don't know that there are any single, bite-sized, and easy answers to any of these questions, but the long view contained in the preceding chapters offers some possible insights. As with other crime genres such as mystery or detective fiction, some observations or interpretations contradict others—true crime both upsets and reiterates the status quo of crime and punishment, for example, and it simultaneously creates and then allays fear. As John Cawelti, the "dean" of popular culture genre scholarship suggests, this is no surprise, because "it is more typical of complex and diverse societies that individual genres become arenas of ideological struggle."[1] Such struggle is visible in true crime as an ongoing dialectic of murder as both mystery and a collection of scientific facts, of women as victims and authors and primary consumers of murder narratives, of killers as both superhuman monsters and simple madmen, and of true-crime creators and consumers as both debased and valiant.

First and foremost, the relentless focus on the killer's biography and psychology in many true-crime depictions marks an obsessive preoccupation with the primacy of individual thought, behavior, and action. The genre gained prominence and market share in the 1980s and 1990s by constructing killers as subjects worthy of minutely focused and lengthy depictions of their lives, motivations, and behavior using the twin lenses of psychology and personal history. True crime presents killers as knowable subjects whose devious and transgressive actions can be understood through narrative dissection. Most true crime forms position an individual act of violence as both an isolated and a knowable event that has a powerful individual actor at its core. Writing in *The New Yorker* in January 2008, Adam Gopnik suggests that the preoccupation with individual experience evinces a "curious double consciousness," because it emerges from a century where people "have been shaped by mass death and a readiness for mass killing." Furthermore, he says that "This imbalance may explain why we give murder such undue weight, why our most popular storytelling apparatus, nightly television, is devoted largely to the lore and legends and compulsive retelling of individual homicides, even though such investigations are a vanishingly small percentage of what policemen really do."[2] The fascination with and focus on individuals in true crime partakes of and further demonstrates this double consciousness; like water dripping on a stone, true crime narrates a mass of murders, story by story, and drop by drop.

Yet true crime also suggests the permeability of the killer's personal identity, and the capacity of the detective—or reader/viewer—to vicariously experience and inhabit another person's identity and personality. The rhetoric of murder narration often includes the tantalizing offer to "get inside the mind" of a killer. This catchphrase, used to describe the experience of reading or viewing true-crime narratives, suggests visiting a physical place rather than attempting to understand or communicate with a person. We can visit the monster and observe with detachment and awe the horror-cluttered room of his mind, but then we leave, untouched by the experience and fundamentally unchanged. Such language also swirls around the act of "profiling" a killer, an increasingly ambiguous occupation that is invested with quasimystical notions of the permeability of both identity boundaries and physical space, suggestions that the killer can be infiltrated and known through psychic processes masquerading as science.

The complex and loaded self-other dialectic in true crime may offer some clues about the genre's appeal to women. That women are primary consumers of the genre is a somewhat anecdotal observation, but it is one based on several strong pieces of evidence and the work of such critics as Laura Browder, whose research into contemporary American true crime readers appears in her article, "Dystopian Romance: True Crime and the Female Reader," published in *The Journal of Popular Culture* in December 2006. Browder reports that "According to publishers, true crime writers, and bookstore owners polled in a preliminary survey, from two-thirds to three-quarters of the readers of these grisly nonfiction accounts are women."[3] Most entries on Ann Rule's Web site "guestbook" come from women, and older women are the Nielsen-reported majority demographic group for the CBS true-crime newsmagazine program *48 Hours Mystery*. Additionally, Browder also writes that "Best-selling true crime author Jerry Bledsoe notes that while on book tours, he invariably encounters mostly women."[4] True crime encourages reader and viewer identification with all three of its key figures to varying degrees, and different people respond differently to the possibilities of sympathizing or identifying with killer, victim, and cop. The strongest inducements cultivate identification with both killer and victim, which for women can be paradoxically subversive.

With her ethnographic survey of female true-crime readers, Browder found that women read true crime for many surprising—and sometimes contradictory—reasons. True crime subverts the strong cultural taboo against women showing interest in violence, for in consuming true crime "women can vicariously experience kinky sex and violence, and survive," or become "armchair killers" themselves.[5] As self-defensive educational texts, the genre is exemplary, for in true crime women can learn what sociopaths are *really* like, and so avoid them while dating (and help their friends, daughters, and female relatives to avoid them as well). Ann Rule sees herself as providing a kind of "social service" for women readers, warning them against controlling men and destructive relationships with her "dystopian romance" narratives. Some survivors of domestic or sexual abuse read true crime for clues about why men enact violence against women, and may see themselves reflected, in both positive and negative ways, in the portrayals of victims, and stories about women who kill children offer a way for women to comprehend the transgression of a primal taboo. The genre is also understood by some of its fans as a larger-scale critique of patriarchal values and male dominance in society, as it depicts the continual policing and punishment of male violence against women. There is no simple reason why women respond so strongly to true crime; indeed, this nexus of reasons may be in effect for a single reader all at once.

It is clear that true crime places great value on individual responsibility for action, and that the genre valorizes personal accountability, integrity, and agency. This idea is made manifest in many different ways in the narratives, from its law-and-order ideology to the way killers are depicted as individual aberrations in the human pattern. In most true-crime narratives, the act of murder is isolated and presented as entirely separate from any social forces apart from the grave flaws in the killer's family of origin, and eventually the demented characteristics of the killer himself/herself. Killers don't kill in true crime because they are desperately poor, or trying to escape the narrow limitations imposed by lower social class status, or as a result of a buildup of frustration about everyday stressors. They kill because they are psychopathic, without conscience, devastatingly selfish, sadistic, or warped. In true crime, killers kill because they want to, a notion that fixes blame squarely on the individual and ignores the emotional or environmental context of the act. Even if the killer was horribly abused as a child or became twisted and mean by neglect and violence visited upon him at a young age, true crime insists that he is still ultimately responsible for his own actions.

The obsessive fascination with the flawed-but-not-blameless individual in true crime reaches its apogee in the figuration of both psychopath and sociopath. The psychopath as a threatening figure emerged from the pages of Hervey Cleckley's *The Mask of Sanity: An Attempt to Clarify Some Issues about the So-Called Psychopathic Personality* in the 1940s, made his debut in the true-crime magazines in the 1950s and 1960s, became fully embodied in such early narratives as *In Cold Blood*, *The Onion Field*, and *Helter Skelter*, and reached his full frightening potential in film versions of these books and such lightly fictionalized depictions as *Henry: Portrait of a Serial Killer* and *Natural Born Killers*. As television true crime has come to eclipse book and film forms, the psychopath has been replaced by the sociopath; that is, he (or she) has been tamed, domesticated, and transformed into a more garden variety killer, particularly in such programs as *Forensic Files*, *The First 48*, and *48 Hours Mystery*. Finally, the Internet both resists the category altogether with The Homicide Report and constructs a true-crime sociopath who is more obsessed with sex than death in many of the blogs, notwithstanding the voluminous coverage of serial killers and the rapaciously violent on the more lurid Web sites.

All this points in one direction: that throughout the 1970s, 1980s, and much of the 1990s, there was enormous anxiety in American culture and society not just about crime, but about a specific type of crime that was interpreted as an indicator of a widespread and irreversible decline in the values or characteristics of care, compassion, and regard for others. In true crime, the terms "psychopath" and "sociopath" are used to indicate the monstrous, completely other, incomprehensible, hidden, irreversibly bad, and unredeemedly dangerous, and the chief identifying mark of this person is the lack of conscience. Conscience—its presence and absence— has become an ordering principle, a way of separating the good from the bad, the benignly mad from the dangerously so. Through its use in true crime, the notion of the psychopath/sociopath has become a metaphorical tool, a way of first making known and then separating the strange, the frightening, disturbing, and finally, the monstrous. The idea that having a conscience in good working order separates the human from the inhuman has risen to prominence dramatically since the 1970s, in true crime, pop psychology, criminology, and popular consciousness alike.

As the epigraph at the opening of this chapter relates, it may be instructive to view the psychopath/sociopath as a metaphor for a "society in decline," and not just as a symbol or a symptom of the same. The increasing and irrational fear about the specific pathological personality whose defining feature is a lack of conscience can be read as a metaphor for larger cultural, sociological, and political trends and preoccupations in American life. One significant change that has many cultural reverberations has occurred in the American self-image. As this country emerged from the moral morass of the Vietnam War in the 1970s, we began to question our status as the protectors of justice, morality, and righteous political order in the world, questions that began with the revelation of such atrocities as the 1968 My Lai Massacre. First reported by journalist Seymour Hersh in late 1969, the mass murder of hundreds of South Vietnamese civilians, largely unarmed women and children, had an enormous impact on America's idea of itself and its actions in the world. The stunning revelation that such depredations and depravities could be carried out as part of ordinary American military procedure laid atrocity, sadism, and blunt horror on our doorstep. The former province of demonized others, most recently Nazis and other "degraded" Europeans in World War II, was now recognized as American territory as well, upsetting dearly held fantasies of G. I. Joe as a world hero and arbiter of righteousness and good.

In the work of Ann Rule, Joseph Wambaugh, Vincent Bugliosi, and other early true-crime creators, these difficult questions about depravity lurking behind normality were brought down to the smaller stage of popular genre writing, where readers could puzzle over such enormous moral questions, now writ small, in private. The emergence of the psychopath as an iconic figure who represents both fear of the demonized other and a gnawing, self-doubting hunch that the other lurks within, thus becomes one of the markers of American life in the post-Vietnam era of the 1970s and 1980s. During this period, the moral monster who is both self and other (*The Stranger Beside Me, The Onion Field*), crazy outsider and one of us (*Helter Skelter, Fatal Vision*) became the central figure in depictions of murderers. In its insistence throughout the 1980s and 1990s that *we* are our own monsters, true crime registered an ideological struggle between America as the benevolent and just global policeman of the World War II era, and a queasy recognition that we were just as capable of depravity, atrocity, and wrong-doing as any Third World dictatorship or renegade nation state. The widespread ascendance of the psychopath/sociopath as an American icon, and now an accepted, if still feared, member of our society, signals a new public self-definition, one that has replaced optimism with cynicism, openness with suspicion, benevolence with unenlightened self-interest.

This new and deeply negative aspect of American identity found its greatest expression in the figure of the serial killer, for as Anita Biressi has noted, "Serial killing has been styled a twentieth-century phenomenon, as a new kind of 'motiveless' or 'pure' murder not driven by jealousy or greed but by existential or metaphysical impulses."[6] "Serial killing," as defined by the FBI and popularly understood, is a consequence of pure appetite and the desire for power over another person, and it resides in an altogether different existential realm than more 'acceptable' justifications for homicide such as insurance money or the "crime of passion." In fact, serial killing is not new—there are records of such deeds throughout recorded human history—but the phenomenon was named in the 1970s and it was constructed in 1980s true-crime murder narratives, both books and films, as a new kind of murder, one that reflected and refracted fears about anonymity, depersonalization, and the consequences of extreme self-interest. Social conservatives, perhaps reacting against the worst excesses of the "me generation" of the 1970s, found a purely self-centered monster on whom to pin its most fantastic nightmares and projections of social decay. Seen as more evidence of a "sick society," serial murder is, as Philip Jenkins writes in his book, *Using Murder: The Social Construction of Serial Homicide*, "presented as a manifestation of the callous and depersonalized nature of the present age, which is contrasted with the supposed harmony and tranquility of bygone days. In this view, we have become a society of strangers."[7] Not just a society of strangers, but—as narrated and created by true crime during this period—one that is fractured, fragmenting, rootless, transient, and increasingly violent.[8]

The statistics on serial killing vary widely according to who is reporting them (the news media, the FBI, various victims' rights organizations, or individual police agencies), but it is now widely agreed upon that the threat was greatly overestimated. Not surprisingly, the fate and fortunes of the FBI were imbricated in the rise of the serial killer as the harbinger of doom within American society. As the Communist threat eased and the most heated part of the Cold War drew to a close during the 1970s and into the 1980s, the FBI began an era of belt tightening and penuriousness that coincided with a drop in public confidence in government institutions and a decline in the FBI's reputation and popularity. The threat posed by serial killers was used by the agency to resuscitate its creaky and ailing image and restore its federal funding, as the term "serial killer" and all it implied leaked into public consciousness. Two widely cited *New York Times* articles were crucial in bringing the serial killer threat into the public arena: the October 28, 1983, report with the headline "35 Murderers of Many People Could Be at Large, U.S. Says," and the January 21, 1984, article "Officials Cite a Rise in Killers Who Roam U.S. for Victims." Both pieces contained influential definitions of serial killing from the FBI and Justice Department warnings about large numbers of serial killers on the loose in America, spiking nascent public fears about random violent crime and an increase in pop culture depictions of such "monsters."

In response to the serial killer threat, programs like VICAP—the federally funded Violent Criminal Apprehension Program—were developed that enabled different agencies and jurisdictions to track similar crimes in various geographical locations.[9] Robert Ressler, the celebrated FBI agent who is widely recognized as one of the fathers of the term "serial killer," admits that his agency was responsible for stirring up unwarranted fears about what appeared to be a new murder epidemic. In his crime-fighter's memoir *Whoever Fights Monsters*, Ressler writes that

> There was somewhat of a media feeding frenzy, if not a panic, over this issue in the mid-1980s, and we at the FBI and other people involved in urging the formation of VICAP did add to the general impression that there was a big problem and that something needed to be done about it. . . . In feeding the frenzy [about serial killing], we were using an old tactic in Washington, playing up the problem as a way of getting Congress and the higher-ups in the executive branch to pay attention to it.[10]

Fully funded once more and fighting a very visible high-stakes battle with the new "enemy within," the FBI was given an enormous boost in popular culture with Jonathan Demme's 1991 film, *The Silence of the Lambs*, which depicted criminal profiler Clarice Starling (portrayed famously by Jodie Foster) engaged in physical and psychological battle with two of the most terrifying screen villains in history. Suddenly, the FBI had its own crime-fighting culture hero to counter the all-powerful psychopathic serial killer—the criminal profiler.

That pop culture rallied around the figure of the profiler as the serial killer's nemesis and literary "double" relates a crucial point about these iconic figures: both are imaginative nonfiction constructions, literary characters who, even when based on actual living people, become placeholders for current manifestations of "evil" and symbolic representatives of a law-and-order ideology of corruption and its containment. As David Schmid points out in his book *Natural Born Celebrities*, "The fact that the popular culture industries embraced and disseminated the FBI's definition of serial murder so quickly and comprehensively suggests that this definition dovetailed neatly with broader patterns of thinking about crime and violence that were current in the United States during the 1980s."[11] The criminal profiler, armed with the powerful weapons of forensic science and superior deductive powers, was posited as the only solution to the problem of serial murder; he also fit neatly into the mold created by Arthur Conan Doyle's Sherlock Holmes and C. August Dupin, the hero-sleuth of Edgar Allan Poe's

"Murders in the Rue Morgue," a story universally recognized as the first in the detective genre. In the 1990s and beyond, the criminal profiler, usually one of a handful of men associated with the FBI's Behavioral Science Unit, would gather as much cultural capital as the serial killer, and would bring new realms of psychological weirdness and graphic intensity into true-crime murder narratives.

The intense interest in serial killing and profiling has now been eclipsed by an equally compelling interest in murder narratives framed by and solved with forensic science. The serial killer threat was never borne out by homicidal reality, and eventually it became clear that the success of criminal profilers rivaled that of psychics used by police—each produce results that are ambiguous at best, useless at worst.[12] As fears and anxieties about roaming psychopaths and serial killers have waned, true-crime murder narratives that rely on mystery and detection through science have ascended, and the more "ordinary" sociopath has become the new figure of threat. Serial killer narratives have been replaced by stories of domestic violence and murder for greed, gain, or hire. The sociopathic individual, with extreme and usually well-hidden narcissism, great charm, selfishness, and a capacity for violence, is the current topic of true-crime fascination. The revelation of the means and motivation for murder, and of the individual depraved personality, is at the compelling center of some of the most popular true-crime narratives, from *Forensic Files* and *CSI* to those crafted on the true-crime blogs.

As a consummate liar, the sociopath in true crime provides an occasion for a practical display of the elusiveness of truth and the ambiguities of postmodern existence. Murder narratives that offer no closure or solution and instead posit competing, equally believable versions of events are increasingly common, particularly in television true crime. The genre has always portrayed psychopaths and serial killers who deny all knowledge of their deeds, but the sociopathic liar seems something else—a closely guarded subject who is also the object of our deepest curiosity: did he, or didn't he, bludgeon his wife? Was it a bizarre accident or a diabolically planned and executed murder? Television viewers search the face of the accused sociopath for emotional signs, study his actions and mannerisms, and seek clues about his truthfulness or deception as he is interviewed or shown in court. Such figures are ciphers for the unease that accompanies postmodern theories about the enmeshment of perception and reality, as well as more practical concerns about the growing body of knowledge that many people are wrongfully convicted of serious crimes. Certain cases, such as the *Fatal Vision* Jeffrey MacDonald family killing or the "staircase murder" portrayed in Jean Xavier-Lestrade's eight-part documentary film of the same name, offer maddeningly unresolved murder narratives that ask the viewer to engage with huge epistemological questions about truth. Whose version of events do we really believe?

As a register of current social fears, true crime now seems to insist on the dangers of the ordinary, the trusted, and the prosaic. Danger is now figured as residing in the most usual of circumstances, and it cannot be countered with police, weapons, or FBI profilers. The genre articulates a discourse about danger and safety, stressing the impossibility, even with the myriad riches and comforts of twenty-first century American middle-class life, of attaining real security. The contemporary obsession with safety in other realms of life has grown alongside true crime; from Ralph Nader's *Unsafe at Any Speed: The Designed-In Dangers of the American Automobile* (1965), which revolutionized consumerism as well as the car industry, to the modern habit of insisting on helmets and safety gear in a range of formerly freer activities, to childproof caps on medicines and safety seals on almost everything consumable, we've become a dangerphobic (and even more litigious) culture. As murder rates have plummeted dramatically in the late twentieth and early twenty-first centuries, the fear of violent crime remains firmly entrenched in the popular imagination. What has changed is that where once it seemed that America was crawling with serial killers, now attention is focused on the sociopath-next-door or the online predator, on the snake in the carefully controlled and manicured garden of strip-mall America. Because of the way its killers are rooted in "reality," however statistically unlikely, true crime can deploy an endless set of variations on the theme of fear, ever-changing and attuned to emerging sensibilities and values.

From its earliest modern forms in the magazines, true crime in popular culture has articulated moral codes while narrating murder, as shifting visual and rhetorical styles have reflected changes in public behavior, decorum, and the limits of acceptability in depictions of crime. Because it is a mass-market popular genre, true crime has always had a working- or lower-class aura, and producers and authors often must defend themselves and their work as having value that transcends the fleeting and sensational spectacle of murder. For true crime, middle-class striving has meant a hardscrabble fight for respectability and acknowledgement, achieved only occasionally with the artistic greatness of a Capote, Mailer, or Morris. The genre itself continues to be viewed as tabloid, degraded, lowbrow entertainment, and its fans as somehow morally suspect or even less intelligent for finding enjoyment in stories about serial killers, sexual sadists, and domestic monsters. There is a valid moral argument in this critique, for there is something truly distasteful in the notion that one person's extreme pain and misfortune serves as another's entertaining diversion. How could such true crime iterations as the "work" of incendiary ambulance-chasing pseudojournalist Nancy Grace on Court TV and CNN, "16 pages of shocking photos!" or the parade of Manson movies possibly have value beyond getting ratings, book sales, or selling movie tickets? Critics of the genre may very well ask, "Does true crime have a moral center?"

One possible response to that question is that crime has served as entertainment for a very long time, particularly in secular society, and what looks like voyeurism or thrill-seeking may actually mask the gut-level human desire to comprehend the irrational. Our modern true-crime formulations can be viewed as extensions of the need to comprehend the "incomprehensible," to look full-on at the worst of human behavior, accept it, and carry on with the business of living. Perhaps turning crime into entertainment is a way to understand the disturbing impulse to enact violence and destruction that persists within human character and community. Perhaps, as with horror movies, the imaginative confrontation with mortal terror and fatal violence that true crime enacts actually maintains some kind of social equilibrium or psychological health. In that case, the "moral center" of true crime is the fact of its existence, and the critique that true crime is somehow immoral fundamentally misunderstands its cultural work.

It is, however, certainly true that some of that cultural work is destructive and profoundly negative. In the ways that murder gets managed, packaged, and consumed as a form of entertainment, some victims are marginalized and others trivialized, and reasoned criticism of the packaging and selling of homicide in the form of books, films, television programs, and Internet material is valid. True crime has developed an ironclad set of conventions and rules, narrative tricks, and tropes whose building blocks are made visible by different kinds of true-crime work like that done by The Homicide Report and *The First 48*. The true-crime refusal to recognize the racial component of contemporary American homicide betrays its origins as a cultural product that validates some, demonizes others, and totally ignores many different kinds of death. If murder is a social, rather than an individual, problem, its proper context is a survey of the scene, not a relentless focus on or "profile" of any single individual killer. Why do we—the human community that both fosters homicide and outwardly rejects it—condone this refusal to focus, this hiding from reality, the massive projection of fantasy about violence that is true crime?

Some recent additions to the genre suggest its evolution away from fantasy and into possible new narrative directions. *The First 48*, The Homicide Report, *Capote*, and *Zodiac* hold promise for a wider-frame depiction of murder and its contexts, as does the true-crime memoir work of Terri Jentz's *Strange Piece of Paradise* (2006), Maggie Nelson's *The Red Parts* (2007), and a strange little book called *There but for the Grace of God* (2007), by journalist Fred Rosen. This book, subtitled with the needlessly sensational phrase "Survivors of the 20th Century's Infamous Serial Killers," tells survivor's stories in their own words, voices that are not often heard in true crime. Ann Rule, although she makes use of the standard true-crime conventions and sometimes contributes to the spectacle of murder, continues to advocate for victims and focus productively on women's experiences of violence. John

Grisham's *The Innocent Man* (2007) is a fine addition to the "justice-gone-wrong" literary subgenre, and the exonerations of wrongly convicted people made possible by The Innocence Project and its subsidiaries may yield some very different true-crime narratives indeed in coming years. One hopes for a mutable and more inclusive true crime that can make greater meaning of violence and brutality, and perhaps, eventually, mediate or prevent some of it.

Finally, Lance Morrow's statement at the head of this chapter suggests that "evil" cannot be comprehended unless it is somehow transformed into a story. In modern American society, murder, atrocity, and the inflicting of needless, excessive harm are understood as primary forms of evil partially because such acts are most regularly transformed into the stories told by true crime. When those things occur, our culture and cognition demands that they be turned into narrative, processed somehow in the form of a story, whether it is a true-crime text, a film, a weekly television series, or an article on a Web site. The rise of true crime from the 1950s magazines to its present various forms both symbolizes and documents an understanding of evil that is by turns subtle and sophisticated, lurid and vulgar, obsessively focused on the individual and always engaged with extremes of feeling, experience, and existence itself. At its heart, and in its most "true" and finest form, true crime narrates humanity's failure, while reassuring us that not everything human has failed.

NOTES

INTRODUCTION

1. These numbers are gleaned from Ben Harrison, *True-Crime Narratives: An Annotated Bibliography* (Lanham, MD: The Scarecrow Press, 1997).

2. Karen Halttunen, *Murder Most Foul: The Killer and the American Gothic Imagination* (Cambridge, MA: Harvard University Press, 1998), 2.

3. Ibid., 29.

4. Ibid., 40.

5. Ibid., 57.

6. David Ray Papke, *Framing the Criminal: Crime, Cultural Work, and the Loss of Critical Perspective, 1830–1900* (Hamden, CT: Archon Books, 1987), xiv.

7. *National Police Gazette*, January 7, 1905, LXXXVI (1430). *American Periodical Series Online*, New York Public Library, June 16, 2006.

8. *National Police Gazette*, November 25, 1905, LXXXVII (1476). *American Periodical Series Online*, New York Public Library, June 16, 2006.

9. *National Police Gazette*, September 10, 1892 LX (783). *American Periodical Series Online*, New York Public Library, June 16, 2006.

10. John Marr, "True Detective RIP," http://www.stim.com/Stim-x/8.1/detective/detective-08.1.html (accessed May 13, 2008).

CHAPTER 1: MAGAZINES

1. Will Straw, Introduction to *Cyanide and Sin: Visualizing Crime in 1950s America* (New York: PPP Editions, 2006).

2. For an idea about how educated elites felt about pulp and crime reading material, see Anita P. Forbes, "Combating Cheap Magazines," *The English Journal*, June 1937, 476–478; Paul F. Lazarsfeld and Rowena Wyant, "Magazines in 90 Cities— Who Reads What?" *The Public Opinion Quarterly*, October 1937; Joe Jennings, "Leisure Reading of Jr. High School Boys and Girls," *Peabody Journal of Education*, May 1929; Geraldine White, "Surveying Reading in a High School Community," *The English Journal*, November 1942.

3. Erin Smith, *Hardboiled: Working-Class Readers and Pulp Magazines* (Philadelphia, PA: Temple University Press, 2000), 45.

4. Erin Smith notes that "H. L. Mencken and George Jean Nathan toyed with the idea of starting a Negro pulp in the 1920s before founding *Black Mask*, but decided that there was not enough money in the black community to support one," *Hardboiled: Working-Class Readers and Pulp Magazines*, 27.

5. Information about print runs and titles from James Surowiecki, "True-Crime Mags' corpse found stuffed under television set!" Salon.com, Media Circus, August 5, 1997, http://archive.salon.com/aug97/media/media970805.html (accessed July 13, 2005), and John Marr, "True Detective, R.I.P.," http://www.stim.com/Stim-x/8.1/detective/detective-08.1.html (accessed May 13, 2008). Those with the longest print runs and greatest popularity (and the largest number of surviving copies in archives) include *True Detective Mysteries* (shortened to *True Detective* in 1941), *Master Detective, Inside Detective, Startling Detective, Real Detective, Official Detective, Crime Detective, Spotlight Detective, Front Page Detective, True Homicide, Confidential Detective, Crime Confessions, Police Dragnet Cases, Smash Detective, Scoop Detective Cases, Headquarters Detective, Detective World,* and *Real Police Stories.*

6. "Topics of the Times," *The New York Times,* January 4, 1946, http://nytimes.com (accessed May 4, 2007).

7. Jay Walz, "State Law of 1884 on Lurid Books Killed by High Court as Too Vague," *The New York Times,* March 30, 1948, http://nytimes.com (accessed May 4, 2007).

8. *Real Detective,* December 1940, 82.

9. *True Detective Mysteries,* March 1934, 34.

10. Bernarr Macfadden, *True Detective Mysteries,* May 1924, 2.

11. Ibid., 2.

12. Jim Bennett, Bernarr Macfadden Web site, "Weakness: A Crime," http://www.bernarrmacfadden.com/macfadden3.html (accessed March 2007).

13. Jim Bennett, Bernarr Macfadden Web site, "A Publishing Empire," http://www.bernarrmacfadden.com/macfadden5.html. (accessed March 2007).

14. Carolyn Strange and Tina Loo, *True Crime, True North: The Golden Age of Canadian Pulp Magazines* (Vancouver, British Columbia: Raincoast Books, 2004), 9.

15. Startling Detective, October 1936, 9; *True Detective Mysteries,* March 1934, 5.

16. *True Detective Mysteries,* June 1928, 9.

17. *True Detective Mysteries,* March 1934, 62–64.

18. *True Detective Mysteries,* June 1928, 56.

19. Erin Smith, *Hardboiled: Working-Class Readers and Pulp Magazines,* 52.

20. *True Detective,* June 1944, 25.

21. *True Detective,* October 1949, 72.

22. *True Detective,* March 1946, 49.

23. *True Detective,* February 1952, 62–64, 73–75.

24. *True Detective,* March 1950, 42.

25. Clive Bloom, *Cult Fiction* (New York: St. Martin's Press, 1996), 15.

26. See Neil Miller, *Sex-Crime Panic: A Journey to the Paranoid Heart of the 1950s* (New York: Alyson Books, 2000).

27. Norman Mailer, "The White Negro: Superficial Reflections on the Hipster," in *Advertisements for Myself* (1959; Cambridge, MA: Harvard University Press, 1992), 343–345.

28. *True Detective*, June 1950, 73.

29. *True Detective*, October 1960, 31.

30. Gregg Olsen and M. William Phelps, Crime Rant blog, May 16, 2007. Guest blog entry by Laura James, "Intersection of True Crime and Pornography," http://www.crimerant.com/?p=798 (accessed January 2008).

31. DetectiveMagazine.com, http://www.detective-magazine.com/ (accessed February 2007).

CHAPTER 2: BOOKS

1. Roger Lane, *Murder in America: A History* (Columbus, OH: Ohio State University Press, 1997), 268–269.

2. All crime statistics are available on the FBI's Web site, Crime in the United States, http://www.fbi.gov/ucr/cius2006/index.html (accessed January 2008). The "murder rate" itself is not an uncontested figure, even though it is gleaned from quantitative data, but is subject to interpretation based on differing political and intellectual perspectives.

3. "The Revolution in Criminal Justice," *Time Magazine* essay, July 16, 1965, http://www.time.com/time/magazine/article/0,9171,833972,00.html (accessed January 30, 2007).

4. Roger Lane, introduction to *Studies in Murder*, by Edmund Pearson (Columbus, OH: Ohio State University Press, 1999), ix–x.

5. Edmund Pearson, "What Makes a Good Murder?" in *Masterpieces of Murder*, ed. Gerald Gross (New York: Avon Books, 1966), 26.

6. Edmund Pearson, "The Borden Case," in *Studies in Murder* (Columbus, OH: Ohio State University Press, 1999), 28–29.

7. Edmund Pearson, "The End of the Borden Case," in *Masterpieces of Murder*, ed. Gerald Gross (New York: Avon Books, 1966), 259.

8. Laura James, "Legends of True Crime Reporting: Winifred Black." Clews blog, June 15, 2006. Reproduction of Winifred Black column entitled, "Only A Woman," from March 1919, http://www.laurajames.typepad.com/clews/2006/06/legends_of_true.html (accessed June 27, 2006).

9. Joel Bartlow Martin, *Why Did They Kill?* (New York: Ballantine Books, 1953), Epilogue.

10. Lucy Freeman, *"Before I Kill More..."* (New York: Crown Publishers, 1955), 65, 71, 241.

11. Ibid., 195–196.

12. Ibid., 221. Compare this with Ann Rule's portrayal of Ted Bundy, especially when he shows his rage one day in court, and she sees underneath his mask for the first time.

13. Truman Capote, *In Cold Blood: A True Account of a Multiple Murder and Its Consequences* (New York: Random House, 1965), 275.

14. George Plimpton, *Truman Capote: In Which Various Friends, Enemies, Acquaintances, and Detractors Recall His Turbulent Career* (New York: Doubleday, 1997), 166.

15. The Boston Strangler case has been controversial since DeSalvo confessed in 1965. Never tried for the crimes for technical reasons, DeSalvo was murdered in prison in 1973, and questions about the veracity of his claims to have killed the eleven "strangler victims" have been questioned by many.

16. The Edgar Allan Poe Awards, or "Edgars," are awards given annually by the Mystery Writers Association for outstanding work in several categories, including (since 1948), "Fact Crime." For more information, see http://www.hycyber.com/MYST/edgars.html.

17. In 1971, NYPD Officer Frank Serpico testified at the Knapp Commission corruption hearings about widespread corruption within the New York City Police Department. In 1973, Peter Maas published *Serpico*, a biographical account of Serpico's experiences in the NYPD. *Serpico* helped change literary depictions of policemen, and led to the increased popularity of sensational, graphic, and lurid treatments of police topics.

18. Joseph Wambaugh in *Playboy Magazine* interview, July 1979, 74, 81.

19. Although it is true that *The New Yorker*, that bastion of Eastern literati, first published *In Cold Blood*, true crime as a distinct genre didn't receive real critical attention until the 1980s, when it could no longer be ignored as a force in the publishing industry.

20. For more on the death of the flourishing and promising hippie culture, see Joan Didion's essays in her books *Slouching Towards Bethlehem* (1968; New York: Noonday Press, 1992) and *The White Album* (New York: Simon & Schuster, 1979).

21. Vincent Bugliosi with Curt Gentry, *Helter Skelter* (1974; New York: Bantam Books, 1995), 552.

22. Ibid., 552.

23. Ibid., 114, Susan Atkins describing the murder of Sharon Tate.

24. Peter N. Carroll, *It Seemed Like Nothing Happened: America in the 1970s* (New Brunswick, NJ: Rutgers University Press, 1982), 313.

25. There are numerous books about Manson, the "family," and the *Helter Skelter* murder events: Ed Sanders' 1971 *The Family* (New York: Thunder's Mouth Press, 2002, revised and updated edition) offers a good alternative to Bugliosi's story and a differing interpretation of the motivation and meaning of the events.

26. For more on the publishing industry during this period, see Kenneth C. Davis, *Two-Bit Culture: The Paperbacking of America* (Boston, MA: Houghton Mifflin Company, 1984); *Mass Market Publishing in America*, ed. Allen Billy Crider (Boston, MA: G.K. Hall & Co., 1982); and Diana Tixier Herald, *Genreflecting: A Guide to Reading Interests in Genre Fiction*, fourth edition (Englewood, CO: Libraries Unlimited, 1995).

27. Bugliosi, *Helter Skelter*, 521.

28. Ibid., 237.

29. Ibid., 606.

30. Ibid., 179.

31. Following the model set with *Helter Skelter*, Bugliosi coauthored his true-crime books, working with Ken Hurwitz on *Till Death Do Us Part* (New York: W.W. Norton & Co., 1978) and Bruce B. Henderson for *And the Sea Will Tell* (New York: W.W. Norton, 1991), a murder narrative set on the tiny Pacific island of Palmyra.

32. Norman Mailer, *The Executioner's Song* (Boston, MA: Little, Brown Company, 1979), 451.

33. Hilary Mills, *Mailer: A Biography* (New York: Empire Books, 1982), 432.

34. David Guest, *Sentenced to Death: The American Novel and Capital Punishment* (Jackson, MS: University Press of Mississippi, 1997), 148.

35. Ibid., 155, 156.

36. Ben Harrison, *True Crime Narratives: An Annotated Bibliography* (Lanham, MD: The Scarecrow Press, 1997).

37. Ann Rule, *The Stranger Beside Me* (1980; New York: Penguin Putnam, 2000), 541.

38. Ibid., 427.

39. 1990s crime statistics showed a steady and sometimes dramatic decline in murder rates nationwide, from an all-time high murder rate of 9.8 in 1991 to a low of 5.5 in 2000 and 2004. FBI Uniform Crime Reports, http://www.fbi.gov/ucr/05cius/data/table_01.html (accessed February 2007). Sociologist Barry Glassner writes, "between 1990 and 1998, when the nation's murder rate declined by 20 percent, the number of murder stories on network newscasts increased 600 percent (*not* counting stories about O. J. Simpson)." *The Culture of Fear: Why Americans Are Afraid of the Wrong Things* (New York: Basic Books/Perseus, 1999), xxi.

40. In a recent article published in *The Journal of Popular Culture* about true-crime readers, Laura Browder writes: "According to publishers, true-crime writers, and bookstore owners polled in a preliminary survey, from two-thirds to three-quarters of the readers of these grisly nonfiction accounts are women." *The Journal of Popular Culture* 39(6), 2006, 929.

41. See Carlton Stowers, *Innocence Lost* (New York: Pocket Books, 1990); Jack Olsen, *"I"—The Creation of a Serial Killer* (New York: St. Martin's Press, 2002); Mark Fuhrman, *Murder in Greenwich: Who Killed Martha Moxley?* (New York: Harper Collins, 1998); Harold Schechter, *Deviant: The Shocking True Story of Ed Gein, the Original "Psycho"* (New York: Simon & Schuster/Pocket Books, 1989); *Deranged* (New York: Simon & Schuster/Pocket Books, 1990); *Bestial* (New York: Simon & Schuster/Pocket Books, 1998); and *Fiend: The Shocking True Story of America's Youngest Serial Killer* (New York: Simon & Schuster, 2000).

CHAPTER 3: FILMS

1. A. H. Weiler, *The New York Times*, April 2, 1959, http://nytimes.com (accessed September 15, 2007).

2. State Supreme Court of Illinois 45 Ill. 2d 434, 259 N.E. 2d 250 (1970), *Nathan F. Leopold, Jr., Appellant, v. Meyer Levin et al., Appellees*, no. 41498, http://www.law.umkc.edu/faculty/projects/ftrials/leoploeb/LEO_SUIT.HTM (accessed September 23, 2007).

3. *Psycho* quote on the "100 Years of Horror" Web site, Psycho page, http://eric.b.olsen.tripod.com/psycho_nov.html (accessed September 17, 2007).

4. Bosley Crowther, "Screen: Graphic Quadruple Murder," *The New York Times*, December 15, 1967, http://nytimes.com (accessed September 28, 2007).

5. Truman Capote, "Ghosts in Sunlight: The Filming of *In Cold Blood*," 1967, *A Capote Reader* (New York: Penguin Books, 2002) 621–627.

6. Ibid., 624.

7. Crowther review of *In Cold Blood*.

8. The Boston Strangler case has been controversial since DeSalvo confessed in 1965. Never tried for the crimes for technical reasons, DeSalvo was murdered in prison in 1973, and questions about the veracity of his claim to have killed the eleven "strangler victims" have been questioned by many.

9. Renata Adler, "Screen: 'The Boston Strangler' Opens," *The New York Times*, October 17, 1968, http://nytimes.com (accessed September 5, 2007).

10. Stephen Prince, ed., *Screening Violence* (New Brunswick, NJ: Rutgers University Press 2000), 35.

11. Vincent Canby, "Screen: 'Manson,' Full-Length Documentary, Opens," *The New York Times*, January 31, 1976, http://movies.nytimes.com/movie/review/ (accessed October 1, 2007).

12. Wayne J. Douglass, "The Criminal Psychopath as Hollywood Hero," *Journal of Popular Film and Television* 8(4) 1981, 30–39.

13. Alessandra Stanley, "TV Weekend: Manson Family's Summer of Death," *The New York Times*, May 14, 2004, http://query.nytimes.com/ (accessed October 1, 2007).

14. Rosemary Baer, *Reflections of a Pseudo-Juror: Reflections on the Manson Trial* (Waco, TX: Word Books, 1972), 72.

15. Quotes from Stephen Rowley, "The Thin Blue Line (Errol Morris), 1988," Cinephobia Review: The Thin Blue Line, *Cinephobia*, 2007, http://www.cinephobia.com/thinblue.htm (accessed October 15, 2007); Janet Maslin, "Anatomy of a Murder: A Real-Life Whodunit," *The New York Times*, August 26, 1988, http://movies.nytimes.com/ (accessed October 15, 2007); and Katherine Dieckmann, "Private Eye," *American Film* 13(1) January/February 1988, 32–38.

16. Errol Morris quoted in Katherine Dieckmann, "Private Eye," 32–38.

17. Linda Williams, "Mirrors without Memories: Truth, History, and the New Documentary," *Film Quarterly* 46(3) (Spring 1993), 9–21, http://www.jstor.org (accessed June 25, 2007).

18. Errol Morris quoted in Lawrence Van Gelder, "At the Movies," *The New York Times*, December 9, 1988, http://nytimes.com (accessed October 20, 2007).

19. Laurent Bouzereau, *Ultraviolent Movies* (Secaucus, NJ: Citadel Press, 1996), 197.

20. Martin Rubin, "The Grayness of Darkness: *The Honeymoon Killers* and its Impact on Psychokiller Cinema," in Christopher Sharrett, ed., *Mythologies of Violence in Postmodern Media* (Detroit, MI: Wayne State University Press, 1999), 60.

21. Jane Caputi, "Small Ceremonies: Ritual in *Forrest Gump, Natural Born Killers, Seven* and *Follow Me Home*", in Christopher Sharrett, ed., *Mythologies of Violence in Postmodern Media* (Detroit, MI: Wayne State University Press, 1999), 153.

22. Rubin, "The Grayness of Darkness: *The Honeymoon Killers* and its Impact on Psychokiller Cinema," 58.

23. Wayne J. Douglass, "The Criminal Psychopath as Hollywood Hero," *Journal of Popular Film and Television* 8(4) 1981, 30–39.

CHAPTER 4: TELEVISION

1. For more on this subject, see the essays in *Entertaining Crime: Television Reality Programs*, eds. Mark Fishman and Gray Cavender (Hawthorne, NY: Aldine De Gruyter, 1998).

2. It is impossible to say with certainty how much of an impact such television shows have on real viewers' attitudes, behavior, and actions. For an overview of the thorny issues involved in this topic and the research to date, see Aaron Doyle, "How Not to Think about Crime in the Media," *Canadian Journal of Criminology and Criminal Justice* 48(6) October 2006, 867–885.

3. There were a number of pro-law enforcement radio programs that were based on "real police files" and produced with police cooperation, including *This is Your*

FBI (1945–1953), *Tales of the Texas Rangers* (1950–1952), the intriguing *Up for Parole* (1950), and *Unit 99* (1957–1958), a very early precursor to *Cops*.

4. Michael J. Hayde, *My Name's Friday: The Unauthorized But True Story of Dragnet and the Films of Jack Webb* (Nashville, TN: Cumberland House, 2001), 18.

5. Ibid., 182.

6. Ibid., 220–221.

7. Gael Fashingbauer Cooper, "Why it's Prime Time for True Crime." MSNBC. com, July 28, 2004, http://www.msnbc.msn.com/id/5216635/print/1/displaymode/1098 (accessed June 15, 2007).

8. Gray Cavender, "In 'The Shadow of Shadows,' Television Reality Crime Programming," *Entertaining Crime: Television Reality Programs*, eds. Mark Fishman and Gray Cavender (New York: Aldine de Gruyter, 1998), 81.

9. Information about *America's Most Wanted* is on their Web site, http://www.amw.com/captures/index.cfm.

10. Gray Cavender, "In 'The Shadow Of Shadows.' Television Reality Crime Programming," 87.

11. Pamela Donovan, "Armed with the Power of Television: Reality Crime Programming and the Reconstruction of Law and Order in the United States," *Entertaining Crime: Television Reality Programs*, eds. Mark Fishman and Gray Cavender. (New York: Aldine de Gruyter, 1998), 117–137.

12. Aaron Doyle, "'Cops': Television Policing as Policing Reality." *Entertaining Crime: Television Reality Programs*, eds. Mark Fishman and Gray Cavender (New York: Aldine de Gruyter, 1998), 114.

13. Steven Brill quoted in "The Development of Court TV." Hedieh Nasheri, *Crime and Justice in the Age of Court TV* (New York: LFB Scholarly Publishing LLC, 2002), 31.

14. Investigation Discovery, "The Criminal Report Daily," http://blogs.discovery.com/criminal_report/ (accessed January 2008).

15. Tricia Despres, "TV's Crime Wave Spreads Across Dial," *Advertising Age* 75(22) May 31, 2004; Academic Search Premier, EBSCOhost, http://web.ebscohost.com (accessed June 27, 2007).

16. Steven Johnson, *Everything Bad is Good for You: How Today's Popular Culture Is Actually Making Us Smarter* (New York: Riverhead Books, 2005), xiii.

17. There are many more true-crime documentary programs than are discussed here, but I have chosen several outstanding and popular examples as representative of the genre. Many programs don't make it past the pilot stage, or are very short-lived.

18. Anita Biressi, *Crime, Fear and the Law in True Crime Stories* (New York: Palgrave Crime Files Series, 2001), 12.

19. Lee Siegel, "Crime Scenes: Why Cop Shows are Eternal," *The New Republic* 228(12) March 31, 2003, 25; Academic Search Premier, EBSCOhost, http://web.ebscohost.com (accessed June 12, 2007).

CHAPTER 5: THE INTERNET

1. Aaron Barlow, *The Rise of the Blogosphere* (Westport, CT: Praeger, 2007), 143–163.

2. Technorati, "About Us," http://technorati.com/about/ (accessed December 1, 2007).

3. Harding, t.o. crime, "Carnival of the True Crime Blogs, 76," May 15, 2007, http://tocrime.blogspot.com/ (accessed November 15, 2007).

4. Sea Woods, "Cyber Cops," *Rolling Stone* 1014, November 30, 2006; Academic Search Premier, Ebscohost, http://web.ebscohost.com/ (accessed November 30, 2007).

5. David Kline and Daniel Burstein, *Blog! How the Newest Media Revolution Is Changing Politics, Business, and Culture* (New York: CDS Books, 2005), 247.

6. Stan Weeber, *In Search of Derrick Todd Lee: the Internet Social Movement That Made a Difference* (New York: University Press of America, 2007).

7. Steve Huff, The True Crime Weblog, November 18, 2007, http://www.truecrimeweblog.com/2007/11/murder-according-to-prophet-of-samael.html (accessed January 18, 2008).

8. http://lostinlimaohio.blogspot.com/; http://amw.com/; http://antimove.blogspot.com; http://missingchild.wordpress.com/; http://billoreilly.com/outragefunnels/ (accessed January 18, 2008).

9. Laura James, "About Me," http://laurajames.typepad.com/about.html (accessed January 18, 2008).

10. Laura James, "Old Clipping of the Week," Clews, November 21, 2007, http://laurajames.typepad.com/clews/2007/11/old-clipping-of.html (accessed December 21, 2007).

11. Web site addresses as follows: http://markgribben.com/; http://www.1947project.com/; http://incoldblogger.blogspot.com/; http://crimerant.com/;http://blackandmissing.blogspot.com/ (all accessed January 18, 2008).

12. Web site addresses as follows: http://www.mycrimespace.com/; http://www.parentsbehavingbadly.com/; http://missingandmurderedchildren.facesofthemissing.org/; http://missingchild.wordpress.com/; http://teachersbehavingbadly.blogspot.com/; http://michellesaysso.blogspot.com/ (all accessed January 18, 2008).

13. Laura James, "Intersection of True Crime and Pornography," Crime Rant, Gregg Olsen and M. William Phelps. May 15, 2007, http://www.crimerant.com/?p=798 (accessed January 18, 2008).

14. Miles Corwin, "Life After Death," *Los Angeles Magazine* Online, January 2008, http://www.lamag.com/ (accessed December 21, 2007).

15. Jill Leovy, "Why Does the Report Talk about Race?" The Homicide Report, http://latimesblogs.latimes.com/homicidereport/2007/06/why_does_the_re.html (accessed December 21, 2007).

16. For more on the topic of urban violence as a public health crisis, see Alex Kotlowitz, "Is Urban Violence a Virus?" *The New York Times Magazine*, May 4, 2008.

17. Jill Leovy, "Why Does the Report Talk about Race?" The Homicide Report, http://latimesblogs.latimes.com/homicidereport/2007/02/welcome_to_the_.html (accessed December 21, 2007).

18. Miles Corwin, "Life After Death," *Los Angeles Magazine* Online, January 2008, http://www.lamag.com/ (accessed December 21, 2007).

19. Jill Leovy, The Homicide Report, comments posted on November 12 and 13, 2007, http://latimesblogs.latimes.com/homicidereport/2007/11/compton-man-sho.html#comments (accessed January 18, 2008).

20. Jill Leovy, The Homicide Report, comments posted on December 22, 2007, and January 7, 2008, http://latimesblogs.latimes.com/homicidereport/2007/12/jonah-alexander.html#comments (accessed January 18, 2008).

21. Jill Leovy, The Homicide Report, comments posted on November 29, 2007, http://latimesblogs.latimes.com/homicidereport/2007/11/watts-murder.html#comments (accessed January 18, 2008).

22. Jill Leovy, The Homicide Report, comments posted on December 2, 2007, http://latimesblogs.latimes.com/homicidereport/2007/11/watts-murder.html#comments (accessed January 18, 2008). Murder seemed to run in Timothy Johnson's family; his older brother Cleamon Johnson, aka "Big Evil," is currently on death row in California, convicted of two first-degree murders.

23. Jill Leovy, The Homicide Report, comments posted on December 5, 2007, http://latimesblogs.latimes.com/homicidereport/2007/11/watts-murder.html#comments (accessed January 18, 2008).

24. Jill Leovy, The Homicide Report, comments posted on December 15, 2007, http://latimesblogs.latimes.com/homicidereport/2007/11/watts-murder.html#comments (accessed January 18, 2008).

25. David Kline and Daniel Burstein, *Blog! How The Newest Media Revolution Is Changing Politics, Business, and Culture* (New York: CDS Books, 2005), 249.

26. Paul LaRosa, The Murder Book, http://tacomaconfidential.typepad.com/the_murder_book_2008/ (accessed January 18, 2008).

27. See http://blogs.orlandosentinel.com/news_homicide/; http://www.city-paper.com/news/story.asp?id=14836 (accessed January 18, 2008). Quote from Willoughby Mariano, *The Orlando Sentinel*, The Orlando Crime Report, http://blogs.orlandosentinel.com/news_homicide/2008/01/index.html/ (accessed January 18, 2008).

28. See http://www.crimeincharlotte.com/ (accessed January 18, 2008).

29. Quote from an e-mail from e-Bay to writer Marty Graham, related in "Making a 'Murderabilia' Killing, *Wired Magazine*, December 8, 2006, http://www.wired.com/science/discoveries/news/2006/12/72259 (accessed January 13, 2008).

CONCLUSION

1. John G. Cawelti, *Mystery, Violence, and Popular Culture* (Madison, WI: University of Wisconsin Press/Popular Press 2004), 96.

2. Adam Gopnik, "In the Mourning Store," *The New Yorker*, January 21, 2008, 81.

3. Laura Browder, "Dystopian Romance: True Crime and the Female Reader," *The Journal of Popular Culture* 39 (2006), 928–953.

4. Ibid., 949, note 4.

5. Ibid., 935.

6. Anita Biressi, *Crime, Fear and the Law in True Crime Stories* (New York: Palgrave Crime Files Series, 2001), 166.

7. Philip Jenkins, *Using Murder: The Social Construction of Serial Homicide* (New York: Aldine de Gruyter, 1994), 123.

8. Popular and scholarly works alike emphasize the perceived transience and "rootlessness" of contemporary American life (since the 1960s) as a factor in murder and murder rates—see Steven Egger, *The Need to Kill: Inside the World of the Serial Killer* (Upper Saddle River, NJ: Prentice Hall, 2003); Steven Egger, *Serial Murder: An Elusive Phenomenon* (New York: Praeger Publishers, 1990); Roger Lane, *Murder in America: A History* (Columbus, OH: Ohio State University Press, 1997); Robert K. Ressler and Tom Schachtman, *Whoever Fights Monsters* (New York: St. Martin's Press, 1992).

9. VICAP, or "Violent Criminal Apprehension Program," is an FBI program that was developed by legendary homicide detective Pierce Brooks in the early 1980s, and became operational in 1985. Robert Ressler consulted with Brooks in the creation of the program. Brooks is an interesting figure in true crime—and in real crime as well. Brooks was a detective, a consultant, and a homicide expert from the 1950s to the 1990s. Incredibly, Brooks was involved in the onion field, Manson (peripherally), Ted Bundy, and Diane Downs cases, as well as many other well-known high profile murders. Like Wambaugh, Brooks also consulted for television, most notably for *Dragnet* and *Dragnet 1969*. He became a close friend of Ann Rule, and he figures prominently in several of her books. Brooks died in 1998.

10. Robert K. Ressler and Tom Shachtman, *Whoever Fights Monsters* (New York: St. Martin's Press, 1992), 203.

11. David Schmid, *Natural Born Celebrities: Serial Killers in American Culture* (Chicago, IL: University of Chicago Press, 2005), 83.

12. For an excellent article on the history and current status of criminal profiling, see Malcolm Gladwell, "Dangerous Minds," *The New Yorker*, November 12, 2007. On the admissibility of criminal profiling testimony in court, see Forensic Solutions, LLP, "Criminal Profiling in Court," http://www.corpus-delicti.com/prof_archives_court.html (accessed January 15, 2008).

BIBLIOGRAPHY

Abbott, Jack Henry. *In the Belly of the Beast: Letters from Prison.* New York: Vintage Books, 1981.

Black, Joel. *The Aesthetics of Murder: A Study in Romantic Literature and Contemporary Culture.* Baltimore, MD: Johns Hopkins University Press, 1991.

Borowitz, Albert. *Blood and Ink: An International Guide to Fact-Based Crime Literature.* Kent, OH: Kent State University Press, 2002.

Breslin, Jack. *America's Most Wanted: How Television Catches Crooks.* New York: Harper Paperbacks, 1990.

Cleckley, Hervey M. *The Mask of Sanity: An Attempt to Clarify Some Issues about the So-Called Psychopathic Personality.* St. Louis, MO: Mosby, 1941.

Fosburgh, Lacey. *Closing Time: The True Story of the "Goodbar" Murder.* New York: Delacorte Press, 1975.

Gilmore, John. *The Tucson Murders.* New York: The Dial Press, 1970.

Gilmore, Mikal. *Shot in the Heart.* New York: Doubleday, 1994.

Glassner, Barry. *The Culture of Fear: Why Americans Are Afraid of the Wrong Things.* New York: Basic Books, 1999.

Graysmith, Robert. *Zodiac.* New York: Berkley Books, 1976.

Herald, Diana Tixier, ed. *Genreflecting: A Guide to Reading Interests in Genre Fiction.* Fourth edition. Englewood, CO: Libraries Unlimited, 1995.

Keyes, Edward. *The Michigan Murders.* New York: Reader's Digest Press, 1976.

Knox, Sara L. *Murder: A Tale of Modern American Life.* Durham, NC: Duke University Press, 1998.

Lesser, Wendy. *Pictures at an Execution: An Inquiry into the Subject of Murder.* Cambridge, MA: Harvard University Press, 1993.

Levin, Meyer. *Compulsion.* New York: Simon & Schuster, 1956.

Malcolm, Janet. *The Journalist and the Murderer.* New York: Vintage Books, 1990.

Martin, Joel Bartlow. *Why Did They Kill?* New York: Bantam Books, 1953.

McGinniss, Joe. *Fatal Vision.* New York: Signet, 1983.

"The Mystery Writers of America," Edgar Awards homepage, http://www.theedgars.com/ (accessed May 2008).

Olsen, Jack. "The Jack Olsen Home Page," http://www.jackolsen.com/ (accessed January 2007).

Pearson, Edmund. "From Sudden Death." *Queer Books.* New York: Kennikat Press, 1970.

Plimpton, George. *Truman Capote: In Which Various Friends, Enemies, Acquaintances, and Detractors Recall His Turbulent Career.* New York: Anchor Books, 1997.

Ramsland, Katherine. *The CSI Effect.* New York: Berkley Boulevard Books, 2006.

Ressler, Robert K., and Tom Schachtman. *Whoever Fights Monsters.* New York: St. Martin's Press, 1992.

Rossner, Judith. *Looking for Mr. Goodbar.* New York: Simon & Schuster, 1975.

Roughead, William. *Classic Crimes.* Ed. Luc Sante. New York: New York Review Books, 2000.

Rule, Ann. *Small Sacrifices.* New York: Penguin, 1987.

———. *Green River, Running Red.* New York: Simon Schuster, 2004.

———. Ann Rule Web Site, http://annrules.com/ (accessed January 2008).

Sanders, Ed. *The Family.* 1971. New York: Thunder's Mouth Press, 2002. Revised and updated edition.

Schechter, Harold. *Deviant: The Shocking True Story of Ed Gein, the Original "Psycho."* New York: Simon & Schuster/Pocket Books, 1989.

———. *Deranged.* New York: Simon & Schuster/Pocket Books, 1990.

———. *Depraved: The Shocking True Story of America's First Serial Killer.* New York: Simon & Schuster/Pocket Books, 1994.

———. *Bestial.* New York: Simon & Schuster/Pocket Books, 1998.

Seltzer, Mark. *Serial Killers: Death and Life in America's Wound Culture.* New York: Routledge, 1998.

Server, Lee. *Danger Is My Business: An Illustrated History of the Fabulous Pulp Magazines, 1896–1953.* San Francisco, CA: Chronicle Books, 1993.

Skal, David J. *The Monster Show: A Cultural History of Horror.* New York: Faber and Faber, 1993.

Smith, Patterson. "True Detective Magazines," http://www.patterson-smith.com/mags.htm (accessed February 2008).

Stasio, Marilyn. "The Killers Next Door: We Can't Get Enough of Them." *The New York Times Book Review,* October 20, 1991, BR46.

Stout, Martha. *The Sociopath Next Door.* New York: Broadway Books, 2005.

Stowers, Carlton. *Innocence Lost.* New York: Pocket Books, 1990.

———. "The Carlton Stowers Homepage," http://www.truecrime.net/carltonstowers/ (accessed February 2007).

Strange, Carolyn, and Tina Loo. "From Hewers of Wood to Producers of Pulp: True Crime in Canadian Pulp Magazines of the 1940s." *Journal of Canadian Studies* 37 (Summer 2002): 11–31.

Tithecott, Richard. *Of Men and Monsters: Jeffrey Dahmer and the Construction of the Serial Killer.* Madison, WI: The University of Wisconsin Press, 1997.

INDEX

About the Author

JEAN MURLEY is Assistant Professor of English at Queensborough Community College, of the City University of New York (CUNY). She has published a review of *Natural Born Celebrities: Serial Killers in American Culture* for the *Journal of Popular Culture* (October 2006), and an essay entitled "Ordinary Sinners and Moral Aliens: The Murder Narratives of Charles Brockden Brown and Edgar Allan Poe" in *Understanding Evil: An Interdisciplinary Approach* (2003), an anthology on contemporary understandings of evil.